DESTROYING LIBYA
AND WORLD ORDER

"Let the free people of the world know that we could have bargained over and sold out our cause in return for a personal secure and stable life. We received many offers to this effect but we chose to be at the vanguard of the confrontation as a badge of duty and honour. Even if we do not win immediately, we will give a lesson to future generations that choosing to protect the nation is an honour and selling it out is the greatest betrayal that history will remember forever despite the attempts of the others to tell you otherwise."

MUAMMAR QADDAFI*

"Qaddafi website publishes 'last will' of Libyan ex-leader", BBC News, 23/10/2011 <http://www.bbc.co.uk/news/world-africa-15420848>

DESTROYING LIBYA AND WORLD ORDER

THE THREE-DECADE U.S. CAMPAIGN TO TERMINATE THE QADDAFI REVOLUTION

BY

FRANCIS A. BOYLE

CLARITY PRESS, INC.

ISBN: 0-9853353-7-8
         978-0-9853353-7-3
E-book: 978-0-9860362-0-0

In-house editor: Diana G. Collier
Cover: R. Jordan P. Santos

Library of Congress Cataloging-in-Publication Data

Boyle, Francis Anthony, 1950-
  Destroying Libya and world order : the three-decade U.S. campaign to reverse the Qaddafi revolution / by Francis A. Boyle.
      p. cm.
  Includes bibliographical references and index.
  ISBN 978-0-9853353-7-3 (alk. paper) -- ISBN 978-0-9860362-0-0 (alk. paper)
  1. United States--Foreign relations--Libya. 2. Libya--Foreign relations--United States. 3. United States--Military relations--Libya.
4. Libya--Military relations--United States. 5. Libya--Politics and government--1969- 6. Libya--International status. I. Title.

  E183.8.L75B68 2013
  327.730612--dc23

                    2013008654

                 Clarity Press, Inc.
           Ste. 469, 3277 Roswell Rd. NE
               Atlanta, GA. 30305 , USA
             http://www.claritypress.com

TABLE OF CONTENTS

Last Will and Testament
Muammar Qaddafi

Introduction / 11

Chapter 1
Using International Law to Analyze
American Foreign Policy Decision-Making / 16

Chapter 2
The Confrontation Between
the Reagan Administration and Libya over
the Gulf of Sidra and Terrorism / 38

Chapter 3
The Reagan Administration's Criminal Bombings
of Tripoli and Benghazi / 66

Chapter 4
Resolving the Lockerbie Dispute
by Means of International Law / 106

Chapter 5
Responsibility to Protect (R2P)
versus International Law / 154

Chapter 6
The 2011 U.S./NATO War Against Libya / 173

Conclusion / 201

Index / 207

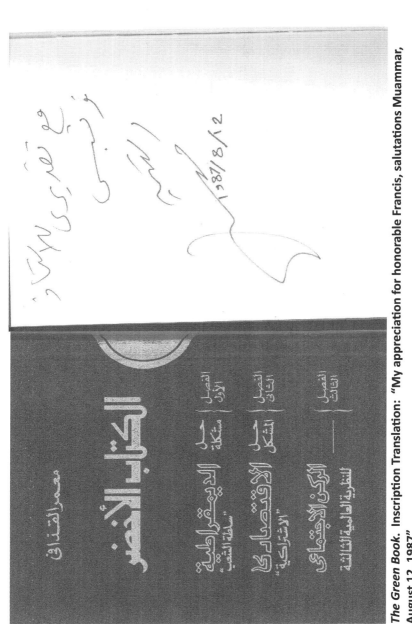

The Green Book. Inscription Translation: "My appreciation for honorable Francis, salutations Muammar, August 12, 1987"

"

(translation from the back cover the 1980 English version of The Green Book)

The thinker Muammar Qaddafi does not present his thought for simple amusement or pleasure. Nor is it for those who regard ideas as puzzles for the entertainment of empty-minded people standing on the margin of life.

Qaddafi's ideas interpret life as it erupts from the heart of the tormented, the oppressed, the deprived and the grief-stricken. It flows from the ever-developing and conflicting reality in search of whatever is best and most beautiful.

Part One of THE GREEN BOOK heralded the start of the era of the Jamahiriya (state of the masses).

Part Two inaugurated an international economic revolution which does away with the old economic structures and brings them down on the heads of the exploiters.

Part Three of THE GREEN BOOK launches the social revolution. It presents the genuine interpretation of history, the solution of man's struggle in life and the unresolved problems of man and woman. Equally it tackles the problem of the minorities and the blacks in order to lay down the sound principles of social life for all mankind.

The living philosophy is inseparable from life itself and erupts from its essence. It is the philosophy of Muammar Qaddafi."

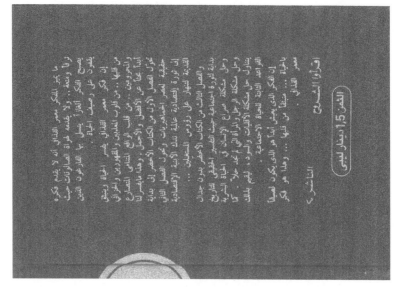

INTRODUCTION

I have unique experience in Libya. To the best of my knowledge, during the 1980s I was perhaps the only American professor to spend a significant amount of time in Libya because of the serial armed hostilities and the imposition of draconian travel prohibitions and economic sanctions inflicted by the Reagan administration. I spent a sum total of four weeks in Libya on three different trips.

In 1985 Libya invited me to conduct a week-long lecture tour and visit. I lectured at universities in Tripoli and Benghazi. I also lectured live on Libyan national television from their studio in Tripoli, and some of my public lectures were broadcasted by Libyan television.

During my first trip to Libya, I spent an entire day visiting their museum dedicated to the documentation of the Holocaust that had been perpetrated upon them by Italy. In 1911 Italy had attacked and invaded the territory we now call Libya and proceeded to occupy it until toward the end of the Second World War. During this period of time (1912-1943), Italy exterminated somewhere "between 250,000 and 300,000" Libyans out of a population of somewhere "between 800,000 and 1 million at the time."[1] About one-third of all Libyans. In proportional terms, this approached the Nazi Holocaust against the Jews. Of course Italy also exterminated Jews and Ethiopians as well as Libyans. These victims included the Italian murder of Libya's acclaimed national liberation hero and martyr, Omar Muktar.

At their request, I would later advise Libya on how to sue Italy over its colonization and outright genocide perpetrated against the Libyans. Protracted negotiations between Libya and Italy eventually led to a settlement of those claims that was concluded between Colonel Qaddafi and Prime Minister Sylvio Berlusconi in 2008, providing for a $5 billion dollar compensation package to be transferred to Libya over twenty years. This token sum was a mere pittance compared to the actual number of human deaths and the amount of physical destruction that Italy had inflicted upon Libya. Nevertheless, that agreement was treacherously repudiated by Berlusconi during the course of his 2011 war against Libya. Berlusconi's illegal and despicable act has re-opened Libya's claims for colonization and genocide against Italy.

During my first trip to Libya, I was surprised to see that women were free and empowered to do anything they wanted all over the country. I asked my government-provided translator about this. He advised: "Qaddafi decreed that women are equal to men. The old men don't like it. But there is nothing they can do about it." As I can attest from my three trips to Libya, under Qaddafi women held up half the sky in that country. I doubt very seriously that the 2011 US/NATO war will advance the cause of women in Libya. Indeed, Libyan women could very well retrogress from Qaddafi's days as, undoubtedly, will the general well being of the Libyan population from its standing in the 2010 U.N. Human Development Index.[2]

In 1987 I returned to Libya for another two weeks after the Reagan administration had bombed Tripoli and Benghazi in 1986 and attempted to murder the entire Qaddafi family sleeping in their home at night. I visited all the bombing sites in the Metropolitan Tripoli area and had a tour of the bombed-out Qaddafi home. I then had a meeting with Colonel Qaddafi in his tent where we discussed what happened to him and his family on the night of the bombing. Qaddafi was a Bedouin from the desert, so he liked to meet guests and conduct business in a pitched tent. It was a practice which he carried out even on travel to the U.N. in New York, for which he was generally ridiculed—though in actuality it represented his determination to maintain his cultural identity, symbolic of his ongoing commitment to his people, rather than to the imperial West.

At the end of that meeting I agreed with Colonel Qaddafi to work with former U.S. Attorney General Ramsey Clark on filing lawsuits in United States federal courts over the bombings against President Reagan, Secretary of Defense Weinberger, Director of the C.I.A. Casey, the U.S. Joint Chiefs of Staff, the U.S. Commander of NATO, the Commander of the U.S. Sixth Fleet, and U.K. Prime Minister Margaret Thatcher, who gave permission to Reagan to use a U.K. base where U.S. bombers were stationed to bomb Libya—together with suing both the United States and the United Kingdom. We lost. Two lawyers against two empires.

In June of 1988 I returned to Libya as their guest in order to attend the session of their Basic Popular Congress meeting in Beida for the adoption of the Great Green Charter for Peace and Human Rights. Interestingly enough, Colonel Qaddafi proposed to abolish the death penalty for Libya. But the Basic Popular Congress rejected his humanitarian initiative: Democracy in action! While there I also provided commentary to C.B.S. Evening News about what precisely was going on and its significance for promoting human rights internally.

Over the years, I would routinely give interviews to Western news media sources about Libya and the prospects for the United States government to overthrow Colonel Qaddafi. I always pointed out that the American government should be careful of what it wished for: Instead of installing a C.I.A. stooge, the United States could get a fundamentalist religious leader sitting on top of Libya's oil fields and occupying that strategic piece of real estate in North Africa and on the southern rim of the Mediterranean right next to Egypt. Colonel Qaddafi's foremost opponents had always been Libya's Muslim fundamentalists who detested him for (1) his secular-nationalist rule deliberately modeled upon his hero and role model, Egypt's Gamal Abdel Nasser; (2) his liberation and empowerment of Libyan women; and (3) Qaddafi's *Green Book* that tried to carve-out a third way between capitalism and communism that was consistent with Islam, but which they nevertheless considered to be heretical. For the most part, Libyans constitute a moderate Sunni Muslim population. Yet in order to overthrow Qaddafi in 2011, the U.S. and NATO states worked hand-in-glove with Libyan and imported foreign Muslim fundamentalists including elements of Al Qaeda and Salafists. Somalia on the Med, anyone?

After the Bush Senior administration came to power, in late 1991 they opportunistically accused Libya of somehow being behind the 1988 bombing of the Pan American jet over Lockerbie, Scotland. I advised Libya on this matter from the very outset. Indeed, prior thereto I had predicted to Libya that they were going to be used by the United States government as a convenient scapegoat over Lockerbie for geopolitical reasons.

Publicly sensationalizing these allegations, in early 1992 President Bush Senior then mobilized the U.S. Sixth Fleet off the coast of Libya on hostile aerial and naval maneuvers in preparation for yet another military attack exactly as the Reagan administration had done repeatedly throughout the 1980s. I convinced Colonel Qaddafi to let us sue the United States and the United Kingdom at the International Court of Justice in The Hague over the Lockerbie bombing allegations; to convene an emergency meeting of the World Court; and to request the Court to issue the international equivalent of temporary restraining orders against the United States and the United Kingdom so that they would not attack Libya again as they had done before. After we had filed these two World Court lawsuits, President Bush Senior ordered the Sixth Fleet to stand down. There was no military conflict between the United States and Libya. There was no war. No one died. A tribute to international law, the World Court, and its capacity for the peaceful settlement of international disputes.

Pursuant to our World Court lawsuits, in February of 1998 the International Court of Justice rendered two Judgments against the United

States and the United Kingdom that were overwhelmingly in favor of Libya on the technical, jurisdictional and procedural elements involved in these two cases. It was obvious from reading these Judgments that at the end of the day Libya was going to win its World Court lawsuits against the United States and the United Kingdom over the substance of their Lockerbie bombing allegations. These drastically unfavorable World Court Judgments convinced the United States and the United Kingdom to offer a compromise proposal to Libya whereby the two Libyan nationals accused by the U.S. and the U.K. of perpetrating the Lockerbie bombing would be tried before a Scottish Court sitting in The Hague, the seat of the World Court. Justice was never done. This book tells the inside story of why not.

When the US/NATO war began against Libya in March of 2011, Colonel Qaddafi immediately disappeared underground, fearing yet another Western attempt to murder him and his family, which later happened. I spent several months engaged in fruitless efforts to get into contact with Colonel Qaddafi to obtain his authorization for filing lawsuits at the International Court of Justice in The Hague against the United States and the NATO states in order to stop their bombing campaign against Libya. All to no avail.

Colonel Qaddafi fought and died for Libya against the West just like his hero Omar Mukhtar had done. Indeed, on the basis of that precedent, I had predicted that Qaddafi would fight to the death for Libya and not flee his country in order to save his own life. Far exceeding my expectations, Colonel Qaddafi resisted the most powerful military alliance ever assembled in the history of the world for seven months. A real modern-day Hannibal!

Colonel Qaddafi ruled Libya like the traditional Arab Shaikh of a Bedouin tribe. Indeed, Libya as a state consisted of an amalgamation of disparate Arab and Tuareg tribes that Qaddafi had melded together into his Jamahiriya system, a state of the masses. The jury is still out on whether or not this now discombobulation of tribes living in Libya can ever be reconstituted as a functioning state after the U.S./NATO war. Libya stands on the verge of a statehood crack-up, as was the U.S./N.A.T.O. intention from the get-go.

Today Libya reminds me of the well-known children's nursery rhyme *Humpty Dumpty*:

> Humpty Dumpty sat on a wall.
> Humpty Dumpty had a great fall.
> All the king's horses and all the king's men,
> Couldn't put Humpty back together again.

ENDNOTES

1   **Dirk Vanderwalle, A History of Modern Libya** 31 (2d ed. 2012).

2   The Libyan Arab Jamahiriya's 2010 HDI of 0.755 is above the average of 0.593 for countries in the Arab States. It was also above the average of 0.717 for high human development countries. Source: <http://hrdstats. undp.org/images/explanations/LBY.pdf>

CHAPTER 1

USING INTERNATIONAL LAW TO ANALYZE AMERICAN FOREIGN POLICY DECISION-MAKING

The current way in which most public international law professors teach international law has become pretty irrelevant to the major problems of contemporary international relations. International law professors must take this great body of black-letter rules that has been handed down to us by our forebears and attempt to make sense of them by applying them to, and testing them by, current problems of international relations. Only in this fashion will our profession continue to maintain some degree of relevance to the contemporary debate over the proper conduct of American foreign policy at the start of the third millenium. Unless we reestablish this integral connection between the study of international law and the practice of international relations, public international law professors will probably become as extinct as the dodo birds that could not fly.

Furthermore, for reasons more fully explained below, it is my firm belief that if any progress is to be made on the numerous problems of contemporary international relations that face the United States and the world at large today, professors of public international law and their erstwhile students must become more actively involved in the current public debate over the great issues of foreign affairs and defense policy. There they must bring to bear their unique training, expertise, and perspective on international problems in an objective, coherent, meaningful, and principled way. Unfortunately, however, it appears that a substantial proportion of the miniscule degree of policy-oriented international legal studies being conducted in the United States of America today seems to consist of parroting whatever the United States Departments of State or Defense utter about problems of international relations and the rules of international law and indeed, how to twist it to fit their needs.

As my teacher of international relations, Hans Morgenthau, who was originally an international lawyer, used to constantly preach: It is the primary duty of professional academics to speak truth to those in power, no matter what the personal consequences—as he had done most courageously during the Vietnam War. He especially intended this admonition to be applied by his students to the members of the United States foreign affairs and defense establishment.

International law professors must never allow patriotism to deflect them from their duty to vigorously defend the proposition that the United States government must preserve and advance its historical commitment to the rules of international law and to the integrity of the international legal order or think that undermining it as may be requested by the United States government would in fact be a patriotic action. As America's Founding Fathers wisely established, the United States of America is supposed to be a society of laws, not of men and women. And as professors of international law we must fight to uphold the rule of law, both at home and abroad. The two are inextricably interconnected.

Hobbism in the American Study and Practice of International Law and Politics

Part of the problem with contemporary international legal studies is due to the fact that shortly after the termination of the Second World War, the study of international relations in the United States was bifurcated into the two disciplines of international political science and international legal studies—primarily by Hans Morgenthau himself. Unfortunately, most international relations scholars of any repute fall into either one or the other of these two categories, and there is little if any personal, intellectual, professional or organizational contacts, movement, or ferment between the respective memberships of these two disparate groups. For that very reason, a substantial percentage of public international law professors know little about international political science in a formal, academic sense, except for what they might have studied in college. Conversely, the overwhelming majority of political scientists not only know nothing about international law, but are in addition possessed by a deep-seated antipathy toward that subject.

As someone who spent ten years of his life becoming formally credentialed in these two disciplines, and then shuttling back and forth between both worlds for over the next three decades, I have detected several characteristics that they share. Among these various common denominators, the most important one for purposes of analysis here is that both international political scientists and public international lawyers essentially perceive the world of both international relations and domestic affairs in Hobbesian terms. To be sure, however, each discipline looks for its seminal reference point to a different part of Thomas Hobbes' *Leviathan* (1651). But the net result is the same for both disciplines.

American political scientists have wholeheartedly embraced the first part of that classic treatise, which proclaims that human nature is basically rapacious and that for this reason the state of nature (which heuristic concept includes international relations) is "solitary, poor, nasty, brutish and short." Whereas American public international lawyers basically operate within the intellectual framework of the second part of *Leviathan*, on the nature of the Commonwealth, which promulgates the cardinal tenets of modern legal positivism that the will of the sovereign is the source of all law; and that therefore where there is no sovereign, there can be no law. Nevertheless, the international lawyers also basically subscribe to the teachings of part one, and the political scientists essentially agree with the teachings of part two, when it comes to both domestic civil society and international relations. Hobbes's *Leviathan* is the intellectual prototype for both international political science and international legal positivism.

In this regard, one could go much farther to argue that Hobbes was the founder of both modern legal positivism and modern political science in Western civilization—such as it is. Yet, the non-Western world never endorsed but was only brutally victimized by European and American Hobbism. Today, the rest of Western civilization has at least formally repudiated Hobbism in favor of a combination of utilitarianism, socialism, and humanism. By contrast, we here in the United States of America still enthusiastically proclaim the continued validity of a political, economic, and psychological theory that is over three hundred and sixty years old as the gospel truth for application to the rest of the world whether they like it or not.

In America we are all obedient Hobbist men and women who live in a basically Hobbist political and economic system while acting in accordance with Hobbist assumptions and prescriptions. During the past three decades or so, the alleged virtues of Hobbism have been glorified by the neoconservatives and their supporters in the news media and before the American people and all humanity. Predictably, therefore, the neoconservatives have also simultaneously demonstrated the fatal vices of Hobbism for all to see. Those who live by Hobbism—whether human beings or societies—will ultimately perish because of Hobbism.

Certainly, there are major differences between American lawyers and political scientists—whether international or domestic—in regard to their respective disciplinary trainings, qualifications, perceptions, analyses, methodologies and prescriptions. But this author submits that both groups essentially endorse the Hobbist perspective on the world of international relations and domestic affairs. This commonality of viewpoint provides a good deal of the reason why universities in the United States produce international relations specialists—whether lawyers or political scientists—who apply the Hobbist approach to the study of international relations and the conduct of American foreign policy. This shared Hobbism, which predominates most legal and political discourse in the United States, is responsible for the sterility that has entered into the study and teaching of both international law and international political science. Even more seriously, Hobbism has become responsible for many of the major crimes, blunders, and tragedies of contemporary American foreign policy decision-making when our Hobbist students have left the groves of academe for the corridors of power in Washington and New York.

Realism versus Neoconservativism

The discipline of international political science is effectively dominated by the political realist school of international relations that was founded by the late Hans Morgenthau and some other "disillusioned liberals" after the end of the Second World War. No point would be served here by elucidating the basic elements of the political realist school, other than to say that these realists essentially subscribed to the Hobbist viewpoint of the world.[1] In particular the realists believed that international law and organizations are essentially irrelevant to the conduct of foreign policy and to the dynamics of international relations. Political realists (and neo-realists) assert that international relations essentially take place in a state of nature where life between nations is "solitary, poor, nasty, brutish, and short."[2] For this reason, political realists argue that there are and can be no rules for the conduct of foreign policy other than the Hobbist "laws of nature," which are essentially prescriptive guidelines for maximizing self-interest and power at the direct expense of everyone else.

At this point in the analysis it is important to clearly distinguish traditional political realism as classically defined and articulated by Hans Morgenthau in *Politics Among Nations* (1st ed. 1948) and what I prefer to call perverted political realism as expounded by the neoconservative movement.[3] Originally, neo-con realism advocated nothing more sophisticated than an across-the-board anticommunist crusade. Then, after the collapse of that shibboleth in 1991, they sought to replace it a decade later with yet another crusade, this time against "terrorism," in order to form the overall basis for the conduct of American foreign policy. Contrast this to the views of Morgenthau and his realist colleagues such as George Kennan, who argued quite convincingly throughout their long and distinguished careers that foreign affairs must not become a crusade, and that anticommunism was no panacea for the numerous conceptual, perceptual and structural defects of American foreign policy decision-making. If he were alive today, I submit Hans Morgenthau would argue the exact same position in relation to the hobgoblin of "terrorism." More Americans die every year from getting struck down by bolts of lightning sent from the skies by Zeus than by terrorist strikes.

Hans Morgenthau would have been appalled to have learned that unscrupulous neoconservative government officials in the Reagan administration and then the Bush Junior administration attempted to legitimate their incompetent, reprehensible, and crusading foreign policies by invoking his sacrosanct theory of "political realism" as underpinning their efforts. If Morgenthau had lived beyond July 19, 1980, he would have been in the vanguard of the anti-Reagan and then later the anti-Bush Junior resistance, just as he was in the vanguard of the opposition to the Vietnam War that was then being waged by the die-hard, crusading anticommunists of the Johnson and Nixon administrations.[4] For similar reasons, it is certainly understandable why some of the most lucid and acerbic criticisms of various aspects of the neoconservative Reagan administration's foreign affairs and defense policies came from the pen of the late George Kennan.

The Irrelevance of Hobbist Legal Positivism

I will not bother here to refute the traditional political realist critique of international law and organizations because I have done so quite extensively elsewhere.[5] But the case remains now as then, that political realists are incorrect to conclude that international law and organizations are irrelevant to the major problems of international relations. Rather, it is more accurate to claim that the traditional Hobbist, legal positivist manner in which international law and organizations have been conceptualized, taught, and propagated by public international law professors is not only destructive to the national interest, but irrelevant to the major conundrums of international relations. The real problem, therefore, is not with international law and organizations per se, but rather with the positivist methodology in which international legal studies, analysis, and training have been traditionally conducted.

Hence, it becomes crucial to distinguish the substantive signifi-cance of international law and organizations for international relations from the positivist methodology of international legal studies. Yet due to their subscription to the Hobbist perspective, political scientists have perhaps unwittingly adopted the traditional Hobbist legal positivist approach to understanding the nature of law and the elements of a legal system, whether domestic or international. According to Hobbist philosophy, the will of the sovereign is the source of all law; so where there is no sovereign, there can be no law. Hence the discourse in American political science which centers around the notion of the hegemon. Thus, political scientists quite naturally concluded by reverse analogy to the domestic legal system where there supposedly exists an absolute Hobbist sovereign, that because there is no such Leviathan over international relations, then there is no such thing as international law except in a purely nominal sense.

Most Hobbist political scientists assume that with respect to the domestic arena of civil affairs, the will of the sovereign is the source of all law and that therefore where there is no sovereign enforcement mechanism, there can be no law. Of course I am in fundamental disagreement with these Hobbist conclusions for reasons more fully explained by my teacher, the late Professor Lon Fuller in his classic treatise *The Morality of Law* (rev. ed. 1969), which is one of the great works of twentieth-century jurisprudence. But putting aside for present purposes the extended debate on this matter between Professor Fuller and the positivist H.L.A. Hart in his *The Concept of Law* (1961), here political scientists fall into the methodological trap described by some of their colleagues by means of the term "the level-of-analysis problem": Namely, they take what might be true for domestic affairs and automatically apply this supposed knowledge to international relations.

According to the Hobbist assumptions generally held by most political scientists, on the domestic level-of-analysis the essence of a municipal government is the existence of an all-powerful sovereign that can coerce obedience to the rule of law against the unbridled wills of its recalcitrant subjects. Therefore, since political scientists do not see an effective world government in operation with the will and the capacity to coerce obedience to the rules of international law by the various governments of the world's nation states, they conclude by analogy that there is no such thing as international law in any meaningful sense. Of course their criteria for determining the meaning and relevance of both municipal law and international law are exclusively Hobbist.

Somewhat curiously, then, the vast majority of political scientists who subscribe to the Hobbist viewpoint on the world are typically more positivistic in their conception of a legal system (whether domestic or international) than their cohorts in the legal studies profession. Indeed, it has been my general experience that even extraordinarily sophisticated political scientists are far more positivistic (and mistakenly so) in their conception of the nature of law (whether domestic or international) than the average practicing lawyer. This is because lawyers have usually had enough practical experience with the actual workings of a legal system to comprehend that its design and operation have little to do with what Hobbes assumed, described, and prescribed. Thus, I would submit that many of Professor Fuller's profound insights into the nature of a domestic legal system inevitably came from the fact that he was originally a student, practitioner, and teacher of the Anglo-American common law of contracts.[6]

As a general proposition, therefore, I would like to suggest that at least with respect to the domestic level-of-analysis, the more you have directly experienced the actual operations of a municipal legal system, the less positivistic you necessarily become in your perception of the nature of law. Conversely, the more highly academic, philosophical, and detached from the real legal world you are, the more likely it is that you become a dyed-in-the-wool Hobbist legal positivist. Since most political scientists know very little about the way municipal legal systems actually work, it is quite understandable why they are so adamantly and positivistically Hobbist in their conception of a legal order--whether domestic or international.

A somewhat similar critique can be made of the many public international law professors who spend their days in their offices thoroughly digesting the contents of the latest edition of the positivistic *American Journal of International Law* rather than in presenting cases to international and domestic courts. Accordingly, the vast majority of international lawyers perceive international relations in strictly Hobbist legal positivist terms. In particular is their positivist conclusion that since the Hobbist social contract is the ultimate source of all domestic law, then by analogical extension to the international system, the explicit or at least inchoate consent of sovereign nation states is the essential precondition for the creation of international law. Hence, for example, their collective but simplistic if not oftentimes erroneous conclusion that United Nations General Assembly resolutions per se do not create rules of international law. Indeed, that is what most U.S. international lawyers are brainwashed to believe by their pro-U.S. government professors in American imperialist law schools.

Likewise, for similarly Hobbist reasons, international legal positivists constantly preach that international law and organizations must be strengthened by improving the enforcement mechanisms of the U.N. Security Council and of regional organizations as temporary measures, which must ultimately be solidified by the creation of a Hobbist world government. On these points, the international legal positivists commit the same level-of-analysis methodological mistakes as have their political scientist counterparts. Moreover, most members of both disciplines either ignore or are unaware of the fact that Hobbes did not recommend or even favor the creation of a world-girdling Leviathan.

Furthermore, under the pernicious influence of the neoconservatives, we have witnessed a most insidious perversion of these Hobbist premises by many American public international lawyers: Namely, that since the U.N. Security Council does not function effectively to accomplish what they perceive to be the foreign policy objectives of the United States government as quite narrowly and selfishly defined, then the rules of international law really do not mean anything; therefore states are free to behave as they wish and the devil can take the hindmost. In other words, the United States government exists in a Hobbist state of nature vis-à-vis its adversaries where it alone must be the judge of what is necessary to defend its "existence" or protect and advance its so-called "national interests," which are certainly not the same thing unless one is gullible enough to believe the fulminations of the neoconservatives. By means of proffering such specious arguments, however, these public international lawyers simply transform themselves into perverted political realists. Witness, for example, the gang of torture lawyers in the neoconservative Bush Junior administration who later gave their imprimatur to his illegal invasion of Iraq.

Many American international lawyers and law professors set out to justify whatever Hobbesian foreign policies the United States government seeks to implement by invoking the rules of international law. But by performing such a sycophantic function, they simply confirm and conform to the well-established criticisms by political scientists that international law is really irrelevant to the effective conduct of foreign affairs since all it consists of is a series of ex post facto rationalizations and justifications for decisions desired or already undertaken by American foreign policy decision-makers for reasons of Hobbesian power politics and economic predation. Thereby, a substantial proportion of the U.S. international legal studies profession have rendered themselves irrelevant to the study and practice of international relations because they have done nothing more than serve as apologists for the United States government's unprincipled foreign policies around the world.

The Irrelevance of the Debate over
International Enforcement Mechanisms

No further point would be served here by continuing this analysis of the various deficiencies of international political science and of the international legal studies profession that are directly attributable to their mutual embrace of Hobbism. Suffice it to say that what is needed is a non-Hobbist or, better yet, an anti-Hobbist way of thinking about international politics, international law, and the dynamic relationships between the two. As a first step, then, this means that both professions must abandon their fascination with the centrality of an international enforcement mechanism as being a prerequisite for establishing an effective system of international law and organizations. The reason why so much time has been expended on all sides debating the existence or nonexistence and the importance of enforcement mechanisms is simply because both political scientists and international lawyers view the international system in Hobbist legal positivist terms in which, by definition, an effective enforcement mechanism is essential for the existence of any legal system, whether international or domestic. For this reason, then, the Hobbist critique of international law reduces itself to a simple tautology.

I will put aside for present purposes the question of whether or not the United Nations Security Council is an effective mechanism for the enforcement of the rules of international law. Certainly the Security Council was originally designed along Hobbist lines to be such an enforcement mechanism; provided there could be unanimous agreement among the five great powers of the world who were designated to be its permanent members, each of which was endowed with a veto power over substantive matters. Yet, according to Hobbes, the sovereign must speak with a voice that is not subject to the vicissitudes of any individual member.[7]

It is obvious, therefore, that the U.N. Security Council was never intended to be a Hobbist world sovereign in the first place. Consequently, it is inappropriate for political scientists and international lawyers to evaluate the performance of the Security Council at maintaining international peace and security by Hobbist criteria: namely, whether it can enforce international law absolutely, at all times, under all circumstances, and against all potential violators. Yet, even when evaluated in accordance with the dictates of *Leviathan*, the U.N. Security Council has operated much more effectively than might have been predicted on that Hobbist basis alone.

In any event, the alleged inability of the Security Council to function as some Hobbist sovereign cannot be properly invoked by American international lawyers to justify the U.S. government's violation of basic norms of international law, including the United Nations Charter and especially its article 2(4) prohibition on the threat and use of force in international relations. Nevertheless, this tactic became a standard-operating-procedure for many American law professors and all U.S. government lawyers during the tenure of the neoconservatives in both the Reagan administration and the Bush Junior administration. These U.S. international lawyers shamelessly debauched and debased the currency of their professional lives by willingly performing such a prostituted role at the behest of their Hobbesian masters.

When analyzed from a non-Hobbist perspective, enforcement per se has little to do with the effectiveness of international law and organizations. Similarly, without falling into the level-of-analysis trap, I would submit that enforcement per se also has little to do with the effectiveness of domestic legal systems. Once again, both lawyers and political scientists are enthralled by the Hobbist legal positivist paradigm that the source of all law--whether domestic or international--is the will of the sovereign, which must be enforced in order to be meaningful.

To the contrary, in my extensive experience as a teacher and a practitioner of U.S. domestic criminal law for over three decades, the reason why ordinary people obey or disobey domestic law has little to do with the existence of sovereign enforcement mechanisms.[8] Rather, most people obey most of the laws most of the time for reasons related to religion, morality, altruism, education, indoctrination, propaganda, and self-interest. Conversely, when citizens consciously decide to disobey the domestic law, the existence of an effective enforcement mechanism might enter into their calculations, but generally fear of punishment will not deter them from their contemplated course of conduct. The Hobbist premise that fear, terror, deterrence, enforcement, and punishment are critical to the existence of a legal system is undoubtedly based upon a mistaken psychological assumption. The Hobbist model of civil society essentially looks to the criminal law enforcement mechanism as the paradigmatic exemplar because men and women are incorrectly assumed to be not much different from vicious beasts of the jungle.

The Hobbist enforcement mechanism of criminal law is an incredibly misleading way to think about the nature of a legal system in a modern civil society. Rather, as Professor Fuller astutely observed, it is more insightful to conceptualize the essence of a domestic legal system by reference to common law, civil law, and commercial law. Professor Fuller's corpus indicates that *any* system of law is most properly understood as creating a facilitative framework of rules in order to permit and enhance the quality of interaction among its participants. Law must not simply be interpreted in its Hobbist legal positivist sense as the making, breaking, and enforcement of rules. Instead, a legal system grows out of the need of the actors involved to do business with each other on a day-to-day basis. Enforcement and sanctions are a part of this system, but they are not essential and, indeed, are perhaps not even critical for the development and preservation of a working legal order. Any system of law, even an incredibly imperfect one, usually proves to be far more beneficial and therefore preferable to each participant than the nonexistence of any legal rules at all. The application of political science game–theory can reach the exact same conclusions.

In the domestic areas of commercial law, civil law, and common law, the legal system is created, obeyed, and complied with for reasons that have little to do with the existence of an external enforcement mechanism and sanctions as such. Rather, such a legal system is essentially self-creating, self-obedient, self-compliant and self-enforcing most of the time on most issues for reasons of rational self-interest. Once again, without falling into the level-of-analysis trap, I would submit that the same is generally true for the system of international law and politics. The existence of legal systems on both the international and domestic levels-of-analysis is better explained by the existential need of their respective actors (whether states, peoples, or citizens) to establish and then to maintain, regulate, and improve their essential and inescapable mutual interactions and interrelationships.

Regime Theory and International Law

At a minimum, therefore, the existence *vel non* of an effective enforcement mechanism is a question that must be kept separate and apart from the issues of whether or not international law exists as a meaningful entity; whether or not states comply with the rules of international law for whatever reasons; and hence, whether or not international law is relevant to the conduct of foreign policy and thus important for the analysis of international relations. Some of these matters have been explored at great length by Professor Roger Fisher in his pathbreaking book, *Improving Compliance with International Law* (1981). In addition to the writings of Professors Fisher and Fuller from the legal profession, I would also like to suggest that we give further consideration to the international political science classic *Power and Interdependence* (1977) by Professors Keohane and Nye, who founded the self-styled "regime theory" school of international relations. A good deal could be learned from the application of regime theory in order to understand the nature of the relationship between international law and international politics.[9]

By now political science regime theorists have established the critical importance of international law and organizations to the areas of international trade, investment, finance, the seas, human rights, etc. But when it comes to questions dealing with the threat and use of force, their general conclusion seems to have been that there is really not a "regime" as defined within that framework of reference; or if there is such a regime, that it is not terribly effective. But once again, these international political scientists were assessing the effectiveness of the international law and organizations "regime" when it came to international conflict in accordance with Hobbist criteria. Hence their conclusion as to the relative ineffectiveness of regime theory to understand the nature of the relationship between international law and politics in such a critical area.

Although it is not my purpose here to apply regime theory to the analysis of the relationship between international law and politics, I would submit that if an analyst were to view that relationship from a non-Hobbist perspective, a good deal of progress could be made toward establishing the existence of an international regime when it comes to regulating the transnational threat and use of force that is fairly effective at maintaining international peace and security today.[10] To be sure, this regime might not be as effective as regimes in the areas of international trade, finance, the seas, human rights, etc.; but it does exist. The start of meaningful progress in the application of regime theory to the threat and use of force in international relations depends upon eliminating all forms of Hobbist assumptions when it comes to the conceptualization of international law and politics as well as their dynamic interaction.

If United States government decision-makers essentially operate on the Hobbist principle that the rules of international law are irrelevant, then what they are doing is acting in a manner that indicates that the United States government does not really care about the expectations held by other states and peoples as to what they believe is the minimal degree of respect and deference to which they are entitled in their relations with the United States government. When this Hobbist attitude is translated into the conduct of American foreign policy, it then quite naturally becomes a prescription for disagreement, difficulties, and conflict with other states and peoples. The U.S. government thus places itself into a position whereby the primary means by which it can achieve its objectives become, through self-fulfilling prophecy, the brute application of political, economic, and military coercion. Needless to say, these latter techniques entail a very high cost to pay, both internationally and domestically, in today's interdependent world.

By contrast, if in the formulation of American foreign policy decision-making, serious attention is paid to the rules of international law, what this will mean is that in essence U.S. government decision-makers will be taking into account the reasonable expectations held by other states and peoples in order to define their objectives (i.e., the ends) and then to accomplish them (i.e., the means). It seems almost intuitively obvious that if this process should transpire, then it would be far easier for the United States government to carry out its foreign policy and achieve its ultimate goals. To be sure, U.S. objectives might have to be scaled down somewhat by taking into account certain criteria of international law (e.g., the inalienable right of the self-determination of peoples); or certain means would have to be discarded in order to achieve American objectives because of the requirements of international law (e.g., the general prohibition on the threat and use of force). From this anti-Hobbist perspective, therefore, maybe the United States government will not obtain everything it wants, but perhaps approximately 85% of the desired objective could be obtained and the countervailing costs both human and material and in good will would have been minimized. To the contrary, as far as the realists and the neoconservatives are concerned, international relations is a zero-sum game.

The American Constitutional Law Regime Controlling the Threat and Use of Force

There is one more point to be made about regime theory per se, which draws upon the rich literature of the political science "linkage-politics" school to understanding the relationship between American domestic politics and its conduct of international affairs: namely, the importance and complexities of the interplay among the President, the Congress, the courts, and the people with respect to the formulation of American foreign policy. The unitary rational-actor model postulated by the political realists and the neoconservatives completely breaks down when it comes to explaining the manner in which American foreign policy is actually made and conducted under its constitutionally mandated system of separation of powers. The United States of America speaks and acts with many voices on foreign affairs. That is all for the better—despite the hallowed teachings of the political realists and the neoconservatives who to the contrary propound a plentitude of dictatorial and imperial powers by the President.

After all, America is supposed to be a constitutional democracy with a commitment to the rule of law both at home and abroad. If the executive branch of the U.S. federal government decides to embark upon a course of egregiously lawless behavior abroad, then it would be a testament to the strength and resilience of American democracy that Congress, the courts, and the American people refuse to go along with it. This dynamic has not been appreciated by most of the self-styled realist and neoconservative analysts of American foreign policy decision-making precisely because of their Hobbesian perspective on the world of both domestic affairs and international relations.

It is an undeniable fact that American foreign policy decision-making has been substantially subjected to the rule of law by the United States Constitution. And this is true whether the realists and neoconservatives like it or not. Despite their Hobbesian predilections, it is the unalterable nature of this "legalist" reality so intrinsic to the United

States of America that must be understood, internalized, and effectuated by its foreign policy decision-makers.

The pernicious thesis incessantly propounded by international political realists and neoconservatives that for some mysterious reason American democracy is inherently incapable of developing a coherent, consistent, and successful foreign policy without Hobbism simply reflects their obstinate refusal to accept the well-established primacy of law over power in the U.S. constitutional system of government. The American people have never been willing to provide sustained popular support for a foreign policy that has flagrantly violated elementary norms of international law precisely because they have habitually perceived themselves to constitute a democratic political society governed by an indispensable commitment to the rule of law in all sectors of their national endeavors, both at home and abroad.

Thus, the U.S. government's good faith dedication to the pursuit of international law and international organizations in foreign affairs has usually proved to be critical both for the preservation of America's internal psychic equilibrium as well as for the consequent advancement of its global position. For these very *realpolitik* considerations, then, historically it has always proved to be in the so-called "national interest" of the United States of America to subject other states to the rule of law as well. Here that which is just and that which is expedient have coincided and reinforced each other.

An American foreign affairs analyst cannot even begin to comprehend the rudiments of U.S. foreign policy decision-making processes without possessing at least a sound working knowledge of international law, and especially of the interpenetration of the international legal regime and the American constitutional regime concerning the threat and use of force. But America's self-styled realist and neoconservative geopolitical practitioners of Hobbesian power politics have demonstrated little appreciation, knowledge, respect, or sensitivity to the requirements of the U.S. constitutional system of government premised upon fundamental commitment to the rule of law, whether at home or abroad. To be sure, it was a tribute to the genius and compassion of the late Hans Morgenthau that he was perhaps the only and archetypal realist who demonstrated a profound appreciation of, and deep respect for, the American democratic system of constitutional government and its commitment to the rule of law in his classic work *The Purpose of American Politics* (1960). Indeed, upon his immigration to the United States, Morgenthau went so far as to obtain an American law degree.

These other self-proclaimed realist and neoconservative American foreign policy decision-makers cannot hope to construct a watertight compartment around their exercise of Hobbesian power politics in international relations without creating a deleterious spillover effect into the domestic affairs of the American people. The Nixon-Kissinger administration was the paradigmatic example of the validity of this phenomenon with its interconnected atrocities of Vietnam and the domestic lawlessness of Watergate. The same can be said for the Reagan administration's Iran-contra scandal. Ditto for the Bush Junior administration's torture scandal.

This spillover phenomenon is produced by the fact that Hobbesian power politics violently contradict several of the most fundamental normative principles upon which the United States of America is supposed to be founded: the inalienable rights of the individual, the self-determination of peoples, the sovereign equality and independence of states, noninterventionism, respect for international law and organizations, and the peaceful settlement of international disputes, etc. Painfully aware of this connection, the American people historically have stridently resisted the practice of Hobbesian power politics by their governmental leaders both at home and abroad.

Yet for at least the past five decades of my active political lifetime, American governmental decision-makers have repeatedly tried to base their foreign affairs and defense policies on such premises. The net result has been the counterproductive creation of a series of unmitigated disasters for the United States, both at home and abroad, as well as the subversion of the entire post-World War II international legal order that the United States constructed, inter alia, at the 1945 San Francisco Conference where it drafted the United Nations Charter in order to protect its own interests and advance its own values. At a minimum, the executive branch of the U.S. federal government must come to understand that the constitutionally mandated separation-of-powers system, together with its concomitant rule of law, must be accepted as an historical fact to be dealt with on its own terms, rather than subverted, ignored, or expressly violated. If the executive branch wishes to design and execute a coherent and consistent foreign policy, then it must take into account and cooperate with the Congress, the people, and to a lesser extent the courts, in the formulation of American foreign policy. The much vaunted goal of developing a truly "bipartisan" approach to foreign affairs cannot be achieved unless and until the U.S. President is willing to recognize the constitutional facts of life that : (1) Congress is an independent and co-equal branch of government; and (2) the President is subject to the rule of law in the conduct of foreign policy as well as of domestic affairs. Failing this, presidential practice of Hobbesian power politics abroad will necessarily require the presidential practice of Hobbesian power politics at home, which in turn will necessarily be resisted by the American people and Congress and the courts.

The Relevance of International Law and Organizations

International law and organizations are simply facts of international politics as well as of U.S. domestic constitutional and political life. Hence, they are incontestable facts that U.S. government decision-makers must routinely take into account in their formulation of American foreign policy, whether in a positive or negative sense—whether they like it or not. Either they must view the rules of international law as something they should attempt to comply with as best as possible under the unique circumstances of an historical situation (e.g., the Cuban missile crisis)[11] or else they must view the rules of international law as something that they have to overcome in order to accomplish their illicit objectives (e.g., Bush Junior's Iraq war).[12] For either reason, however, the rules of international law are therefore "relevant" to the formulation and conduct of American foreign policy in what I would call these "functionalist" terms.

Let us assume, however, that the United States government really pays absolutely no meaningful attention whatsoever to the rules of international law when it formulates its foreign policy; but instead only invokes those rules and panders to international organizations on an ex post facto basis in order to justify whatever decision it has taken for Hobbist reasons. Does this then mean that the rules of international law are indeed irrelevant? Once again, I submit that the answer to this question for all of us as teachers, students, and analysts of international relations is definitely in the negative. International law and organizations would still remain critically relevant for any concerned citizen living in a democracy with a constitutional commitment to the rule of law for the purpose of formulating his or her own opinion on whether to support or to oppose specific foreign affairs and defense policies, and to determine their legitimacy.

Invariably it is the case that the United States government will publicly attempt to justify its foreign policy in terms of international law and organizations or, more broadly put, in terms of what is legally/morally right or wrong for the management of domestic, allied, and international public opinion. It may be the case that the actual motivation for a policy had been considerations of Hobbesian power politics. But it would be extremely difficult, if not impossible, to sell pure, unadulterated Hobbism to the American people and Congress as the proper basis for the conduct of United States foreign policy.

Hence, U.S. government decision-makers oftentimes resort to legalistic subterfuges by pleading principles of international law in order to disguise their *realpolitik* foreign policy decisions. This was certainly the case for the most part of both the neoconservative Reagan and Bush Junior administrations. Of course this phenomenon simply confirms the worst suspicions held by political scientists that international law and organizations are therefore really irrelevant to the conduct of American foreign policy and international relations as a whole. But once again, the definition of "relevance" depends upon whether the analyst's perspective and criteria are Hobbist or functionalist.

Even if American government decision-makers pay absolutely no meaningful attention at all to the rules of international law, nevertheless they will and indeed must attempt to justify their policies to U.S. domestic and international public opinion by invoking its norms. This permits a foreign policy analyst who possesses a rudimentary working knowledge of international law and organizations to apply these criteria to the government's stated rationalizations in order to determine whether or not the policy can be justified as the government has put forward. If it cannot, then obviously the analyst must realize that he or she is not being told the truth and therefore something else must be going on behind the scenes that is quite different from what U.S. government officials are saying in public. By thus using the principles of international law and organizations as an analytical tool, the student, scholar, and concerned citizen can first identify such legalistic deceptions, and then proceed to pierce through the veil of legal and moral obfuscations put forth by U.S. government officials in order to grasp the real heart of what the policy is all about. Such analysts might not like what they find when they get there--Hobbesian power politics. But at least a substantive knowledge of international law and organizations would have enabled them to pierce the fog of perception management.

In addition, many foreign states also try to justify their policies to the United States government as well as to the American Congress and people by invoking the rules of international law and resorting to international organizations. Therefore, American foreign policy decision-makers, academic foreign policy analysts, and concerned American citizens need to be able to evaluate those foreign claims in accordance with the standard recognized criteria of international law. If the claims of the foreign government fall within what I would call the "ballpark" of international legality, then the U.S. government, private-sector foreign policy analysts, and the American people should be willing to give these foreign claims the benefit of the doubt and do their best to accommodate them within the overall conduct of American foreign policy to whatever extent is feasible.

On the other hand, when the foreign policy of the foreign state does not even fall within the "ballpark" of international legality, then it really is entitled to no recognition or support on America's part and U.S. foreign policy decision-makers should be wary of associating their government with it in any way, shape or form. To the extent that American foreign policy decision-makers do so associate the U.S. government with the illegal policies of a foreign government, a basic knowledge of international law will put congressional, academic, and private-sector foreign policy analysts as well as concerned American citizens in a better position to intelligently criticize this policy. Conversely, the same analytical methodology would also hold true when the United States government adopts an adversarial stance against a foreign government whose policies basically comport with the rules of international law.

Furthermore, once foreign policy analysts (congressional, students, scholars, citizens) have figured out the true nature of U.S. foreign policy by evaluating it in accordance with the standard recognized criteria of international law, if it is Hobbist, then they can proceed to construct an alternative policy that is based upon normative considerations of international law and organizations. Unfortunately, however, most international political scientists of the realist school and most international lawyers of the positivist school really have no constructive alternatives to offer anyone. The realists simply state that all is a matter of power and interest, which means reliance upon political and economic coercion, and ultimately upon the threat and use of U.S. military force. Whereas the legalists lament the fact that international law cannot be enforced and there is thus little that can be done except let the devil take the hindmost. In the final analysis, both schools lead to the same Hobbist prescriptions. Of course the same principles of analysis hold true *ex proprio vigore* for the neoconservatives.

It is never satisfactory for American foreign policy analysts just to criticize the U.S. government's decisions. Rather, they owe it to our students, to the American people and Congress, to U.S. government decision-makers themselves, as well as to foreign states and peoples, to develop a constructive alternative approach toward resolving the major problems of international relations. How many times have we heard the refrain, especially during the tenures of the neoconservative Reagan and Bush Junior administrations, that there are really only two alternative courses of conduct: Either the threat and use of U.S. military force in a particular situation; or else the "adversaries" of the United States of America (communists or terrorists or both) will prevail? There is, however, a third alternative to Hobbism and doing nothing. It consists of deploying the rules of international law and the procedures of international organizations for the peaceful settlement of international disputes. This is true Internationalism as opposed to Isolationism.

Prologue

The rules of international law provide useful criteria by which U.S.

government decision-makers can, do, and should formulate their foreign affairs and defense policies. This does not mean, however, that the rules of international law are so clear that all the U.S. government has to do is to apply them in order to achieve its objectives. Rather, in my opinion, the rules of international law typically tell U.S. government decision-makers what they should *not* do in order to avoid foreign affairs blunders, disasters, and atrocities. Similarly, in a more progressive sense, the rules of international law and the techniques of international organizations for the peaceful settlement of international disputes usually provide a guiding way out of some of the most urgent and pressing dilemmas that confront American foreign policy decision-makers in today's interdependent world.

International law and organizations also comprise a most powerful analytical tool for professional foreign policy experts (whether congressional, lawyers, political scientists, historians, or economists) to use for the purpose of first explaining and then evaluating the conduct of American foreign policy as well as the behavior of other nation states--whether allied, friendly, neutral, nonaligned, or overtly hostile. The rules of international law can provide objective criteria for making both predictions and value judgments as to the feasibility, the propriety and the ultimate success or failure of interactive foreign policy behavior among nation states. Finally, the rules of international law can likewise be used by concerned citizens living in a popularly elected democracy with a constitutional commitment to the rule of law in order to serve as a check-and-balance against the natural abuses of power endemic to any form of government when it comes to the conduct of foreign affairs and defense policies.

To be sure, international law and organizations are no panacea for the numerous problems of contemporary international relations. But they do provide one promising medium for extricating the American foreign policy decision-making establishment from the oppressive Hobbist morass that has enmired it for at least the past five decades of my active political lifetime. By conceptualizing international law and organizations in these functionalist terms, we can objectively demonstrate their relevance to the study and analysis of international relations, as well as to the future conduct of American foreign policy. In the process, we can hopefully point the way for new directions in the study and practice of international politics, law, organizations, and regimes toward the start of the third millennium of humankind's parlous existence.

This book applies my functionalist, Fullerian, and anti-Hobbesian framework of analysis for international law and organizations elaborated above in order to develop a comprehensive history and critique of American foreign policy toward Libya from when the Reagan administration came to power in January of 1981 until today in the immediate aftermath of the Obama administration's orchestrated NATO War against Libya, that is for over the past three decades. Chapters 2 and 3 deal with the repeated series of military conflicts and crises between the United States and Libya over the Gulf of Sidra and international terrorism during the eight years of the neoconservative Reagan administration. Chapter 4 explains and analyzes the Lockerbie bombing allegations and dispute by the United States and the United Kingdom against Libya that started with the realist Bush Senior administration, continued through the neoliberal Clinton administration, and was finally wound up by the neoconservative Bush Junior administration in order to gain access to Libya's oil. Then in 2011 the neoliberal Obama administration directly took over Libya's oil fields under the pretext of the so-called Responsibility to Protect (R2P) doctrine illustrating its fraudulent manipulation of international humanitarian law that might have been and in any future application should be critiqued by means of the very kind of accurate reading of international law that I have been advocating above.

Chapter 5 then proceeds to analyze and debunk the doctrines of R2P and its immediate predecessor, "humanitarian intervention," in accordance with the standard recognized criteria of international law. Chapter 6 then takes this debunking analysis and applies it specifically to the U.S./NATO war against Libya under the R2P rubric during the neoliberal Obama administration in 2011. The Conclusion will set forth my reflections on where the world stands today after September 11, 2001 and the consequent American "global war on terrorism" for which the oil-laden Libya had always been designated to be a primary target starting since the late neoliberal Carter administration, and primarily because of that oleaginous reason alone. It took three decades for the United States government spanning and working assiduously over five different presidential administrations (Reagan, Bush Senior, Clinton, Bush Junior, and Obama) to overthrow and reverse the 1969 Qaddafi Revolution in order to reconquer and re-subjugate the Libyan people and seize their oil fields, as well as to re-establish an American neo-colonial outpost in North Africa for the express purpose of projecting power onto that continent where all human life itself began—the cradle of civilization.

This book tells the story of what happened, why it happened, and what was wrong with what happened from the perspective of an international law professor and lawyer who tried for over three decades to stop it and to promote a better future for Libya and the Libyans as well as improved, peaceful and better relations between them and the United States. At the end of the day, I failed. But for the historical record, I submit it is worthwhile for me to tell this story. As George Santayana said: "Those who cannot remember the past are condemned to repeat it." [13] And as Thucydides said long before him, I offer this book to "those inquirers who desire an exact knowledge of the past as an aid to the interpretation of the future, which in the course of human things must resemble if it does not reflect it."[14] For thanks to the United States government, humanity is now reliving *The Peloponnesian War* in a thermonuclear age and on a global basis. That twenty-seven-year-long series of wars that were summed up by Thucydides into one cataclysm was the original Long War of Western civilization.

Will the Imperial American Republic suffer the same fate as the Imperial Athenian Democracy? Will World War III be far behind? Will humanity suffer the same fate as the dinosaurs? Will the Planet Earth become a radioactive wasteland?

The present danger is Hobbesian power politics. The only known antidote is international law, international organizations, and the peaceful settlement of international disputes. Otherwise the future of humankind will be left to the brutal and bloody hands of geopolitical Hobbists such as the realists, the neo-realists, and the neoconservatives.

In this thermonuclear age, humankind's existential choice is that stark, ominous, clear, and compelling. As global citizens we must not hesitate to apply this imperative anti-Hobbesian regimen immediately before it becomes too late for the entire world. There will be no International War Crimes Tribunal like Nuremberg after World War III. Only humankind's deafening silence for the rest of eternity—a Last Will and Testament to our cosmic folly. Humanity's future is in the hands of you, the reader.

ENDNOTES

1   *See* **F. Boyle**, *The Law of Power Politics*, 1980 **Univ. Ill. L** F. 901.

2   **T. Hobbes, Leviathan** 100 (M. Oakeshott ed. 1962).

3   *See* **F. Boyle**, *Neo-cons, Fundies, Feddies & Con-Artists*, **Atlantic Free Press**, April 3, 2010.

4   **Louis B. Zimmer, The Vietnam War Debate: Hans J. Morgenthau and the Attempt to Halt the Drift into Disaster** (2011)

5   *See* **F. Boyle, World Politics and International Law** (1985).

6   Indeed, I was most fortunate to have studied Professor Fuller's Casebook on **Contracts** for my entire first year course on that subject at Harvard Law School under the late Professor Philip Areeda during the 1971-1972 academic year. Then I later took Professor Fuller's course on *The Sociology of Law* that he had co-taught with Talcott Parsons during the 1975-1976 academic year.

7   **T. Hobbes, Leviathan** 128 (M. Oakeshott ed. 1962).

8   *See generally* **F. Boyle, Defending Civil Resistance Under International Law** (1987) *and* **Protesting Power: War, Resistance and Law** (2009).

9   *See also* **R. Keohane, After Hegemony** (1984); **International Regimes** (S. Krasner ed. 1982); Haggard & Simmons, *Theories of International Regimes*, 41 Int'l Org. 491 (1987).

10   *See* **F. Boyle**, *International Law and the Use of Force: Beyond Regime Theory*, **in Ideas and Ideals: Essays on Politics in Honor of Stanley**

Hoffmann 376 (L. Miller & M.J. Smith eds. 1993).

11   *See, e.g.,* **A. Chayes, The Cuban Missile Crisis** (1974).

12   *See* **F. Boyle**, **Destroying World Order** (2004) *and* **Breaking All the Rules** (2008).

13   **George Santayana**, I **The Life of Reason** 284 (1905).

14   **The Complete Writings of Thucydides: The Peloponnesian War** 14 (Modern Library College ed. 1951).

CHAPTER 2

THE CONFRONTATION BETWEEN THE REAGAN ADMINISTRATION AND LIBYA OVER THE GULF OF SIDRA AND TERRORISM

What Is Terrorism?

Upon its ascent to power in January of 1981, the Reagan administration forthrightly proclaimed its intention to replace President Carter's purported emphasis on human rights with a war against international terrorism as the keystone of its foreign policy.[1] The Reagan administration's specious argument was that terrorism constituted the ultimate denial of human rights and therefore, in a classic nonsequitur, somehow justified the renewal of military and economic assistance for the then repressive regimes in Argentina, Guatemala, Chile, and the Philippines,[2] as well as warranting the destabilization of Colonel Qaddafi's rule in Libya, among other such nefarious projects.[3] This inversion of priorities for the future conduct of American foreign policy was perversely misguided and should have been immediately repudiated by the American people.

"Terrorism" is a vacuous and amorphous concept entirely devoid of any accepted international legal meaning, let alone an objective political referent.[4] The standard cliché that "one man's terrorist is another man's freedom fighter" is not just a clever obfuscation of values. It indicates that the international community has yet to agree upon a legal or political meaning for the term "terrorism." For example, even the U.N. Ad Hoc Committee on International Terrorism could not agree upon a definition for the word "terrorism."[5] Yet due to the transnational character of "terrorist" violence, the establishment of multinational consensus and international cooperation is the only way that wanton attacks directed against innocent civilians around the world can be adequately combatted.[6]

The pejorative and highly inflammatory term "terrorism" has been used by the governments of the United States, Britain, the Soviet Union/Russia, Israel, and apartheid South Africa, among others, to characterize acts of violence ranging the spectrum of human and material destructiveness from common crimes to wars of national liberation. One state's invocation of a holy war against international terrorism may constitute effective governmental propaganda designed to manipulate public opinion into supporting a foreign policy of aggression premised on considerations such as Hobbesian power politics. But it cannot serve as the basis for conducting a coherent and consistent global foreign policy in a manner that protects and advances a state's legitimate national security interests in accordance with the requirements of international law.[7]

For example, the Reagan administration was elected in part on the specious claim that the Carter administration's general "softness" had been responsible for an alleged increase in international terrorist attacks during the latter's tenure. Thus, shortly after entering office, Director of Central Intelligence William Casey ordered the C.I.A. to conduct a study on international terrorism designed to document their unsubstantiated campaign rhetoric. But when finally produced, the C.I.A. study did not list enough terrorist incidents to support the administration's assertions. Not being content with the truth, Casey ordered the C.I.A. to change its definition of terrorism in a manner that would substantiate the Reagan administration's irresponsible claims. Whereupon the C.I.A. broadened its definition of "terrorism" and dutifully complied with Casey's ukase by issuing a new report that doubled the number of terrorist attacks documented in the previously rejected report.[8]

The truth of the matter was that starting in the mid-1970's there had occurred a significant decline in the number of so-called terrorist attacks against the United States by the various Palestinian groups operating out of the Middle East. This was because the United States government had worked very hard at the United Nations, the International Civil Aviation Organization, and the International Committee of the Red Cross (I.C.R.C.) negotiations at Geneva and in all other available forums to convince the P.L.O. as well as Arab states that terrorism was counterproductive in the sense that it would not help advance their cause but rather would retard it in the estimation of U.S. and European public opinion. By the end of the decade, that message had gotten through.[9]

Despite these serious reservations about the practical utility of employing the term "terrorism" and its numerous derivatives, I will use it here even though that term obscures more than it clarifies. For analytical purposes, I would prefer to talk about "transnational violence perpetrated by non-state actors against members of the civilian population for political reasons." Nevertheless, for want of a better term, I will use the words "terrorism" and "terrorists," but only because they have entered into popular acceptation, and always subject to the above reservations and qualifications. We must never forget that the overwhelming majority of terrorist acts—whether in number or in terms of sheer human and material destructiveness—have been committed by strong states against weak states, as well as by all governments against their own citizens: State Terrorism.

The Israeli Origins of the Reagan Administration's War Against International Terrorism

With the advent of the Reagan administration in 1981, the overall foreign policy of the United States government toward the Middle East dramatically changed. The Reagan administration became the most vigorously pro-Israeli government that had ever been experienced in the United States of America up to that point in time. Large numbers of the foreign affairs and defense appointees brought in by the Reagan administration were themselves ardent supporters of the state of Israel: the neoconservatives. Operating under the mistaken assumption that what was good for Israel was by definition good for the United States, they put the interests of Israel first and those of the United States second when it came to the formulation of American Middle East foreign policy.

The Israelis had always been arguing a very tough line against international terrorism even though, in fact, what they actually did was quite different from what they said they were doing. Although successive Israeli governments had said that a state should never negotiate with international terrorists, the fact of the matter was that Israeli leaders had always so negotiated when innocent Israeli lives were at stake. This is not to say that such negotiations occurred to the exclusion of or even in preference to the implementation of military options. But rather, that successive Israeli governments had always been willing to strike deals with known "international terrorists" if they believed there was a reasonably good chance that this would result in the safe release of their own people. When it came to the lives of their citizens, Israeli actions had always been far more humanitarian than Israeli words and propaganda.

Not so with the Reagan administration, which was so enamored of the tough Israeli rhetoric that it proceeded to pattern American Middle East foreign policy on what the Israelis said was their approach to fighting their war against international terrorism. Thus, under the aegis of the Reagan administration, America and the world witnessed the progressive Israelization of U.S. foreign policy toward the Middle East. The Reagan administration proceeded to adopt the same type of philosophy, rhetoric, tactics and at times illegal and reprehensible behavior that Israel's Begin/ Sharon government was then practicing against Arab states and peoples throughout the region.

But as my Professor of International Relations, Hans Morgenthau, was fond of saying about U.S. deference to the wishes of the South Vietnamese government: "This is a case of the tail wagging the dog!" The United States and Israel occupy very different positions concerning the means whereby to best secure their respective national interests and promote their different value systems. For the Reagan administration to have pursued a policy premised upon the illegal threat and use of military force simply turned America even further into a garrison state like Israel, especially in the Middle East.

Terrorism as a Response to the Invasion of Lebanon

The above considerations put into context the reason why there occurred a resurgence of so-called terrorist actions against U.S. citizens, and against airplanes, facilities, programs, etc. affiliated with the United States government located abroad during the tenure of the neoconservative Reagan administration. As a direct result of the 1982 Israeli invasion of Lebanon, more than 20,000 people were killed. The vast majority of the victims were Palestinians and Lebanese Muslims who were quite wantonly destroyed by means of weapons, equipment, supplies, money, and diplomatic and political support provided by the United States government to Israel and to the "Christian" Phalange militia during the course of the invasion and its aftermath. The Arab peoples of the Middle East held the United States government fully responsible for all atrocities against the civilian population of Lebanon that were undeniably perpetrated by the Israeli army and air force as well as the Phalange militia. Under basic principles of international law, they certainly had a perfect right to do so.

Common article 1 to the Four Geneva Conventions of 1949 required that a party to the Conventions such as the United States must not only "respect" the Conventions itself but also "ensure respect" for the terms of the Conventions by other contracting parties such as Israel "in all circumstances."[10] The United States government completely failed to perform its obligations under the Geneva Conventions to make sure that the Israelis obeyed the laws and customs of warfare during the course of their invasion of Lebanon by means of denying them access to U.S. weapons, equipment, and supplies. Indeed, from all the indications in the public record, it appeared that instead, the United States government consented and connived in advance to this illegal invasion.[11]

As a result of the 1982 Lebanon invasion, the entire P.L.O. infrastructure was destroyed and as a result, the ability of Arafat and his particular organization, Al Fatah, to control the other Palestinian groups was significantly diminished. These anti-Arafat Palestinian groups proceeded to undertake a series of terrorist attacks against U.S. interests around the Mediterranean that were launched from their respective headquarters in the Syrian-controlled Bekaa valley or in Damascus itself. In addition, the Shiites in Lebanon also proceeded to undertake terrorist attacks against Americans by means of hijacking airplanes, kidnapping U.S. citizens, assassinations, bombings and atrocities of this nature, whereas prior to Israel's 1982 invasion, the Shiite population of Lebanon had been basically quiescent. Thereafter, U.S. support for both the Israeli invasion and the latter's continued occupation of southern Lebanon provided the immediate reason why these devoutly religious people decided to fight back against the interests of the United States and Israel in whatever primitive manner they could. Hence Hezbollah became a national liberation movement.

The American people could not even begin to comprehend how to deal with the problem of international terrorism in the Middle East unless they first came to grips with the fact that the Reagan administration was directly responsible for the perpetration of one of the great international crimes in the post World War II era against the Palestinians and Muslim peoples in Lebanon. Only if America is willing to face up to its collective responsibility under international law for this crime against humanity can it then proceed to make some progress on the problem of international terrorism. Until that time, Americans will continue to become targets of attack by these frustrated and aggrieved individuals throughout the Middle East and the Mediterranean.

The Reagan Administration's War Against International Law

The Reagan administration pursued a unilateralist antiterrorism policy that was essentially predicated upon the illegal threat and use of U.S. military force in explicit and knowing violation of article 2(4) of the United Nations Charter.[12] Their preferred measures included military retaliation and reprisal, preemptive and preventive attacks, kidnapping suspected terrorists, hijacking aircraft in international airspace, destabilization of governments, fomenting military coups, assassinations, and indiscriminate bombings of civilian population centers, etc. Predictably, the results proved to be quite negligible in terms of accomplishing their purported objectives and most counterproductive for the purpose of maintaining international peace and security. Witness the needless deaths of over 300 U.S. marines and diplomats in Lebanon as a direct result of the Reagan administration's illegal military intervention into that country's civil war in order to prop-up a supposedly pro-Western regime that was imposed by the Israeli army. Both of the latter were guilty of inflicting barbarous outrages upon the Palestinians and Muslim peoples of Lebanon.

The foremost proponents of such reprehensible counterterrorism policies were Secretary of State George Shultz and his Legal Adviser, former U.S. federal district judge Abraham Sofaer. One of the great ironies of the Reagan administration proved to be the fact that its Secretary of State was consistently far more bellicose than its Secretary of Defense, Caspar Weinberger. Indeed, what little restraint that was demonstrated by the Reagan administration when it came to the illegal threat and use of military force generally originated from the Pentagon, not the State Department. Whenever Shultz failed to obtain his foreign policy objectives by means of diplomacy, his standard fallback position was to call for the threat and use of U.S. military force--whether in Lebanon, the Persian Gulf, Central America and the Caribbean, Libya, or to combat international terrorism.[13] If the U.S. government and American citizens became special targets for attack by international terrorist groups, this phenomenon was directly attributable in substantial part to the Reagan administration's primary reliance upon the illegal threat and use of military force as an ultimately self-defeating substitute for its bankrupt foreign policies--especially toward the Middle East.

The Perversity Behind the Shultz Doctrine

The operational premise behind the so-called Shultz Doctrine was that the Reagan administration should fight international terrorism by means of American sponsored counterterrorism. This rationale constituted a most pernicious assault upon the U.S. government's historical commitment to upholding the rules of international law and promoting the integrity of the international legal order. Just because some of the adversaries of the United States might pursue patently illegal policies in their conduct of belligerent hostilities provides absolutely no good reason why the American government should automatically do the exact same thing. The United States of America has to analyze the equation of international relations in light of both its own vital national security interests and its own cherished national values.

In particular, America cannot abandon or pervert its national values simply because its adversaries might not share them. Likewise, America cannot ignore its vital national interest in preserving the rules of international law and upholding the integrity of the international legal order simply because its adversaries might not share that exact same interest. If America mimics international terrorists, then America gradually becomes like them and eventually becomes indistinguishable from them in the eyes of its allies, friends, neutrals, and, most tragically of all, its own citizens. During the tenure of the Reagan administration, the United States government became just as terroristic and Hobbesian in its conduct of foreign affairs as many of America's international adversaries undoubtedly were.

The Sofaer Corollary

The paradigmatic example of the Reagan administration's mirror-image reasoning process with respect to international terrorism was provided by the then new Legal Adviser to the United States government in a speech he gave before a plenary session of the American Society of International Law Convention devoted to the World Court on April 10, 1986, shortly after President Reagan had decided to bomb the Libyan cities of Tripoli and Benghazi.[14] There former Judge Abraham Sofaer did his best to justify a perverse innovation in the theory of international law and the practice of international relations: namely, that the United States government possesses some god-given right to resort to the use of military force in alleged self-defense as unilaterally determined by itself alone.

In light of the fact that earlier that same day the Society had commemorated the Fortieth Anniversary of the Nuremberg Tribunal, it was striking and indeed saddening that the Legal Adviser was making an argument similar to that put forth in defense of the Nazi war criminals before the Nuremberg Tribunal in 1945 with respect to the non-applicability of the Kellogg-Briand Pact of 1928.[15] This "Paris Peace Pact" had formally renounced war as an instrument of national policy. However, when signing the Pact, Germany entered a reservation to the effect that it reserved the right to go to war in self-defense as determined by itself. So when in 1945 the Nazi war criminals were indicted for crimes against peace on the basis of the Kellogg-Briand Pact, they basically argued that the Second World War was a war of self-defense as determined by the German government, and therefore that the Nuremberg Tribunal had no competence to determine otherwise because of Germany's self-judging reservation. Needless to say, the Tribunal summarily rejected this preposterous argument and later convicted and sentenced to death several Nazi war criminals for the commission of crimes against peace, among other international crimes. Seven decades after Nuremberg, the critical question becomes whether America will preserve its fundamental commitment to the rule of law both at home and abroad, or abandon all pretense of honoring the rule of law, whatsoever.

The Hypocrisy Behind the Reagan Administration's Antiterrorism War Against Libya

Starting in January of 1981 a lot of hot air had been expended in the United States about how the American government should best deal with the so-called problem of international terrorism. Most of this discourse was completely self-serving. The Reagan administration proceeded to act in a manner similar to that of a doctor treating only the symptoms of a disease, rather than the root causes of the disease itself. For example, if the United States government seriously wished to alleviate the interrelated problems created by international terrorist actions directed against American interests around the world, then the first and most effective step it could have taken in this direction would have been to finally implement the international legal right of the Palestinian people to self-determination and a state of their own. Further, all the vices, defects, and hypocrisies characteristic of the Reagan rhetoric on terrorism can be demonstrated by reference to its aggressive actions toward Libya from the very outset of the former's tenure in office.[16] The outstanding series of crises between the United States and Libya over the latter's alleged support for international terrorism presents the paradigmatic example of the fatally flawed and dissembling nature of the Reagan administration's self-styled war against international terrorism.

On January 7, 1986 President Reagan conducted a news conference in which he announced that sanctions were being taken against Libya because there existed "conclusive" evidence that Colonel Qaddafi was involved in two terrorist attacks that occurred on December 27 near El Al ticket counters at airports in Rome and Vienna, resulting in the loss of twenty lives, five of whom were American.[17] The commandos killed in Rome carried notes justifying the attack as a reprisal for the Israeli air raid on the P.L.O. headquarters near Tunis in August of 1985, which in turn was justified as a reprisal for the P.L.O. assassination of Israeli "tourists" in Cyprus. This latter incident was, in turn, justified on the grounds that the so-called tourists were really Mossad agents monitoring the movement of P.L.O. fighters from Cyprus to Lebanon for the purpose of directing Israeli naval operations designed to intercept them on the high seas.[18] Etc., ad infinitum and ad nauseam.

President Reagan claimed that while responsibility for the Rome and Vienna attacks "lies squarely" with the Abu Nidal organization (whomever it *really* worked for!), "these murderers could not carry out their crimes without the sanctuary and support provided by regimes such as Col. Qaddafi's in Libya."[19] Consequently, the President ordered that all economic transactions between the United States and Libya essentially be terminated and that all Americans living or working there must leave by February 1 upon pain of criminal prosecution.[20] The next day the President ordered a freeze of Libyan assets held in the United States as well as Libyan assets held in subsidiaries of U.S. banks located abroad.[21] Somewhat curiously, however, an exemption from this economic pullout was later given to U.S. oil companies doing business in Libya, though under public pressure it was later withdrawn effective June 30.[22]

Destroying Libya and World Order

All of this transpired in an atmosphere of increasingly bitter rhetoric between the two countries. The Reagan administration immediately dispatched two aircraft carrier task forces to the Gulf of Sidra and Colonel Qaddafi responded by stating that in the event of an armed attack upon Libya he would send suicide squads into the streets of the United States to strike targets there.[23] Perhaps the lowest point in the public debate was reached by Senator Howard Metzenbaum when he suggested in a television interview that the United States government should give serious consideration to assassinating Colonel Qaddafi.[24] Little did he know that the Reagan administration had already decided affirmatively to do so.[25]

After two sets of U.S. naval maneuvers outside the Gulf of Sidra during January and February of 1986, and with the arrival of a third naval task force organized around the aircraft carrier *America*, the Reagan administration was finally prepared to penetrate the Gulf of Sidra south of the closing line which Libya had drawn across its mouth at 32°30" in 1973.[26] This calculated decision precipitated a military conflict between the United States and Libya on March 24, 1986 that lasted over a period of three days and resulted in the successive destruction of two Libyan naval craft, one SAM-5 missile site, and the loss of approximately thirty Libyan sailors.

Shortly after the completion of this U.S. military action against Libya, a bomb exploded on a T.W.A. commercial passenger jetliner flying between Rome and Athens, killing four Americans. The group that took responsibility for the bomb attack called it an act of retaliation for U.S. military aggression against Libya, though no evidence established a Libyan connection to this attack and U.S. officials expressed doubt that Libya had ordered the bombing.[27] This was followed by the explosion of a bomb at a discotheque in West Berlin frequented by American soldiers, resulting in the death of two U.S. servicemen and a Turkish woman as well as injuries to scores of other U.S. soldiers.[28] The Reagan administration promptly blamed Colonel Qaddafi for this latest anti-American attack, and ordered two U.S. aircraft carrier battle groups back to the Gulf of Sidra for further action.[29]

On April 14, 1986, the Reagan administration launched a bombing run against various targets in and near Tripoli and Benghazi, the two major metropolitan areas in Libya, by means of U.S. Air Force bombers stationed in England and U.S. naval aircraft from the carriers off the Gulf of Sidra.[30] The nighttime attack (occurring at 2:00 a.m. April 15, Libyan time) utilized British-based F-111 bombers equipped with "terrain avoidance radar" that were accompanied by EF-111 electronic jamming planes.[31] The 18 F-111s were refueled four times in flight by KC-10 and KC-135 fuel tankers during their 2,800 nautical mile journey. A circuitous route down the eastern coast of Europe and through the Straits of Gibraltar was necessitated by the fact that the governments of France and Spain had refused overflight permission.[32]

While the F-111s approached Tripoli, A-6 bombers and A-7 and F-18 attack aircraft from the U.S.S. *America* and *Coral Sea* stationed near the Gulf of Sidra prepared to attack targets in Benghazi. These naval aircraft fired dozens of Shrike and high-speed antiradiation missiles (HARMS) to destroy the radar capabilities of Libyan antiaircraft batteries, while the EF-111s jammed Libyan electronic defenses. Laser-guided "smart bombs" fired from the F-111s and the A-6s struck at five targets around Tripoli and Benghazi, including the home and headquarters of Qaddafi at the El Azziziya barracks in Tripoli. Reports indicated that the damage inflicted in these attacks actually could have been much greater in as much as seven of the 32 attacking aircraft aborted their missions. One F-111 and its two-member crew were reported to have been the only casualties experienced by U.S. forces during this operation.[33]

These attacks resulted in the deaths of approximately 40 people and injury to approximately 200 more, almost all of whom were civilians.[34] In response to the severity of these bombing raids, various terrorist groups in the Middle East and Europe took vengeance upon the United States and Great Britain. In the aftermath of the April raid, these groups carried out a fairly large number of bombings, assassinations, and armed attacks against American and British citizens, diplomatic missions, and business interests around the world: the shooting of an American communications specialist at the U.S. embassy in the Sudan; the shooting deaths of two British school teachers and an American near Beirut; the abduction of a London-based Worldwide Television News bureau chief in Beirut; the thwarted bombing attempt of an El Al airplane about to leave London's Heathrow airport for Tel Aviv; and a firebombing incident at a U.S. Marine compound in Tunis, among others.[35]

Thus, haughty predictions uttered by members of the U.S. government that the bombings of Tripoli and Benghazi would somehow reduce the incidence of terrorist attacks against Americans proved to be wrong.[36] In direct reaction thereto, the Reagan administration decided to maintain U.S. aircraft carrier task forces in the vicinity of the Gulf of Sidra for the indefinite future.[37] These task forces and their complement of aircraft continued to engage in provocative military maneuvers near, in, and around Libya and the Gulf of Sidra.[38]

Prior to all these events, I had spent one week in Libya as a guest during May of 1985 to discuss the current state of U.S.-Libyan relations and what if anything could be done to improve them. Most probably, I had been one of the very few professional American academics to have so visited Libya for this purpose since the Reagan administration invalidated U.S. passports for travel to that country in December of 1981.[39] Although having traveled to Libya in a manner that was explicitly approved by a State Department letter to me, for obvious reasons I did not wish to draw much attention to the fact that I had been there. Nevertheless, in light of the ominous development of events that occurred between the United States and Libya after Rome and Vienna, in mid-January of 1986 I decided to break my silence and publicly offered whatever insights I might have been able to shed upon the then escalating crisis in U.S.-Libyan relations.[40] I started a one-man national campaign to prevent the looming major military attack against Libya by the Reagan administration. I failed.

Both at the time and in retrospect, it was obvious that the Reagan administration purposely moved toward initiating this major military confrontation with Qaddafi, and utilized whatever pretexts it could invent under international law and otherwise to justify such provocative measures to the American people in a bid to obtain their active support for an undeclared or even formal war. There existed no justification for this belligerent policy under basic principles of international law, and no underlying rationale according to fundamental considerations of U.S. national security interests. Direct U.S. military action against Libya only proved to be counterproductive in terms of maintaining international peace and security in the Middle East; of mobilizing currently existing forms of Libyan internal opposition to Qaddafi; and of avoiding a potential military confrontation between the United States and the Soviet Union in the Mediterranean. U.S. military intervention to destroy Qaddafi proved to be a monumental blunder for the future course of American foreign policy toward Arab states and Muslim peoples around the world.

To put it bluntly, whatever benefit might be derived therefrom, the overthrow of Colonel Qaddafi was not worth the life of even one U.S. serviceman, let alone the two men America already lost in April of 1986. I challenged any member of the Reagan administration to elaborate a rational and convincing argument to the contrary without blustering about some U.S. god-given imperative to destroy international terrorism despite the rules of international law. As the Reagan administration's aggressive policy toward Libya proceeded unchecked by the American people, the Gulf of Sidra could have readily become the 1986 equivalent of the Gulf of Tonkin.

The 1981 Gulf of Sidra Incident

The first point that must be kept in mind with respect to developing any sound comprehension of the prolonged crises in U.S.-Libyan relations was that the Reagan administration had been attempting to overthrow Qaddafi since the former came into power in January of 1981.[41] One of the very first projects ever submitted by C.I.A. Director William Casey to the Congressional Committee dealing with the oversight of intelligence activities and covert operations was a plan to overthrow Qaddafi.[42] To the best of my knowledge, that had been standing U.S. policy since the Reagan administration came into office, and they attempted to carry out this illegal endeavor both directly by themselves and indirectly by means of working with various Libyan exile groups around the world,[43] as well as by fomenting numerous internal military coups against Qaddafi.[44]

This fact puts into context claims by the Reagan administration that Qaddafi sponsored assassination attacks against Libyan exiles around the world, including in the United States. In light of the previous history of U.S. supported coups, one could not blame Qaddafi for believing that the Reagan administration's obvious and admitted attempt to overthrow him would include within that plan his murder or assassination. In this regard, witness what had already happened to Diem in Vietnam, Lumumba in the Congo, Allende in Chile, the Kennedy administration's numerous attempts to assassinate Castro, and more recently, repeated attempts to assassinate leaders of the Sandinista government in Nicaragua following the strategy outlined by the Reagan administration in its infamous *Contra "Psyops" Manual.* If the Reagan administration really would have liked to have seen an end to so-called terrorist attacks against Libyan exiles in the capitals of Europe that it attributed to Libya, then perhaps it should have first terminated its plan to overthrow, murder, and assassinate Qaddafi and using such groups as a means toward that end.

At this point in the analysis it becomes necessary to understand what happened back in the summer of 1981 during the first Gulf of Sidra incident if we want to comprehend the later stages of the outstanding series of crises between the United States and Libya.[45] As mentioned above, one of the very first steps undertaken by the Reagan administration upon its assumption of power was to adopt a plan calling for the overthrow of Qaddafi. As part of that plan, it contemporaneously reversed the Carter administration's policy of not sending the Sixth Fleet into the Gulf of Sidra in order to forcefully contest the Libyan's claim to treat the latter as "internal waters."[46]

Pursuant thereto, in February of 1981 the Reagan administration began planning for Sixth Fleet military maneuvers to be held that summer, this time below 32°30' north latitude, the so-called "line of death" described by Qaddafi.[47] As one Reagan administration official put it, they decided to penetrate the Gulf "because the principle of the open seas is important--and because we wanted to tweak Qaddafi's nose."[48] The 1981 Gulf of Sidra incident was a clear-cut military provocation by the Reagan administration that was purposefully designed to provoke Qaddafi into a major military conflict in the hope and expectation that a decisive defeat could initiate a military coup that would result in Qaddafi's deposition.

As best as can be reconstructed from the public record and my research in Libya, what happened in the summer of 1981 was this: The Sixth Fleet was ordered to go on maneuvers into the Gulf of Sidra. It proceeded into what the Libyans claim to be their internal waters, and the United States government called high seas. The validity of their respective claims under international law will be analyzed below. Suffice it to say here that the Libyans were especially concerned by the fact that the U.S. ships and then later their fighter aircraft were sent upon hostile military maneuvers in the direction of the major Libyan oil installations located around the southern rim of the Gulf. Of course oil represents Libya's only major economic resource apart from underground water.[49]

The Reagan strategy was that Libya would be forced to defend itself against this hostile military threat by sending up its entire air force to combat the Sixth Fleet and its accompanying aircraft, whereupon the Sixth Fleet would easily destroy the entire Libyan air force, thus precipitating an internal military coup against Qaddafi, who was not in the country at the time. The former task could have been easily accomplished by utilizing the same type of sophisticated technology that the Israeli government successfully employed during its 1982 invasion of Lebanon to destroy most of the Syrian air force in one afternoon without experiencing any casualties in return.[50] In this regard the so-called Hawkeye command plane would have had the most critical role to play in vectoring U.S. jet fighters against enemy aircraft before the latter were even aware that they were under attack. Despite the Reagan administration's fatuous claims to the contrary, such aircraft do not simply serve a surveillance purpose, but represent a formidable offensive threat.

But the Libyans were smart enough not to fall into Reagan's trap. Instead, they marshalled their airplanes above the cities of Tripoli and Benghazi as well as over the oil fields, waiting for a U.S. attack to occur. Keeping the Libyan aircraft over land would afford them some protection by the short-range Soviet surface-to-air missiles then in the possession of the Libyans, whereas a fight over the Gulf of Sidra would have pitted clearly inferior Libyan jet fighters directly against advanced American fighter aircraft under the supervision of the Hawkeye system.

As the fabled F-14 Tomcats approached to within approximately 30 miles of the Libyan coastline and oil installations, Libya apparently sent out two Sukhoi jet fighters to intercept them and ward them off from engaging in any further penetration of disputed Libyan airspace. It was those two Libyan planes that were shot down by the Tomcats in a totally unequal fight. Yet the Libyans could still not be provoked and continued to hold the rest of their planes in reserve over land. It was Libya's wise decision not to be drawn into an all-out fight with Sixth Fleet aircraft above the Gulf of Sidra that led to the termination of the crisis at this particular point in time.[51]

I should point out that the United States government itself maintains an air defense identification zone (ADIZ) around its own borders, in some places extending outward three hundred miles from its shores.[52] Therein any unidentified aircraft will be intercepted by U.S. jet fighters and escorted out of this zone, or forced to land, or else presumably destroyed. Based upon its own precedent, the U.S. government was estopped to deny that Libya had a right to do the exact same thing, especially in order to protect its vital oil fields from imminent threatened destruction. After all, both the United States government and several other members of the international community claim the right to establish such air security zones on the grounds of "national security" despite the provisions of the Chicago Convention to the contrary.[53] Sauce for the goose is sauce for the gander.

Who Fired First?

The Reagan administration's account of the aerial combat between U.S. and Libyan fighters over the Gulf of Sidra in the summer of 1981 defied credulity.[54] First, all military analysts agreed that the Tomcats completely outclassed the Sukhois in all relevant military characteristics. It would have been a suicide mission--pure and simple--for the Libyan Sukhois to have fired first upon the American Tomcats. Despite Qaddafi's rhetoric as well as propaganda by the Reagan administration to the contrary, the vast majority of Libyan people are not "Muslim fanatics" who are prepared to commit suicide attacks in the pious expectation that this will gain them immediate entry into Paradise.

Second, the Reagan administration's claim that the Sukhois fired first upon the Tomcats is highly suspect. The Reagan administration's account runs to the effect that the Sukhois fired their heat-seeking missiles first while directly approaching the Tomcats. But it would make no sense at all to fire heat-seeking missiles in the direction of oncoming aircraft. Normally, such missiles have to be fired *behind*, not in front of, enemy aircraft in order to have any chance at all of homing onto their target. Moreover, it is also extremely doubtful that the Sukhois could have been able to maneuver behind the superior Tomcats, and the Reagan account never said they attempted to do so. In the unlikely event that they had even tried, due to the superior performance and sophisticated technological defenses of the Tomcats, it would have been extraordinarily difficult for the Sukhois first to have outmaneuvered and then to have destroyed the Tomcats. Hence all the more reason for the Sukhoi pilots *not* to have fired first upon the Tomcats.

Irrespective of who fired first, the vectoring of Tomcats in attack formation toward the Libyan oil installations around the Gulf of Sidra constituted a clear-cut violation of article 2(4) of the United Nations

Charter prohibiting the threat or use of force against the territorial integrity or political independence of a state. The U.S. provocation also violated the article 2(3) requirement that it settle this dispute with Libya over the status of the Gulf of Sidra in a peaceful manner. Under these circumstances, the Libyans had a perfect right to defend themselves by necessary and proportionate means against this U.S. "armed attack" or, to follow the French version of the Charter, "armed aggression" under article 51 thereof.

Use It or Lose It?

Whatever the legal merits of the Gulf of Sidra dispute between the United States and Libya, international law certainly provided no justification for the Reagan administration to have continually sent the Sixth Fleet in there in order to provoke a military confrontation for the expressed purpose of overthrowing Colonel Qaddafi. The argument by the Reagan administration that it had to send the fleet into the Gulf periodically in order to demonstrate that the United States government did not recognize Libya's claim to the Gulf was utter nonsense. When the Libyans attempted to draw a closing line across the Gulf of Sidra back in 1973, the United States government publicly stated that it would not recognize the legal validity of this action. Under contemporary standards of international law, that was certainly enough to preserve whatever rights of access the U.S. government might purportedly have to the Gulf of Sidra.

The Reagan administration nevertheless attempted to justify such provocative military maneuvers by relying upon the alleged customary international law doctrine popularly known as "use-it-or-lose-it."[55] Yet, whatever validity and meaning this alleged doctrine might have had prior to the promulgation of the United Nations Charter in 1945, it can no longer be construed in a manner to authorize hostile military action in explicit violation of articles 2(3) and 2(4). Undaunted by such legal technicalities, the Reagan administration quite consistently and most disingenuously invoked this pre-Charter doctrine in order to spread a thin veneer of legal respectability around its otherwise belligerent policies for the consumption of U.S. domestic and international public opinion.

Article 33 of the United Nations Charter enunciates the basic rule of customary international law that parties to any dispute likely to endanger international peace and security must first exhaust all peaceful means to achieve a solution. This requirement would include negotiation, enquiry, mediation, conciliation, arbitration or judicial settlement, among other such procedures. The dispute between the United States and Libya over the Gulf of Sidra was a clear-cut legal issue that could have been easily resolved by the International Court of Justice or by an international arbitration tribunal. But the Reagan administration willfully rejected all overtures made by Qaddafi to peacefully settle the longstanding crises between the United States and Libya over the Gulf of Sidra as well as his alleged support for international terrorism.[56]

A World Court Option

Indeed, despite the fact that the official Libyan position was that the Gulf of Sidra was part of their sovereign territory and therefore its status was not susceptible to international adjudication or arbitration, one of the reasons for which I was invited to Libya in 1985 was to discuss the potential for Libya to bring a complaint against the United States in the International Court of Justice over this matter. Such a lawsuit would have required Libya to have accepted the compulsory jurisdiction of the World Court under article 36(2) of its Statute, to which the United States government was a party at the time.[57] If this had occurred, Libya could have proceeded against the United States under Statute article 36(2)(b), which gives the Court jurisdiction in all legal disputes concerning "any question of international law." Here the narrow issue would have been whether or not Libya was entitled to claim the Gulf of Sidra as internal waters.

In addition, the Libyans could have also sought from the World Court an indication of provisional measures of protection under Statute article 41 to the effect that the United States government would be obligated to refrain from any threat or use of force in order to contest the Libyan claim to the Gulf of Sidra while the matter was *sub judice*. In this regard, the World Court's previous indication of provisional measures in the *Nicaragua* case was directly on point.[58] I explained to the Libyans that the World Court's indication of provisional measures in the *Nicaragua* case played an important role in the internal debate within the United States over restraining the Reagan administration's military aggression against Nicaragua, particularly with respect to inhibiting funding for the *contras* by Congress. There was no guarantee that the same would happen with respect to Libya, a far more difficult case in the estimation of U.S. public opinion. Nevertheless, a World Court suit along these lines was at least worth a try since the Reagan administration clearly intended to take further military action against Libya by means of using the disputed status of the Gulf of Sidra as a pretext.

At the time of my visit, the Libyans were quite skeptical that the Reagan administration could be expected to live up to any World Court decision. This was because of the latter's January 15, 1985 decision to withdraw from any further proceedings in the *Nicaragua* case because of the Court's 26 November 1984 determination that it did indeed have jurisdiction to entertain Nicaragua's complaint against the United States on the merits.[59] For the same reason, in October of 1985, the Reagan administration then completely repudiated the compulsory jurisdiction of the International Court of Justice, rendering my proposed lawsuit against it by Libya over the Gulf of Sidra impossible under I.C.J. Statute article 36(2)(b).[60]

By contrast, the Libyans had a fairly good track record at submitting disputes to the International Court of Justice. In the recent past, for example, Libya had settled disputes with Malta and Tunisia over the delimitation of their respective continental shelves by means of World Court adjudication.[61] In a similar vein, it would have been possible for the United States government to have offered to conclude a *compromis* with Libya for the submission of the dispute over the status of the Gulf of Sidra to the International Court of Justice under article 36(1) of its Statute. But the odds of this occurring during the Reagan administration were infinitesimal precisely because the latter wished to preserve an outstanding dispute over the Gulf of Sidra as a convenient pretext for renewing direct military action against Libya for the purpose of overthrowing Qaddafi whenever deemed expedient.

The Status of the Gulf of Sidra

When I visited Libya in May of 1985, I told the Libyans that the Reagan administration clearly intended to attack them again in the event that another pretext could be found. I cautioned that although they certainly had a perfect right to defend themselves under international law, in the event Reagan provoked them, they should not engage in any type of counter-provocations against Reagan because he was an extremely dangerous man. The Reagan administration would only use their counter-provocations in order to escalate tensions into major overt hostilities that they were not really in much of a position to defend themselves against. In my opinion at the time, the immediate pretext for another U.S. attack upon Libya would be over the Gulf of Sidra. The Libyans claimed that they have a right to draw what international lawyers call a closing line across the headlands of the Gulf of Sidra and therefore treat the Gulf as their internal waters, not as high seas or even territorial waters. Under international law, internal waters are treated just as if they were an integral part of the land and are completely subject to the territorial sovereignty of the coastal state.[62] The same would be true for airspace above internal waters.

Thus, there is no right of "innocent passage" through internal waters. This would be in contrast to the territorial sea, where international law does recognize a right of innocent passage.[63] But even this latter right would not include within its scope the Sixth Fleet on maneuvers or transiting in any manner designed to threaten the security or independence of the coastal state as it had repeatedly done to Libya.[64] Moreover, there is no right of innocent passage for U.S. jet fighters to transit the airspace above the territorial sea of another state for any reason.

The Libyans claimed, and the United States recognized their right to claim, a twelve mile territorial sea. Hence, according to the Libyan claim, the Sixth Fleet, including its aircraft, would only be able to traverse the high seas that are located twelve miles seaward of the closing line drawn across the Gulf of Sidra.[65] It would not be "innocent passage" for the Sixth Fleet to maneuver through these territorial waters, and there would certainly be no right for U.S. fighter aircraft to penetrate the column of airspace above these territorial waters for any reason. And even when U.S. battleships and fighter aircraft went on hostile maneuvers outside the Gulf on the high seas and in international airspace as recognized by Libya, this still constituted a blatant violation of article 2(4) of the U.N. Charter since such maneuvers represented a threat of force directed against Libya's territorial integrity (i.e., the Gulf of Sidra as internal waters) and political independence (i.e., the overthrow of Qaddafi).

On the other hand, the United States government took the position that the Libyans were not entitled to draw a closing line across the Gulf of Sidra because it would, simply put, violate the closure rules enunciated in article 7 of the 1958 Geneva Convention on the Territorial Sea and Contiguous Zone.[66] Unfortunately for the Reagan administration's argument, Libya was not a party to that Convention and, unlike the Geneva Convention on the High Seas of 1958, the former Convention does not even purport that it is simply declaratory of customary international law on this subject. Moreover, article 7(6) of the Territorial Sea Convention expressly exempts "historic bays" and "historic waters" from its closure rules.

According to the U.S. interpretation of international law, the Libyan territorial sea would basically extend out seaward for twelve miles from around the coast along the rim of the Gulf of Sidra. Correlatively, the rest of the Gulf would constitute high seas in which the Sixth Fleet and its jet fighters would be able to traverse, maneuver, and engage in whatever types of provocative military operations it wanted. In this regard the best the Reagan administration could argue with respect to the obvious articles 2(3) and 2(4) violations was the customary international law doctrine of "use-it-or-lose-it." Even this argument would not include the right to launch military aircraft on hostile maneuvers in the general direction of Libyan oil fields so long as they allegedly do not approach to within twelve miles of the land.

Of course, the United States government itself would never put up with this type of provocative military behavior on the part of any other state. As mentioned before, America has established air defense identification zones (ADIZ) around the country whereby it unilaterally claims the right to regulate any aircraft that approaches to within a certain distance of its territory despite the fact that under the Chicago Convention U.S. airspace only extends to the column of air above its claimed territorial sea, which at the time was three miles. On December 28, 1988 President Reagan unilaterally extended the breadth of U.S. territorial waters from 3 to 12 miles. Moreover, it is clear that the United States government would never tolerate any foreign state, let alone a superpower, engaging in provocative naval maneuvers and potentially hostile air operations right in the middle of a large bay thoroughly enclosed on three sides by U.S. territory in close proximity to major strategic-economic facilities during a crisis situation or otherwise.

The Doctrine of Historic Bays/Waters

The way the United States government has traditionally prevented this from happening is to draw a closing line between the headlands of such bays on the basis of the customary international law doctrine known as "historic bays" or "historic waters."[67] Under this doctrine, generally put, if the coastal state can prove that it has traditionally treated the bay as if it were an integral part of the land, then it would be entitled to draw a closing line across the mouth of the bay even if it exceeded whatever are the internationally recognized criteria for drawing such closing lines. Thus it could treat the bay as internal waters, that is, as if it were part of the land. Hence the historic bay would be completely subject to the coastal state's sovereign control and there would be no right of innocent passage across it for ships or aircraft from other states. Thus, for example, in the case of the United States coast, the territorial sea would have been measured three miles (later twelve miles) seaward of the closing line across the historic bay or historic waters.

The doctrine of historic bays/waters has been used by the United States government to enclose bodies of water that exceeded two times the breadth of America's claimed territorial sea on both its Atlantic and Pacific coasts.[68] In addition, the existence of this doctrine as a matter of customary international law has also been expressly recognized by decision of the United States Supreme Court.[69] It is also recognized in article 7(6) of the 1958 Geneva Convention on the Territorial Sea and Contiguous Zone, to which the United States is a party though Libya is not.[70] Nevertheless this latter fact is irrelevant because the doctrine of historic bays/waters is a well known principle of customary international law that Libya would have been entitled to rely upon in any event.[71]

I do not at this point wish to express a definitive opinion at all as to whether or not the Libyans were entitled to draw that closing line across of Gulf of Sidra. But I do wish to point out that they certainly had a plausible claim to draw that closing line under well recognized principles of international law that had been fully subscribed to by the United States government itself. This is a straight-out legal question that could have easily been resolved by the International Court of Justice or by an international arbitration tribunal.

For example, the World Court readily dealt with a similar problem in the *Norwegian Fisheries Case*.[72] This litigation concerned the question of whether Norway was entitled to draw a straight base line system around the outside of the islands surrounding its indented coastline and treat the waters between the coast and the baselines as its internal waters under the doctrine of historic waters.[73] The World Court held that under the circumstances there involved Norway was entitled to establish its straight base line system.

Thus, the disputed status of the Gulf of Sidra could have provided no legitimate excuse for the United States government to send the Sixth Fleet into the Gulf on hostile maneuvers in the general direction of Libya's main economic resources located in the oil fields. If the Reagan administration had been sincerely interested in settling the dispute over the legal status of the Gulf of Sidra in a peaceful manner, I suspect the Libyans might have been prepared to consider a proposal that both sides conclude a *compromis* specifically submitting the matter for resolution to the International Court of Justice, or to a mutually acceptable international arbitration tribunal.

Undoubtedly, Libya would have demanded that the scope of the *compromis* be broadened to include U.S. military actions against it from January through April of 1986. But if the Reagan administration truly believed that its policies toward Libya during those months genuinely comported with the requirements of international law (as it vigorously maintained in public) and that it had "conclusive" or "irrefutable" evidence of Qaddafi's sponsorship for international terrorism (the intelligence source for which had already been admittedly compromised), then it should have been happy to submit the entire outstanding conflicts between the United States and Libya over international terrorism and the status of the Gulf of Sidra to the International Court of Justice. But the chance of that happening was substantially less than the slight possibility that the Reagan administration would have actually obeyed the World Court's final decision on the merits in favor of Nicaragua that was rendered on June 27, 1986.[74]

Indeed, Libya publicly offered to submit the Reagan administration's allegations of its sponsorship for international terrorism to the International Court of Justice or to any other mutually acceptable international tribunal and to pay damages if a judgment were rendered against it.[75] The only way to have tested the Libyans on these points would have been to make them a fair and reasonable offer. But in my opinion, the primary reason why the Reagan administration did not want to do this was to preserve the Gulf of Sidra and the cause of "international terrorism" as convenient pretexts over which it could easily provoke Qaddafi into a military conflict for the purpose of overthrowing him. The adamant refusal of the Reagan administration to pursue any means for the peaceful settlement of these disputes with Libya simply betrayed the fact that it never proceeded in good faith on such matters.

Planning for War

The validity of this latter proposition can be demonstrated by reference to the 1986 Gulf of Sidra incident, the planning for which can be traced to the summer of 1985. It has now been revealed that in July of that year a meeting of the National Security Council determined that another round of forceful military action was to be taken by the U.S. government for the purpose of overthrowing Colonel Qaddafi. Pursuant thereto, Admiral Poindexter, then the Deputy National Security Adviser and later the President's National Security Adviser, traveled to Egypt over Labor Day weekend in order to convince President Hosni Mubarak to invade Libya as part of a joint military action in conjunction with the United States.[76]

The Reagan theory was that since they had been unable to overthrow Qaddafi in a coup, the only way that he could be physically eliminated from power would be by an outright armed invasion. Since the number of U.S. military forces that could be brought to bear directly on the situation would not be sufficient to do the job, the U.S. government would have to rely upon the Egyptian army to do America's dirty work for it. Remember that former Egyptian President Anwar Sadat had invaded Libya once before in 1977 with the approval of the allegedly nonbelligerent Carter administration.[77]

As best as can be gleaned from the public record, the Reagan administration made repeated overtures throughout the fall of 1985 to get the Egyptians to go along with this hare-brained scheme. Pursuant thereto, it launched a policy of escalating political, economic, and military measures against Libya in order to prepare the way for the Libyan military establishment to overthrow Qaddafi. Thus, when Colonel Qaddafi failed to attend the fortieth commemorative session of the United Nations General Assembly in October of 1985, the Reagan administration contended he feared to leave the country because of the threat of an internal military coup. Nothing could have been further from the truth. At the time, Qaddafi rather feared that he would be assassinated either in New York or on his way to or from United Nations Headquarters by the C.I.A. or Libyan exile groups working in conjunction with them. *I had personally so advised Colonel Qaddafi not to attend for that reason.*

The proof of this matter was that while the U.N. commemorative session was taking place, Qaddafi flew to Moscow where he requested the further provision of military assistance from the Soviet Union in return for increased shipments of Libyan oil.[78] Shortly thereafter, it was revealed in the *Washington Post* that the Reagan administration was indeed taking steps to overthrow Qaddafi, and the President expressed his great irritation at whoever was responsible for this leak to the press.[79]

Immediately thereafter, America witnessed the military results of Qaddafi's visit to Moscow. The Soviet government finally responded affirmatively to Qaddafi's outstanding request for the emplacement of longer-range Soviet SAM-5's around the Gulf of Sidra, which were put under the operation and control of Soviet troops.[80] The impetus for this request went back to the first Gulf of Sidra military confrontation between the United States and Libya during the summer of 1981. Given this prior incident and the reports of a newly authorized U.S. intervention, Qaddafi had every right under international law to secure such SAM-5s in order to defend Libya from renewed U.S. military aggression. Likewise, the Soviets had a perfect legal justification to give Qaddafi the SAM-5s pursuant to the right of collective self-defense recognized by article 51 of the United Nations Charter.

The Reagan administration's importunate overtures toward Egypt eventually resulted in the production of a plan calling for joint military action by the United States and Egypt against Libya toward the end of 1985. This military operation would have involved a ground invasion by Egyptian troops, supported by air, logistical and communications assistance from the United States. One version of events maintained that Egyptian President Hosni Mubarak stubbornly refused to go along with these U.S. invasion plans despite vigorous support for them by his Defense Minister, General Abu-Ghazala. Another theory had it that Egypt apparently cancelled the invasion plans in October of 1985 because of the Reagan administration's incredibly stupid and counterproductive decision to have a U.S. jet fighter aircraft hijack an Egyptian passenger plane carrying the hijackers of the *Achille Lauro* cruiseship on their way for trial in Tunisia for the murder of Leon Klinghoffer despite the advice of Defense Secretary Weinberger and in explicit and knowing violation of basic rules of international law.[81] In any event, the U.S. public's overwhelmingly favorable reaction to this blatant example of aerial piracy probably encouraged the Reagan administration to go ahead with its longstanding plans to depose Qaddafi by means of unilateral military action, if possible, on the basis of the first pretext that could be found. This, of course, became the impetus for laying the blame for the infamous terrorist attacks at the Rome and Vienna airports on December 27, 1985 on Libya .

ENDNOTES

1   At a Jan. 27, 1981 press conference, Secretary of State Alexander Haig declared: "International terrorism will take the place of human rights . . . The greatest problem to me in the human-rights area today is the area of rampant international terrorism." **B. Woodward, Veil** 93 (1987).

2   *See, e.g.,* Jacobs, *The Reagan Turnaround on Human Rights*, 64 **Foreign Aff.** 1066, 1069 (1986).

3   *See* Hersh, *Target Qaddafi*, **N.Y. Times Mag.**, Feb. 22, 1987, at 17.

4   For a short history of the search for a definition, *see* **F. Boyle, World Politics and International Law** 136-39 (1985).

5   *See Report of the Ad Hoc Committee on International Terrorism*, 34 U.N. GAOR Supp. (No. 37) at 11, UN. Doc. A/34/37 (1979).

6   For a look at past efforts at combatting international terrorism, *see* League of Nations 1937 Convention for the Prevention and Punishment of Terrorism, *opened for signature* Nov. 16, 1937, League of Nations Doc. C.546(I).M.383(I) (1937), *reprinted in* 7 **Hudson, International Legislation** 862 (1941); 1972 United States Draft Convention for the Prevention and Punishment of Certain Acts of International Terrorism, *reprinted in* 67 **Dept. State Bull.** 431 (1972).

7   It has been pointed out that "terrorism has come to replace Communism as a way of legitimizing U.S. military action." *See Introduction* to **Mad Dogs: The U.S. Raids on Libya** 3 (M. Kaldor ed. 1986).

8   *See Terrorism: Dubious Evidence*, **Economist**, May 9, 1981, at 28 (C.I.A.'s fatuous redefinition of "terrorism"); *C.I.A.,* **Economist**, July 4, 1981, at 26.

9   *See* **World Politics and International Law**, *supra* note 4, at 136-54.

10   Geneva Conventions of 1949, 6 U.S.T. 3114, T.I.A.S. No. 3362, 75 U.N.T.S. 31 (wounded and sick in field armed forces); 6 U.S.T. 3217, T.I.A.S. No. 3363, 75 U.N.T.S. 85 (wounded and sick in forces at sea); 6 U.S.T. 3316, T.I.A.S. No. 3364, 75 U.N.T.S. 135 (prisoner of war treatment); 6 U.S.T. 3516, T.I.A.S. No. 3365, 75 U.N.T.S. 287 (protection of civilians in wartime). *See also* International Convention on the Prevention and the Punishment of the Crime of Genocide, Dec. 9, 1948, 78 U.N.T.S. 277 (1951). Israel is a party to the Genocide Convention.

11   *See* **World Politics and International Law**, *supra* note 4, at 230-49.

12   **United Nations Charter**, art. 2, para. 4 provides:
All Members shall refrain in their international relations from the threat or use of force against the territorial integrity or political independence of any state, or in any other manner inconsistent with the purposes of the United Nations.

13   For an example of Shultz urging that the U.S. take action to "raise the cost" of terrorism, see N.Y. Times, Jan. 13, 1986, at A8, col. 3.

14   *See* 80 **Am. Soc'y Int'l L. Proc.** 204 (1986). *But see* Schachter, *Introduction: Self-Judging Self-Defense*, 19 **Case W. Res. J. Int'l L.** 121 (1987).

The decision to bomb Libya was made on April 5. *See* Hersh, *supra* note 3, at 74.

15   Kellogg-Briand Pact, Aug. 27, 1928, 46 Stat. 2343, T.S. No. 796, 94 L.N.T.S. 57. Article 1 provided: "The High Contracting Parties solemnly declare in the names of their respective peoples that they condemn re-course to war for the solution of international controversies, and renounce it as an instrument of national policy in their relations with one another."

16   The existence of a White House plan to overthrow Qaddafi was reported by the *New York Daily News* on May 17, 1981. *Newsweek* in its August 3, 1981 edition provided a more detailed account of the plan including C.I.A. involvement and plans to use disinformation, countergovernment challenges, and paramilitary activities to engineer the overthrow of Qad-dafi. *See A Plan to Overthrow Kaddafi*, Newsweek, Aug. 3, 1981, at 19. *See also* McConnell, *Libya: Propaganda and Covert Operations*, **Coun-terSpy,** Nov. 1981 - Jan. 1982, at 20, 33; *Libyan Witch-Hunt: The War at Home*, **CounterSpy**, Feb.-Apr., 1982, at 31; N.Y. Times, June 3, 1981 (C.I.A. plots to assassinate Qaddafi); **New Statesman**, Aug. 21, 1981, at 13; Wash. Post, Mar. 22, 1981 *and* Aug. 20, 1981; Failgot, *The Plot to Unseat Qaddafi*, **The Middle East**, Aug. 1981, at 34 (French-Egyptian joint assassination plan); Wright, *The Politics of Liquidation: The Reagan Administration Policy Toward the Arabs*, **Arab World Issues** (Occasional Papers: Number 10, 1986); Hersh, *Target Qaddafi*, **N.Y. Times Mag.**, Feb. 22, 1987, at 17; **B. Woodward, Veil** (1987).

17   Text of President Reagan's Press Conference of Jan. 7, 1986, **Cong. Q.**, Jan. 11, 1986, at 93, *reprinted in* 25 **I.L.M.** 175 (1986) [hereinafter President's Press Conference].

18   *See* Wash. Post, Dec. 29, 1985, at A1, col. 6.

19   President's Press Conference, *supra*.

20   Exec. Order No. 12543, 51 Fed. Reg. 875 (1986) [hereinafter Exec. Order]. Authority for the President's order was premised upon both the International Emergency Economic Powers Act, 50 U.S.C. §§1701-1706 (Supp. 1985), and the National Emergencies Act, 50 U.S.C. §§1601-1651 (Supp. 1985). Under the two acts the President was required to find that the policies and actions of Libya constituted an unusual and extraordi-nary threat to the national security and foreign policy of the United States. The President was then authorized to declare a national emergency in order to respond to that threat. For an explanation of criminal sanctions imposed pursuant to the President's order, *see* Libyan Sanctions Regula-tions, Final Rules, 51 Fed. Reg. 1357 (1986) (codified at 31 C.F.R. pt. 20). *See also* Economic Sanctions to Combat International Terrorism, U.S. Dep't State Spec. Rep. No. 149 (July, 1986). For a series of documents presenting, in chronological order, the evolution of sanctions against Libya, *see* 25 **I.L.M.** 1 (Jan. 1986).

21   Exec. Order 12544, Jan. 8, 1986, *reprinted in* **Cong. Q.**, Jan. 11, 1986, at 94 *and in* 25 **I.L.M.** 181 (1986). According to the Commerce Depart-ment's Bureau of Economic Analysis, direct investment in Libya from the United States was valued at $440 million, while Libya's direct invest-ment in the United States was estimated at $2 million. N.Y. Times, Jan. 7, 1986, at A8, col. 2.

22   *See, e.g.,* N.Y. Times, May 6, 1986, at A4, col. 3. *See also Hearing and Markup Before the Committee on Foreign Affairs and its Subcommittee on International Economic Policy and Trade, House of Representatives*, 99th Cong., 2nd Sess. at 49 (1986) (Treasury Dept. announces that oil companies must terminate Libyan operations).

23   **Newsweek**, Jan. 20, 1986, at 15.

24   "[M]aybe we're at that point in the world where Mr. Kaddafi has to be eliminated." **Newsweek**, Jan. 20, 1986, at 17.

25   *See* Hersh, *supra* note 16, at 17.

26   *See generally* **Facts on File**, March 28, 1986, at 201-202.

27   *See generally* **Facts on File**, Apr. 4, 1986, at 217.

28   N.Y. Times, Apr. 6, 1986, at A1, col. 6.

29   **Facts on File**, Apr. 11, 1986, at 243-44.

30   **Facts on File**, April 18, 1986, at 258, col. 1. For other accounts of the attack, *see Reagan's Raiders*, **Newsweek**, Apr. 28, 1986, at 26; *Targeting Gaddafi*, **Time**, Apr. 21, 1986, at 18. For an overview of what transpired in the days immediately before the April 14 attack upon Libya as well as the events of that day itself, *see* **Democratic Policy Committee, Special Report, The Not-So-Secret Raid Against Libya: The Administration Ignores the Principles of Secrecy and Surprise**, May 7, 1986 (containing reports of Secretary of Defense Caspar Weinberger's apparent opposition to the use of military force).

31   **Facts on File**, Apr. 18, 1986, at 258.

32   124 **Aviation Week & Space Tech.**, Apr. 21, 1986, at 19.

33   *See generally* **Facts on File**, Apr. 18, 1986, at 258-59.

34   Declaration of the Assembly of Heads of State and Government of the Organization of African Unity on the Aerial and Naval Miitary Attack Against the Socialist People's Libyan Arab Jamahiriya by the Present United States Administration in April 1986, Letter dated 17 July 1987 from the Permanent Representative of the Libyan Arab Jamahiriya to the United Nations addressed to the Secretary-General, Addendum, U.N. Doc. A/42/412/Add.1 (July 24, 1987).

35   *See* **Facts on File**, Apr. 18, 1986, at 259.

36   *See, e.g.*, **Newsweek**, Apr. 28, 1986, at 19.

37   *See* **Newsweek**, Apr. 28, 1986, at 19.

38   *See* **Newsweek**, Apr. 28, 1986, at 19.

39   Bialos & Juster, *The Libyan Sanctions: A Rational Response to State-Sponsored Terrorism?*, 26 **Va. J. Int'l L.** 799, 804-05, 829 (1986).

40   *See, e.g.,* Champaign-Urbana News-Gazette, Jan. 23, 1986, at A2; **Africa Events**, Feb. 1986, at 41; Champaign-Urbana News Gazette, Apr. 24, 1986, at A4; **Africa Events**, May/June 1986, at 51.

41   *See* Hersh, *supra* note 16, at 17. Qaddafi's overthrow was a major item on the agenda of the first meeting of Reagan's National Security Council in January, 1981. Oberdorfer, *How U.S. Decided to Pressure Gadhafi*, Wash. Post., Aug. 29, 1986, at 18.

42   *See A Plan to Overthrow Kaddafi*, **Newsweek**, Aug. 3, 1981, at 19. *See also* **B. Woodward, Veil** at 94-87, 157-60 (1987).

43   *See* **B. Woodward, Veil** 411 (1987).

44   *See, e.g.,* Hersh, *supra* note 16, at 22 (C.I.A. had advance knowledge of Libyan commander's unsuccessful attempt to assassinate Qaddafi in 1981).

45   *See, e.g.,* Francioni, *The Gulf of Sirte Incident (U.S. v. Libya) and International Law*, 5 **Y.B. Int'l L.** 85 (1980-81); Spinnato, *Historic and Vital Bays: An Analysis of Libya's Claim to the Gulf of Sidra*, 13 **Ocean Dev. & Int'l L.J.** 65 (1983/84); Francioni, *The Status of the Gulf of Sirte in International Law*, 11 **Syracuse J. Int'l L. & Com.** 311 (1984); Francioni, *Peacetime Use of Force, Military Activities, and the New Laws of the Sea*, 18 **Cornell Int'l L. Rev.** 208 (1985).

46   In negotiations with Libya, the Carter administration had agreed that U.S.

naval and air exercises would not enter into the area of the Gulf of Sidra claimed by Qaddafi. *See* Wright, *Libya and the West: Headlong Into Confrontation?,* 58 **Int'l Aff.** 13, 15, 23 n.58 (1982).

47   In 1973, Libya announced that it claimed the territory of the Gulf of Sidra south of Latitude 32 degrees 30 minutes as internal waters. *See* Ratner, *The Gulf of Sidra Incident of 1981: A Study of the Lawfulness of Peacetime Aerial Engagements,* 7 **Yale J. Int'l L.** 59, 64 (1984); 78 **Revue Générale de Droit International Public** 1177 (1974).

48   *See* **Newsweek**, Aug. 31, 1981, at 11; *Tripoli, in a Protest Note, Accuses U.S. of International Terrorism,* N.Y. Times, Aug. 20, 1981, at A1, col. 4; Oberdorfer, *How U.S. Decided to Pressure Gadhafi,* Wash. Post, Aug. 29, 1986, at 18.

49   Oil accounts for more than ninety-nine per cent of Libya's export earnings. *See* Intoccia, *American Bombing of Libya: An International Legal Analysis,* 19 **Case W. Res. J. Int'l L.** 177, 180 n.33 (1987).

50   *See generally* **W.T. Mallison & S. Mallison, Armed Conflict in Lebanon, 1982: Humanitarian Law in a Real World Setting** 11 (1985).

51   *See generally* **Aviation Week and Space Tech.**, Aug. 24 *and* Aug. 31, 1981; **Newsweek**, Aug. 31, 1981; Int'l Herald Trib., Aug. 20 *and* 21, 1981;Wash. Post, Aug. 20 *and* 22, 1981. *See also*, Ratner, *supra* note 47; Neutze, *The Gulf of Sidra Incident: A Legal Perspective,* 108 **Proc. U.S. Naval Inst.** 26 (1982); **J. Cooley, Libyan Sandstorm** 267 (1982).

52   *See* Note, *Air Defense Identification Zones: Creeping Jurisdiction in the Airspace,* 18 **Va. J. Int'l L.** 485, 509 (1978) [hereinafter Air Defense]. *See also* **L. Bouchez, The Regime of Bays in International Law** 11 (1963).

53   Chicago Convention on International Civil Aviation, Dec. 7, 1944, 61 Stat. 1180, T.I.A.S. No. 1591, 15 U.N.T.S. 295.

54   *See* Winchester, *Why Reagan Set the Tomcats on "The World's Most Dangerous Man,"* Sun. Times (London), Aug. 23, 1981, at 6; Ratner, *supra* note 47.

55   *See, e.g., Who Will Protect Freedom of the Seas?,* **U.S. Dept. State, Current Pol.** No. 855, at 2 (July 21, 1986) (address by John D. Negroponte, Asst. Sec'y of State) [hereinafter Negroponte] ("The rights and freedom of the sea will be lost over time if they are not used").

56   *See Quaddafi Overtures Rejected by U.S.,* Wash. Post, Apr. 2 1986, at 1; **B. Woodward, Veil** 186 (1987) (rejection of Qaddafi's 1981 overture for a channel to U.S. during hysteria over so-called "Libyan hit squads"); N.Y. Times, Aug. 16, 1987, at 12, col. 1 (U.S. spurned Libya's May 1986 offer of communication through third parties). *See also* Libya's offer to submit allegations of its support of terrorism to the International Court of Justice or any U.S. or Western European court, contained in a Letter to the United Nations Secretary General, U.N. Doc. A/41/496 S/18253, July 31, 1986.

57   Statute of the International Court of Justice, June 26, 1945, 59 Stat. 1055, T.S. No. 993, 3 Bevans 1153, 1976 Y.B.U.N. 1052, art. 36(2):The states parties to the present Statute may at any time declare that they recognize as compulsory ipso facto and without special agreement, in relation to any other state accepting the same obligation, the jurisdiction of the Court in all legal disputes concerning:
 a. the interpretation of a treaty;
 b. any question of international law;
 c. the existence of any fact which, if established, would constitute a breach of an international obligation;

        d. the nature or extent of the reparation to be made for the breach
        of an international obligation.

58   *Military and Paramilitary Activities In and Against Nicaragua* (Nicar. v. U.S.), 1984 I.C.J. 169 (Interim Protection Order of May 10).

59   *Military and Paramilitary Activities In and Against Nicaragua* (Nicar. v. U.S.), 1984 I.C.J. 392 (Judgment of November 26).

60   *See* Sofaer, *The United States and the World Court*, **U.S. Dept. of State Current Pol.** No. 769 (address before Senate Foreign Relations Committee Dec. 4, 1985).

61   *See Case Concerning the Continental Shelf* (Libyan Arab Jamahiriya v. Malta), 1985 I.C.J. 13 (Judgment of 3 June); *Case Concerning the Continental Shelf* (Tunisia v. Libyan Arab Jamahiriya), 1982 I.C.J. 18 (Judgment of 24 February); Note, 27 **Harv. Int'l L. Rev.** 304 (1986).

62   Francioni, *Peacetime Use of Force, Military Activities, and the New Laws of the Sea*, 18 **Cornell Int'l L.J.** 203, 212 (1985).

63   Convention on the Territorial Sea and the Contiguous Zone, Apr. 29, 1958, art. 14, 15 U.S.T. 1606, T.I.A.S. No. 5639, 516 U.N.T.S. 205.

64   "Passage is innocent so long as it is not prejudicial to the peace, good order or security of the coastal State." Convention on the Territorial Sea, *supra*, art. 14(4).

65   Intoccia, *American Bombing of Libya: An International Legal Analysis*, 19 **Case W. Res. J. Int'l L.** 177, 183-84 n.67 (1987).

66   Article 7 provides in its entirety:

        1. This article relates only to bays the coasts of which belong to a single State.

        2. For the purposes of these articles, a bay is a well-marked indentation whose penetration is in such proportion to the width of its mouth as to contain landlocked waters and constitute more than a mere curvature of the coast. An indentation shall not, however, be regarded as a bay unless its area is as large as, or larger than, that of the semi-circle whose diameter is a line drawn across the mouth of that indentation.

        3. For the purpose of measurement, the area of an indentation is that lying between the low-water mark around the shore of the indentation and a line joining the low-water marks of its natural entrance points. Where, because of the presence of islands, an indentation has more than one mouth, the semi-circle shall be drawn on a line as long as the sum total of the lengths of the lines across the different mouths. Islands within an indentation shall be included as if they were part of the water areas of the indentation.

        4. If the distance between the low-water marks of the natural entrance points of a bay does not exceed twenty-four miles, a closing line may be drawn between these two low-water marks, and the waters   enclosed thereby shall be considered as internal waters.

        5. Where the distance between the low-water marks of the natural entrance points of a bay exceeds twenty-four miles, a straight baseline of twenty-four miles shall be drawn within the bay in such a manner as to enclose the maximum area of water that is possible with a line of that length.

        6. *The foregoing provisions shall not apply to so-called "historic" bays, or in any case where the straight baseline system provided for in article 4 is applied.* [Emphasis added.]

See generally Francioni, *The Status of the Gulf of Sirte in International Law*, 11 **Syr. J. Int'l L. & Com.** 311, 314-15 (1984); **L. Bouchez, The Regime of Bays in International Law** 15, 108, 115 (1963); **G. Westerman, The Juridical Bay** (1987).

67   "By 'historic waters' are usually meant waters which are treated as internal waters but which would not have that character were it not for the existence of an historic title." *Fisheries Case* (U.K. v. Nor.), 1951 I.C.J. 116, 130 (Judgment of Dec. 18). *See* Goldie, *Historic Bays in International Law--An Impressionistic Overview*, 11 **Syr. J. Int'l L. & Com.** 211 (1984).

68   *See* **M. Strohl, The International Law of Bays** 264 (1963) (Delaware Bay); *id.* at 276-83 (Chesapeake, Monterey, Santa Monica, and San Pedro Bays).

69   *See, e.g., United States* v. *Louisiana*, 470 U.S. 93, 105 S.Ct. 1074 (1985).

70   Convention on the Territorial Sea, *supra* note 63, art. 7(6).

71   *See also* Ellafi, *Settlement of International Disputes: The Libyan-American Confrontation over the Gulf of Sirt* (Paper prepared for presentation at the ninth annual scientific meeting of the International Society of Political Psychology, Amsterdam, June 30-July 2, 1982); *Juridical Regime of Historic Waters, Including Historic Bays*, U.N. Doc. A/CN.4/143 (1962); Historic Bays, U.N. Doc. A/CONF.13/1 (1957).

72   *Fisheries Case* (U.K. v. Nor.) 1951 I.C.J. 116. (Judgment of Dec. 18) [hereinafter Fisheries Case].

73   The baseline is the point of separation between a country's internal waters and the territorial sea. From that point is measured the extent of a country's territorial waters, e.g. 3 or 12 miles from the line, over which it asserts legal control. Different demarcation procedures when applied to unique geographical situations (i.e. the Gulf of Sidra) quite naturally result in disparate territorial claims. *See* **N. Leech, C. Oliver, and J. Sweeney, The International Legal System** 153-154 (1973).

74   *Military and Paramilitary Activities In and Against Nicaragua* (Nicar. v. U.S.), 1986 I.C.J. (Judgment of June 27).

75   *See* Libya's Letter to the United Nations Secretary General, U.N. Doc. A/41/496 S/18253, July 31, 1986.

76   *See* **B. Woodward, Veil** 411-12 (1987); *State Dep't Acted to Block U.S.-Egypt Attack on Libya*, Wash. Post, Feb. 20, 1987, at A1, col. 1; *U.S. Said to Plan for Aid to Egypt in Attacking Libya*, N.Y. Times, Feb. 21, 1987, at A1, col. 3; First Principles: National Security and Civil Liberties, July, 1986, at 11-12 (citing Wash. Post 3/26/86, 4/2/86, 4/18/86, N.Y. Times 4/3/86, 4/17/86, 4/18/86, 4/26/86); *U.S., Egypt Begin Joint Maneuvers*, Wash. Post, Aug. 25, 1985, at 14, *reprinted in* U.S. Department of Defense, Current News, Aug. 25, 1985, at 4, col. 1.

77   McConnell, *Libya: Propaganda and Covert Operations*, **CounterSpy**, Nov. 1981-Jan. 1982, at 29.

78   *See* N.Y. Times, Oct. 2, 1985 at A10, col. 1 (Qaddafi cancels plans to attend); N.Y. Times, Oct. 12, 1985, at A11, col. 4 (Qaddafi in Moscow).

79   Lardner, *Byrd Says Rash of Leaks Preceded Strike on Libya*, Wash. Post, May 14, 1986, at 28.

80   **Africa Events**, May-June 1986, at 15.

81   *See UI Law Professor: U.S. Owes Egypt Apology for Grabbing Jet, Terrorists*, Champaign-Urbana News Gazette, Oct. 19, 1985, at A-3.

CHAPTER 3

THE REAGAN ADMINISTRATION'S CRIMINAL BOMBINGS OF TRIPOLI AND BENGHAZI

The Terrorist Attacks at Rome and Vienna

It is now very clear from even a cursory examination of the world press that Qaddafi was not responsible for the attacks in Rome and Vienna. Indeed, the Ministers of the Interior from both Italy and Austria publicly stated as much.[1] Moreover, when presented with so-called "conclusive" evidence of Qaddafi's involvement by U.S. Deputy Secretary of State John Whitehead, the Foreign Ministers of the Federal Republic of Germany and of Greece disagreed with his assessment.[2] Nor was this so-called evidence sufficient to convince U.K. Prime Minister Margaret Thatcher, who was Reagan's great ally and friend, to take any measures against Qaddafi with respect to these allegations. By contrast, Thatcher publicly stated at the time that any proposed or contemplated U.S. military "retaliation" against Qaddafi would violate basic principles of international law.[3]

As best as can be reconstructed from the public record, it appears that the people who carried out these attacks were Palestinians who had been recruited by the renegade Abu Nidal organization from the Sabra and Shatilla refugee camps located in the environs of Beirut, Lebanon.[4] These were the same camps where in September of 1982 about two thousand completely innocent Palestinian and Lebanese old men, women and children were brutally massacred by units of the Phalange militia with the connivance of the Israeli army.[5] In addition, the United States government had given a pledge of protection for these refugees as part of a deal to secure the withdrawal of P.L.O. troops from Beirut under the aegis of U.S. Marines.[6]

Instead of living up to the terms of this commitment, the U.S. government prematurely evacuated American Marines from Beirut, did not prevent the Israeli army from invading the city contrary to the latter's express promise, and then did nothing to terminate the ongoing massacre until it was too late to make any difference. For these reasons then, those Palestinians living in the Sabra and Shatilla refugee camps held the governments of the United States and Israel fully responsible for the massacres. Under general principles of international law and particularly the Fourth Geneva Convention of 1949, that was a perfectly correct and reasonable conclusion for them to have reached.

To be sure, the fact that Israel and the United States were legally responsible for the perpetration of these and other heinous war crimes upon innocent civilians in Lebanon can neither justify nor excuse the fact that these victims' friends, relatives, and neighbors allegedly responded by committing acts of terrorism upon civilian nationals of the United States and Israel. But this observation can certainly help us to understand what happened at Rome and Vienna--and why. These attacks were not simply random and inexplicable acts of violence directed against the United States and Israel, as the Reagan administration tried to deceive the American people into believing. Rather, these attacks were apparently acts of revenge and reprisal specifically designed to retaliate for the blatantly illegal and callously inhumane policies that the United States and Israel had pursued in Lebanon since at least the 1982 invasion of that country – if not well before.

The Palestinians who carried out the attacks at Rome and Vienna were allegedly trained by the anti-Arafat, anti-P.L.O. Abu Nidal organization in Lebanon's Bekaa Valley in territory then subject to the occupation and control of Syria, not Libya. From there they traveled to Damascus, Syria (not Libya) where Abu Nidal maintained his headquarters with the permission of the Syrian government, not Libya. From Damascus they traveled to Belgrade and then launched the attacks. Indeed, the captured terrorists said that Syrian agents accompanied them all the way to Rome.[7] In addition, there were grounds to suspect that the Abu Nidal Organization also acted under instructions from Western intelligence agencies.

In any event, it is clear that Colonel Qaddafi had little if any connection to what happened at Rome and Vienna. The Reagan administration clearly and purposefully manipulated these two unfortunate incidents as a pretext to move one step closer toward military action against Qaddafi in order to overthrow him. As previously explained, that had been the Reagan administration's standing policy from its very outset in 1981.

Reagan Sanctions Against Libya

The subsequent set of sanctions imposed by the Reagan administration against Libya were clearly intended to create a prolonged and degenerating crisis with Qaddafi that would ultimately culminate in some type of major military conflict. This can be verified by a brief analysis of the nature of and rationale behind that latest set of U.S. sanctions against Libya. The Reagan administration's disingenuous arguments for imposing these sanctions could not obscure the fact that they were neither necessary nor warranted by the attacks at Rome and Vienna.

First came the Reagan administration's order that all Americans must depart from Libya by February 1, 1986 or face criminal prosecution. Those American citizens living and working in Libya were in absolutely no danger at all from the Jamahiriya.[8] Indeed Libya was happy to have as many Americans there as wanted to come to Libya, and bent over backwards to be very careful and protective of Americans. From everything I had read and experienced in Libya, the Americans there were happy to stay and did not want to leave. Quite frankly, the Reagan administration unjustifiably disrupted the lives of these innocent U.S. citizens in order to pursue its patently illicit foreign policy objectives.

There was no danger to Americans living and working in Libya unless, of course, the United States government was planning to take military action against Qaddafi, which it subsequently did. In the event such major military conflict resulted in the outbreak of war between the two countries, then of course any Americans in Libya could quite legitimately be treated and interned as enemy aliens for the duration of hostilities. Hence, the major threat to the safety of American citizens in Libya came from Reagan, not Qaddafi. Indeed, during my second trip to Libya, Reagan sent the U.S. fleet back to Libya's coast, and their entire leadership fled into the desert with their families in dire fear for their lives. I was left alone to my own devices for several days wandering around the streets of Tripoli wondering whether Reagan was going to bomb me there or else while sleeping in my hotel at night.

The second dangerous development was the Reagan administration's freeze on Libyan assets here in the United States as well as on assets held by subsidiaries of U.S. banks located abroad that violated fundamental principles of international law. As far as I could tell when I visited Libya, American assets there were in absolutely no jeopardy at all from Qaddafi. The Libyans were very happy to have as much American economic investment as they possibly could in the country, and constantly asked me why U.S. corporations and banks did not want to come and do more business in Libya. I had to explain to them that it was not the business community's decision but rather the Reagan administration that wanted to impede and prevent U.S. businessmen from engaging in any form of economic transactions with Libya.

The Reagan administration imposed the assets freeze primarily as a provocative measure in the expectation that Qaddafi would retaliate in kind by expropriating U.S. assets in Libya. The Reagan administration's apparent hope was that Qaddafi's confiscation of U.S. assets would simply serve to further escalate tensions between the United States and Libya. Most probably, the Reagan administration calculated that this scenario could have developed somewhat along the lines of the extended crisis that occurred in U.S.-Cuban relations after Castro's ascent to power, which eventually culminated in the Bay of Pigs invasion of 1961.

Under the customary international law doctrine known as retorsion,[9] Qaddafi had every right to seize U.S. economic assets in Libya in order to guarantee the return of Libya's assets that had been illegally frozen by the United States government. But such an expropriation did not occur precisely because Qaddafi genuinely wished to defuse the crisis over Rome and Vienna. Once again, it was the Reagan administration that rushed head-long toward war despite Libya's repeated efforts to prevent hostilities.

In this regard, the third and most disturbing element of the early 1986 stage in the crisis became of course the immediate dispatch of two aircraft carrier task forces to the Gulf of Sidra. The *Coral Sea* and its support ships were sent from Italy to engage in hostile military maneuvers in the vicinity of the Gulf of Sidra. Also the battle group organized around the aircraft carrier *Saratoga* sailed through the Suez Canal with Egyptian permission in order to join the *Coral Sea* on maneuvers near the Gulf of Sidra.[10] Meanwhile, the naval task force organized around the aircraft carrier *America* proceeded from Norfolk, Virginia in order to be on station in the Mediterranean.[11]

Hostile military maneuvers by these three aircraft carrier battle groups near the Gulf of Sidra for the specific purpose of precipitating armed conflict with Libya in order to overthrow Colonel Qaddafi violated article 2(4) of the United Nations Charter. In addition, such maneuvers constituted a threat to the peace, breach of the peace, and act of aggression under Charter article 39 that warranted the imposition of "enforcement measures" against the Reagan administration by the U.N. Security Council under Chapter 7. Nevertheless, the Reagan administration was completely undeterred because the U.S. government's veto power would have prevented the U.N. Security Council from taking any effective measures designed to help protect Libya against U.S. military aggression. Libya would be forced to defend itself all alone.

The 1986 Gulf of Sidra Incident

Once all these naval ships and fighter aircraft were in place and most American citizens were out of Libya it was then a very simple matter for the Reagan administration to push Qaddafi into a direct military conflict. Indeed, U.S. officials indicated that one of the main reasons why U.S. citizens were called home was so that the U.S. government would have a free hand to take military action against Qaddafi in the event another pretext could be found without having a significant number of American citizens still in Libya as potential hostages.[12]   The January 20, 1986 issue of *Newsweek* contained a story in which the top deputy to then National Security Adviser John Poindexter stated that the Reagan administration was preparing to take military action against Qaddafi and would do so as soon as some other pretext could be found.[13]

The emplacement of large numbers of U.S. military forces operating off and in the Gulf of Sidra was an illegal and purposefully provocative policy that predictably created a military confrontation with Libya. By purposefully engaging in such military brinksmanship the Reagan administration knowingly but foolishly surrendered the initiative for starting a war to Qaddafi in the misguided hope and expectation that he would do so. But once again, Qaddafi was smart enough not to fall for Reagan's trap.

The Reagan administration once again argued that it had a right under international law to send the Sixth Fleet into the Gulf of Sidra in order to guarantee access to what it claimed to be international waters. For reasons previously explained, this alleged justification was a legal fiction pure and simple. The "high seas" argument was cynically manipulated by the Reagan administration in order to create a thin veneer of legal respectability to build U.S. public support for a policy that was clearly designed to provoke a military encounter with Qaddafi that would lead to his overthrow.

During the first two sets of maneuvers in January and February the U.S. Navy did not enter into the Gulf itself. But with the arrival of the third aircraft carrier battle group, the Navy was ready for a large-scale military action against Qaddafi and thus entered the Gulf of Sidra during the third set of maneuvers in late March.[14] Based on their behavior during the 1981 maneuvers, when the U.S. aircraft flew into the Gulf of Sidra, they probably were moving in the direction of Libya's oil facilities on its southern rim. Indeed, one report in the London *Sunday Times* indicated that U.S. fighters actually penetrated Libyan airspace even as recognized by the United States government itself.[15] The Reagan administration gave Qaddafi no alternative but to defend himself from potential aerial bombardment by firing his SAM-5 missiles at the approaching U.S. high performance jet combat aircraft. Under these circumstances, Libya had a perfect right under international law to defend itself from hostile military action by the United States government under article 51 of the United Nations Charter.

The U.S. naval jet aircraft then destroyed the SAM-5 site near Sirte. In addition, U.S. naval ships destroyed at least two and possibly three Libyan naval craft in the Gulf, with the loss of approximately 30 Libyan sailors. Even the accounts of these encounters put forth by the Reagan administration tend to indicate that the Libyan naval craft were not actually engaged in hostile maneuvers directed against the U.S. naval vessels that had penetrated the Gulf of Sidra. Rather, the Libyan ships were attacked because U.S. Admiral Kelso had already declared that the U.S. fleet would automatically regard as hostile any Libyan forces departing Libyan territorial waters or Libyan airspace.[16] In other words, Libyan ships were destroyed because Qaddafi had the nerve to try to defend himself against oncoming U.S. jet aircraft by firing SAM-5 missiles upon the latter. It does not appear by any stretch of the imagination that the U.S. Navy's wanton attack upon the Libyan naval ships and sailors can be justified in accordance with any conceivable doctrine of legitimate self-defense, all of which depend upon fulfilling the basic requirements of necessity and proportionality.

As occurred in the 1981 Gulf of Sidra incident, however, once again Libya could not be drawn out by the Sixth Fleet into large-scale aerial combat and prudently kept its aircraft in reserve and most of its ships in port. And apparently, once again, the Reagan administration was seriously disappointed that it could not provoke Qaddafi into a major military conflict for the purpose of producing his deposition. Vice President George Bush publicly stated as much shortly thereafter while on a tour of Middle Eastern states.[17]

The 1986 Gulf of Sidra incident was clearly designed to provoke Qaddafi, if not to engage in outright combat, then certainly to respond by means of a terrorist attack against American interests in retaliation for this large-scale destruction of Libyan lives and property. Hence the United States government purposefully proceeded into the Gulf of Sidra knowing full well that either Qaddafi or his supporters or his sympathizers around the world would respond to this aggression in one fashion or another, thus creating a pretext for further and more serious military action against Libya. In other words, the Reagan administration was fully and knowingly responsible for setting into motion a chain of events that predictably resulted in death and destruction for hundreds of innocent human beings in Berlin, Tripoli, Benghazi, and elsewhere.

Libyan Alleged Responsibility for the Berlin Discotheque Bombing?

Thus on April 2, a T.W.A. jet airliner on its way from Rome to Athens exploded, killing four American citizens. There was no evidence to indicate that Colonel Qaddafi was involved in this explosion. Rather, once again, the evidence pointed to the Abu Nidal organization operating out of Damascus, Syria, not Libya.[18] Then on April 5 a West Berlin discotheque frequented by American soldiers stationed there was bombed. The Reagan administration stated that it had irrefutable evidence that the bombing had been carried out by the Libyan People's Liaison Bureau in East Berlin acting on orders issued in Tripoli.

The American people should have been extremely skeptical of any such claims by the Reagan administration that they did indeed have such incontrovertible evidence. The Reagan administration had said the same thing with regard to the attacks in Rome and Vienna, yet this claim had turned out to be untrue. In specific regard to the Berlin incident, Reagan administration officials also admitted that they had lied when they claimed that they had absolute proof that Tripoli cabled its Bureau in East Berlin after the discotheque attack in order to praise the diplomats for the bombing.[19] In other words, this report was blatant disinformation intended to deceive public opinion in the United States and Europe into supporting further aggressive military action against Qaddafi.

Later on it was revealed in the *New York Times* that the persons whom the West German police detained for the discotheque bombing had connections with groups operating out of Syria, not Libya.[20] Indeed, all the evidence that emerged into the public record about the discotheque bombing pointed once again in the direction of the Abu Nidal organization in Syria, not Libya. The only evidence put forward for the American people to go on was the Reagan administration's claim that its alleged intercepted cable-traffic between Tripoli and the People's Bureau in East Berlin had somehow established Libyan responsibility for the April 5 bombing. We were expected to accept their obviously self-interested word for its existence, translation, meaning, and significance.

Before the American people supported any further military measures against Qaddafi, they should have demanded hard evidence from the Reagan administration as to Libya's direct involvement in terrorist acts. For example, when the Reagan administration said they had evidence that the Soviet Union shot down K.A.L. Flight 007 in 1983, they actually produced the intercepted transcripts of the discussions between the Soviet jet pilot and his ground controllers. Even then, the Reagan administration persisted in the bogus claim that those intercepts proved the Soviets actually knew they were shooting down a civilian airplane, despite the fact that U.S. intelligence agencies at that very moment possessed data establishing that the Soviets actually believed, however negligently, that they were shooting down a spy plane.[21] The Reagan administration purposely distorted the meaning of the released intercepts in order to create massive public revulsion in the United States and Europe against the so-called "evil empire" that could then be utilized and exploited for additional anti-Soviet purposes.

In light of the Reagan administration's unsavory manipulation of the "evidence" on Soviet responsibility for the destruction of K.A.L. 007, the American people should have demanded to see direct evidence of Libyan support for the Berlin discotheque bombing before they supported his terror bombings of Tripoli and Benghazi. The fact that the Reagan administration refused to produce such evidence despite the fact that the intelligence source had already been compromised tended to indicate that the evidence was not as incontrovertible as they said it was. The same can be said for most of the other unsubstantiated Reagan administration allegations of Libyan sponsorship for acts of terrorism against American targets.

Contradictory Evidence from the Pentagon

The discotheque-bombing "evidence" rested exclusively upon so-called intelligence reports, but neither the public nor the press had any independent means of confirming the accuracy of these reports or whether they were subject to other interpretations. Indeed, an official publication produced and widely disseminated by the U.S. Department of Defense itself shortly after the bombings of Tripoli and Benghazi raised serious questions about the credibility of this alleged evidence.[22] This extraordinarily unusual compilation, translation, and dissemination of several directly contradictory foreign press dispatches by means of an official Pentagon publication suggests that the Department of Defense continued to maintain serious reservations about the Reagan administration's incredibly belligerent agenda for military actions against Libya.[23]

For example, according to this Pentagon publication, an April 8, 1986 dispatch by the German Press Agency (G.P.A.) reported that the special commission set up by the German government to trace those behind the bomb attack at the discotheque in Berlin "has no indications that Libyans placed the bomb."[24] The head of the State Protection Department, Manfred Ganschow, said that he could not confirm the contents of an article pre-released by BILD newspaper naming a Libyan as a likely suspect.[25] Investigations were indeed being conducted in the direction of Arab terrorism, but only in that direction, according to Ganschow.[26] He also stressed that nothing was known of an alleged monitored conversation between Tripoli and East Berlin.[27]

Another G.P.A. dispatch dated April 8, 1986 reported that German government circles confirmed the receipt of U.S. documents about an alleged involvement by Libya in the discotheque attack: "These documents contain clues and suspicious factors, but no real proof."[28] This was corroborated by an Agence France Press (A.F.P.) dispatch dated April 8, 1986 which reported that the West German government had not ruled out possible Libyan involvement in the discotheque blast, but had no proof.[29]

In another G.P.A. dispatch dated April 11, 1986, Manfred Ganschow said that two Libyans who tried to travel from the East Berlin Libyan People's Bureau into West Berlin on March 27, 1986 had not been involved in the discotheque attack: "He described reports that they were 'behind' the attack as 'pure speculation.' There was no such knowledge."[30] Another G.P.A. dispatch of April 12, 1986 reported that the Free Democratic Party (F.D.P.) politician Burkhard Harsch said that to his knowledge no information existed to prove the involvement of a foreign state in the Berlin attack.[31] At the time, the F.D.P. was part of the coalition government that ruled in Germany by virtue of an alliance with Chancellor Helmudt Kohl's Christian Democrats and Franz Joseph Strauss' Christian Social Union party.

An April 15, 1986 dispatch from the *Los Angeles Times* reported that when U.S. Ambassador to the United Nations Vernon A. Walters made a whirlwind tour of London, Bonn, Paris, and Rome before the bombings of Libya in order to present the so-called cable evidence to allied government leaders, those in Italy and West Germany were apparently not persuaded and specifically urged the United States to avoid military action, though Chancellor Kohl said there was "some evidence" linking Libya to the disco-bombing.[32] According to London's *Financial Times*, it was not until two days *after* the bombing, on April 17, 1986, that the West German government claimed "somewhat sheepishly that it too now had clear proof of Libyan involvement in West Berlin discotheque bombing on April 5."[33] The "proof" which Bonn then claimed to have (as opposed to the mere pointers referred to in preceding days) appeared to have been intercepts by West German intelligence of the same radio messages between Tripoli and the Libyan People's Bureau in East Berlin immediately before and after the discotheque attack whose significance Bonn had already discounted when presented by Walters.[34]

Most probably what happened was that the "conclusive" and "irrefutable" evidence of Qaddafi's sponsorship of the Berlin discotheque bombing never existed. But once the U.S. bombing attacks upon Tripoli and Benghazi had occurred, as an accommodation to his great personal friend Ronald Reagan, Chancellor Kohl reversed the German government's position to proclaim that the evidence was there. Nevertheless, a U.P.I. dispatch of May 23, 1986 reported that the West Berlin Justice

Department said that two of the three Palestinian suspects arrested in the nightclub attack confessed that they got their explosives from the *Syrian* Embassy in East Berlin--not the East Berlin Libyan People's Bureau as the Reagan administration had insinuated.[35]

Prelude to War

Hence my earlier assertion that the Gulf of Sidra could have readily become the Gulf of Tonkin for the 1980s--or early 1990s. It has now been documented that the Gulf of Tonkin "incident" as contemporaneously described never took place but rather was fabricated by the Johnson administration in order to obtain support from Congress for a major increase in U.S. military involvement in Vietnam.[36] Similarly, as will be discussed in more detail below, it is now undeniable that the Reagan administration manufactured evidence with respect to alleged Libyan sponsorship for international terrorism in order to manipulate U.S. public opinion and the Congress into supporting direct U.S. military action against Libya for the purpose of destroying Qaddafi and terminating his Revolution.

Even assuming that the Reagan administration did indeed have clear and convincing evidence that Qaddafi had ordered the bombing at the West Berlin discotheque, this could be viewed an attempt by Libya to retaliate for the wanton destruction of 30 Libyan sailors in the Gulf of Sidra two weeks earlier. Under those circumstances, the discotheque attack would have been clearly designed to kill and injure American soldiers stationed in West Berlin in reprisal for the Libyan sailors who were maliciously and unnecessarily killed by U.S. aggression against their homeland. This argument is not intended to justify either act. Rather, the events indicate that since the Reagan administration undertook the 1986 Gulf of Sidra incident in full awareness that it would provide cause for some form of retaliation against Americans, it would have had to share an amount of the blame for the discotheque casualties at least equivalent to that of the real perpetrators.

The discotheque bombing conveniently served as just another pretext for the Reagan administration to undertake drastic military measures against Qaddafi, a course of action that had been already decided upon long before. As early as January 1986, the Reagan administration had asked the French government to permit British-based planes to overfly French territory on their way to strike against Qaddafi.[37] As far as the Reagan administration was concerned, it was really irrelevant who was ultimately responsible for the Berlin discotheque bombing. In any event, this act of hostility directed against American soldiers could not possibly have served as any justification under international law for the Reagan administration's decision to bomb civilian targets in and near the Libyan cities of Tripoli and Benghazi.

Misinterpreting the International Legal Right to Self-Defense

President Reagan himself attempted to justify this April 14, 1986 bombing operation on the grounds of self-defense as recognized by article 51 of the United Nations Charter.[38] In his news conference, Secretary of State George Shultz also invoked the right of "self-defense."[39]   This is a completely erroneous and inaccurate interpretation of the doctrine of self-defense that has historically been recognized by the United States government: retaliation is never the same as self-defense![40] Yet the 1986 bombing attacks on the targets in Libya were clearly stated to be in retaliation for the bombing of the Berlin discotheque on April 5.[41]

The alleged justification under article 51 of the United Nations Charter was just another legal artifice concocted by the Reagan administration, only this time for public consumption in England, not America. The *New York Times* revealed that Reagan officials first planned the bombing of Libya and only later sought to invoke article 51.[42]   The decision to refer to article 51 was prompted by pressure from British Prime Minister Margaret Thatcher.[43]

Earlier in the year, Thatcher was publicly asked if military retaliation against Libya would be acceptable. She had responded in the negative on the grounds that this would be a violation of international law.[44] Of course she was right! By mid-April Thatcher felt she needed at least some plausible legal justification to be uttered by the United States government in order to explain this obvious reversal of her highly publicized and undoubtedly correct opinion on the illegality of military retaliation issued just a few months before.

As best as can be figured out from the public record, what happened was that the Reagan administration went to Thatcher and probably argued that the U.S. government had supported Britain during the war over the Falklands/Malvinas and therefore expected Thatcher's support in return by her giving permission to use NATO air bases in England for the purpose of staging a bombing attack against Libya. Thatcher had fairly serious objections to the wisdom of this course of action, and apparently vigorously opposed a bombing mission until the President personally requested her support for military action that the U.S. government clearly intended to take anyway. In addition, the U.S. Senate Foreign Relations Committee was currently considering a proposed U.S.-U.K. Supplementary Extradition Treaty that would retroactively abolish the outstanding extradition treaty's exception for political offenses. Thatcher desperately wanted the supplemental treaty passed in order to obtain the extradition of I.R.A. members who had fled to the United States.[45] Under these circumstances, she probably felt there really was no other option but to comply with Reagan's wishes.

Nevertheless, Thatcher insisted that the U.S. government at least refer to the Charter article 51 right of self-defense in order to provide what some British officials called a "fig leaf" behind which she could then attempt to justify her actions in Parliament and to the British people. This artifice was not terribly successful, thus creating a very serious political crisis for Margaret Thatcher. Shortly thereafter, however, Thatcher did indeed obtain her anti-I.R.A. treaty from the U.S. Senate primarily because of the support she gave to Reagan on the Libya bombings.[46]

Retaliation Is Not Self-Defense!

Let us assume, for the sake of argument, that Libya was indeed "responsible" for the Berlin discotheque bombing (which it probably was not) and that the Reagan administration never possessed a preexisting intention to destroy Qaddafi under any pretexts available and by whatever means possible (which it undoubtedly did). Under these limited and nonexistent circumstances, the April 14 devastation wreaked upon Tripoli and Benghazi by the Reagan administration could arguably have been a case of what international law professors call actions of peacetime retaliation and reprisal.[47] Yet, from the time of the signing of the United Nations Charter in 1945, the United States government had always taken the position that retaliation and reprisal were not legitimate measures of self-defense under article 51.

To the contrary, this provision of the Charter made it quite clear that self-defense could only be exercised in the event of an actual or perhaps at least imminent "armed attack" against the state itself. By definition, this would not include peacetime retaliation and reprisal since they occur after the fact. Hence, under the regime of the United Nations Charter as historically interpreted by the U.S. government, peacetime retaliation and reprisal were clearly illegal and thus prohibited.

The original U.S. government adherence to a restrictive interpretation of the right of self-defense found in Charter article 51 was due to its belief that it was in the best interest of America to minimize the scope for the threat or use of force by other states in the world community as much as possible. An expansive reading of the doctrine of self-defense to include retaliation and reprisal would gratuitously provide ample grounds for many other states to come up with all sorts of justifications and pretexts for engaging in the threat and use of force that could significantly undermine international peace and security, thus threatening the vital national security interests of the United States and its allies in the peaceful maintenance of a favorable postwar status quo. Until the advent of the Reagan administration, the United States government had generally favored the stability produced by the peaceful settlement of international disputes to the instability generated by the unilateral threat and use of military force.

The Progressive Israelization of American Foreign Policy

Even during the dark days of the Vietnam War, the U.S. government never formally abandoned its attachment to the legal proposition that retaliation and reprisal were prohibited by international law. Prior to the events of 1986, this policy position had been most recently reaffirmed by the United States government with respect to Israeli retaliatory attacks into surrounding Arab states. The Israeli government maintained that its actions were in retaliation and reprisal for attacks on civilian targets in Israel or occupied Palestine and therefore could be justified under the doctrine of self-defense as recognized by article 51 of the United Nations Charter. The United States government strongly disagreed, and refused to accept the Israeli interpretation of the article 51 right of self-defense so as to include the latter's retaliatory and later preemptive strikes.

The disagreement over this point was politically significant because the United States and Israel had and still have an arms supply agreement which provides that American weapons, equipment and supplies can only be used in legitimate self-defense as determined by article 51 of the U.N. Charter or as part of an enforcement action authorized by the United Nations Security Council.[48] In addition, this was and still is a requirement of the United States domestic law known as the Arms Export Control Act.[49] Therefore, an attempt had to be made by Israel's American supporters to get the Department of State to change its formal position on the illegality of retaliation and reprisal.

In 1973-74, Eugene V. Rostow--who had been Undersecretary of State in the Johnson administration, was later to serve as the Director of the Arms Control and Disarmament Agency (ACDA) in the Reagan administration, and was a vigorous supporter of the state of Israel--requested that the Department of State change its policy on retaliation and reprisal. Pursuant to Rostow's request, the State Department did look into the matter. Yet the State Department concluded that there were no good grounds for the United States government to change its longstanding policy that retaliation and reprisal were not legitimate exercises of the right of self-defense and, therefore, were prohibited by international law.[50]

Essentially, what happened in 1986 was that the neoconservative Reagan administration unofficially adopted the Israeli interpretation of article 51 of the United Nations Charter as including retaliation and reprisal despite the fact that the State Department had specifically refused to do so over ten years before. Under the auspices of the Reagan administration, and in particular its passionately pro-Israel Legal Adviser, Abraham Sofaer, the United States witnessed the start of what would be the progressive Israelization of American foreign policy when it came to utilizing the illegal threat and use of military force to accomplish its foreign policy objectives, especially in the Middle East. It was not surprising, therefore, that American embassies around the world had to transform themselves into armed bunkers in order to provide some degree of protection from retaliatory terrorist attacks.

The Reagan administration's wholesale terrorism inflicted upon Arab states and Muslim peoples simply encouraged the latter to respond by sponsoring or engaging in acts of retail terrorism against American airplanes, facilities, and citizens around the world. America became even more of a garrison state like Israel; while in turn, such a mutual identification of interests, values, attitudes, mentality, and position suited the overall objectives of Israeli foreign policy quite effectively. Yet another case of the tail wagging the dog.

The Violent Settlement of International Disputes

The second point that must be kept in mind with respect to the argument by the Reagan administration that the April 14 bombings could be justified as an act of self-defense under the United Nations Charter was that the U.S. government made absolutely no attempt to solve this dispute with Qaddafi over his alleged support for international terrorism in a peaceful manner as required by article 33 of the U.N. Charter. Starting in late December and early January, numerous attempts were made by Libya to contact the United States government in an effort to sit down and negotiate in order to head-off a military conflict.[51] In one way or another, the prime ministers of Italy and Malta and the governments of Saudi Arabia and Belgium also attempted to avoid a military confrontation by transmitting Libyan messages, offering to mediate, or by calling for conferences of the then E.E.C. and Mediterranean states to deal with the problem of international terrorism.[52] But as the Reagan administration quite forthrightly admitted, it had absolutely no intention of talking to, or negotiating and compromising with Qaddafi over anything.[53] In their opinion, there was nothing to discuss because, quite simply put, they wanted Qaddafi's head on a platter.

I personally found it appalling that the United States government would launch a bombing operation during the middle of the night on Qaddafi's family compound located in metropolitan Tripoli. To the best of my knowledge, whatever terrorist training operations might allegedly occur in Libya did not occur at this compound. Rather, the compound was Qaddafi's home where he lived with his wife and children. He also received visiting dignitaries and heads of state in this compound. According to the subjective criteria applied by the Reagan administration, the White House would be a far more significant "terrorist command center" than Qaddafi's compound was or ever could be.

The compound itself was located right in the heart of metropolitan Tripoli surrounded by large numbers of civilian homes, offices, shops, etc. The Reagan administration must have known that to launch a complicated bombing operation on the compound in the middle of the night when visibility would have been significantly diminished could only have resulted in a significantly large loss of innocent human lives. Yet in their ruthless attempt to murder Qaddafi and his entire family, the Reagan administration was fully prepared to sacrifice innocent Libyan civilians in order to achieve this abhorrent goal. If that was the attitude of the United States government officials toward innocent civilian lives in Libya, then I believe that realistically they could have expected no more respect on the part of Libya or its supporters or its sympathizers around the world for innocent American lives. Nevertheless, it was a tribute to Qaddafi's sense of humanity that he did not undertake a terrorist campaign against American civilians to avenge his family and compatriots. Rather, Qaddafi decided to authorize lawsuits in the United States federal court system against the United States and the United Kingdom together with the leading U.S. and U.K. government officials responsible for their criminal bombings of Tripoli and Benghazi, as will be explained below.

Assassination Is a War Crime

It seems pretty clear from the public record that the attack on the compound was obviously intended to murder Qaddafi and his entire family no matter what the costs. This goal was the culmination of the Reagan administration's basic foreign policy objective toward Libya going all the way back to its very start in 1981 when they put Qaddafi at the top of their hit list. It clearly violated the Reagan administration's own standing Executive Order that prohibited U.S. participation in assassinations, thus demonstrating the need for that Order to be replaced by a formal statute with tough criminal sanctions.[54]

It was the official policy of the United States government that assassination of anyone, let alone a head of state or head of government, was a violation of the laws and customs of warfare and therefore a war crime. This prohibition goes all the way back to the Hague Regulations of 1907, which prohibit killing of adversaries in armed conflict by means of treachery. This minimal standard of international behavior was later incorporated into the U.S. Army Field Manual 27-10 *The Law of Land Warfare* (1956).[55] This official position of the United States government on the requirements of international law for the conduct of warfare was drafted anonymously by the late Richard R. Baxter, Professor at the Harvard Law School and later Judge of the International Court of Justice. This author was privileged to have studied international law, including the laws of war, with Professor Baxter from 1974 to 1976.

The Field Manual prescribes the appropriate standards of international law and U.S. domestic law applicable to such situations that have long been recognized as valid by the United States government. According to paragraph 498 thereof any person, whether a member of the armed forces or a civilian, who commits an act which constitutes a crime under international law is responsible therefore and liable to punishment. Such offenses in connection with warfare include what are commonly known as "war crimes." Paragraph 499 defines the term "war crime" to be the technical expression for a violation of the law of war by any person or persons, military or civilian. Every violation of the law of war is a war crime.

According to paragraph 31 thereof, political assassination is a violation of the law of war. And pursuant to paragraph 500, conspiracy, direct incitement, and attempts to commit as well as complicity in the commission of such war crimes are similarly punishable as war crimes. According to paragraph 501, any U.S. government official who had actual knowledge, or should have had knowledge, through reports received by him or through other means that troops or other persons subject to his control were about to commit or committed war crimes and failed to take the necessary and reasonable steps to insure compliance with the law of war or to punish violators thereof was similarly guilty of a war crime.[56] Finally, paragraph 510 thereof denies the defense of "act of state" to such alleged war criminals by providing that the fact a person who committed an act which constitutes a war crime acted as the head of state or as a responsible government official does not relieve him from responsibility for his act.

Thus all civilian officials and military officers in the United States government who either knew or should have known that the Reagan administration intended to assassinate Qaddafi and participated in the bombing operation are "war criminals" according to the U.S. government's own official definition of that term. The American people should not have permitted any aspect of their foreign affairs and defense policies to be conducted by acknowledged "war criminals." They should have insisted upon the impeachment, dismissal, resignation, and prosecution of all U.S. government officials guilty of such war crimes. Nevertheless, U.S. public opinion had been so effectively brutalized by five years of Reaganism that over three-quarters of the American people rallied to the support of their demented leadership over the destruction, injuries, and death it had inflicted upon hundreds of innocent civilians in Tripoli and Benghazi.

Terrorism and War

These observations place the Reagan administration's so-called war against international terrorism in a completely different light. The Reagan administration consistently manipulated the whole concept of some need to fight a war against international terrorism in order to put various bills through Congress that would constitute serious infringements upon the civil rights and civil liberties of people here in the United States. Other legislative proposals attempted to give the Reagan administration congressional authorization to engage in the threat and use of force in clear-cut violation of basic principles of international law as well as of the terms of the United States Constitution and other provisions of U.S. domestic law.

For example, the Reagan administration had long sought to repeal the War Powers Resolution[57] precisely because it was specifically designed to prevent presidential war abuses when it came to the threat and use of U.S. military force in order to forestall the development of another Vietnam War along the lines of the Gulf of Tonkin scenario. Thus, immediately after the Libyan bombings, the Reagan administration attempted to amend the War Powers Resolution out of existence by introducing a piece of legislation that essentially exempted presidential military action from the most important requirements of the statute so long as it was purportedly designed to combat international terrorism against the United States. At least two sponsors of this legislation, Senator Robert Dole and Senator Jeremiah Denton, said the measure would authorize the assassination of anyone, including a foreign head of state, who organizes, attempts, commits, procures, or supports the commission of an act of terrorism against United States citizens.[58] Presumably this would have constituted a congressional license for President Reagan to order the murder of Qaddafi, Hafez al-Assad of Syria, Ayatollah Ruhollah Khomeini of Iran, Daniel Ortega of Nicaragua, Fidel Castro of Cuba, Saddam Hussein of Iraq and any other leaders of foreign states that the United States government might seriously disagree with so long as they or it are alleged to support "international terrorism." Most ominously, we must remember that from its very outset in 1981 the Reagan administration vigorously yet disingenuously proclaimed that the Soviet Union was responsible for a good deal of the terrorism directed against American interests around the world.

The outbreak of the First World War provides a very compelling example of the principle at stake here. This conflagration started because of a terrorist attack at Sarajevo by a Serbian nationalist against Archduke Francis Ferdinand, who was heir-apparent to the throne of the Austro-Hungarian empire. With the backing of Germany, Austria-Hungary issued an ultimatum to Serbia, which in turn was supported by Russia. Eventually the world went to war and approximately 20 million people were killed.[59] At the 1919 Paris Peace Conference, however, the Allied Powers put the responsibility for the outbreak of the war squarely upon the shoulders of the Central Powers by means of article 231 of the Treaty of Versailles.[60]

This experience with "international terrorism" a century ago should have established the validity of the proposition to the satisfaction of the entire international community that the assassination of even a head of state or heir-presumptive to a throne was insufficient grounds for going to war or resorting to the threat or use of military force. Yet the Reagan administration foolishly and quite contemptuously tried to rewrite the tragic lessons of modern history. As George Santayana wrote: "Those who cannot remember the past are condemned to repeat it."[61] Except that at this point in the thermonuclear age, there will most probably not be a peace conference at the end of World War III.

The Disinformation Campaign Against Libya

In late November of 1986 the U.N. General Assembly finally passed a resolution soundly condemning the April bombings of Libya as a violation of international law. The resolution, sponsored by 27 states, also called upon the United States "to refrain from the use or threat of force" against Libya and said that Libya had the right to "appropriate compensation for the material and human losses inflicted."[62] The General Assembly passed this resolution after it had been revealed that the Reagan administration purposely launched a "disinformation campaign" designed to deceive the U.S. news media and the American people as well as Qaddafi into believing that it was going to take further military action against him.

As reported in the *Washington Post*, the Reagan administration engaged in a "war of nerves" with Qaddafi in the hope of "scar[ing] him into an irrational reaction."[63] The plan was the product of meetings between Secretary of State George Shultz and C.I.A. Director William Casey that had occurred in late July. It called for the Reagan administration to promote the renewal of the threat of international terrorism allegedly posed by Qaddafi in order to orchestrate his downfall. The plan was to include pressures of an economic, military, political, and psychological nature.[64] The plan appeared to have been revised several times throughout the summer during various meetings of the so-called Crisis

Pre-Planning Group—truly Orwellian: planning crises!—and the National Security Planning Group, a subsidiary body of the National Security Council. Fortunately, the existence of the disinformation campaign was leaked to the press by disaffected elements of the Reagan administration who had no desire to see another round of military action against Libya.

Nevertheless, at least originally the American news media dutifully propagated the Reagan administration's party line that there existed further evidence of Libya's support for international terrorism. To be sure, once it was revealed that the Reagan administration had concocted a disinformation campaign against Qaddafi, the press then engaged in a torrent of criticism directed against its authors. But in this regard, the American news media's harsh reaction was not much more than rank hypocrisy for the media limited their criticism only to the events of August and September, 1986.

The U.S. news media never really explained to the American people that the Reagan administration had been engaging in an organized disinformation campaign against Libya and Qaddafi since 1981. I suspect the reason why was that the media did not wish to admit that they had been duped into becoming either witting or unwitting accomplices to the Reagan administration's plans to overthrow Qaddafi for the preceding five years. There has yet to be produced a comprehensive and detailed study of how the U.S. news media had been deceived and manipulated by the Reagan administration from its very outset in 1981 in order to propagate disinformation against Qaddafi that could be used to build support among the American people and Congress for military aggression against Libya for the purpose of producing his deposition. This author doubts very seriously that the U.S. news media will ever attempt to correct the public record and thus admit its own negligence and culpability in these matters. The U.S. mainstream news media has always been *Manufacturing Consent* (Chomsky and Herman: 1988) for war by the United States government.

The Overthrow of Qaddafi

Even if the Reagan administration had succeeded in overthrowing Colonel Qaddafi, the question would then have become who would take his place? Libya was effectively governed by a Revolutionary Command Council (R.C.C.). Although the members of the Council were not in complete agreement with Colonel Qaddafi on all key issues, nevertheless they did seem congruent on basic points. If Qaddafi were to be overthrown or assassinated the one major change that could be anticipated to be made might have been the abandonment of Qaddafi's *Green Book* as the philosophical basis for political and economic decision-making in Libya.

Moreover, even assuming that a joint U.S.-Egyptian military invasion of Libya had led to the complete destruction of the Revolutionary Command Council and its replacement by a civilian leadership, I submit that this would still not have solved what the Reagan administration perceived to be the "Libyan problem." Any civilian leadership that was installed in Libya at the behest or with the connivance of the United States government would have possessed absolutely no legitimacy in the eyes of the vast majority of the Libyan people, and would have to be sustained in power by a continued U.S. presence. Whether the United States government liked it or not, Qaddafi was incredibly popular with the common people of Libya. And for good cause. He distributed vast amounts of oil income that had come into the Libyan treasury during his tenure to the common people of Libya by one means or another.

Before the Qaddafi coup against King Idris the Libyan people lived in a situation of dire poverty despite the inflow of oil money because of the royal family's corruption. Qaddafi completely reversed this situation. As a direct result of the Qaddafi Revolution, the Libyan people acquired excellent and subsidized housing, education, and health care. Libya maintained a very high standard of living for its citizens that was comparable to that found in many of the Mediterranean countries in Europe. Qaddafi gave Libyans the highest per-capita standard of living on the Continent of Africa.

Despite the manifest weight of the evidence to the contrary, the Reagan administration sorely deluded itself into believing that all they would have to do in order to instigate the Libyan people or military into rising up against and deposing Qaddafi would be to destroy the Libyan air force and perhaps engage in some other types of hostile actions against military and economic targets in Libya. This delusion was somewhat akin to that which possessed the Kennedy administration when it authorized the surrogate invasion of Cuba in the naive expectation that the Cuban people would rise up and depose Castro.

This was not to deny that there were indeed significant sources of opposition to Qaddafi within the urban educated elite of Tripoli and Benghazi. Indeed, from the perspective of many in this group, Qaddafi was a fairly unsophisticated Bedouin bumpkin from the desert who it was their misfortune to have ruling them. Nevertheless, when the United States government made military threats or took military action against Qaddafi, it forced all sectors of Libyan society to rally to his support against what they perceived to be imperialist intervention by a superpower. Moreover, as witnessed in the aftermath of the 1986 events, the same happened throughout the Arab world. Many Arab leaders who bore absolutely nothing but animosity and contempt for Qaddafi were nevertheless forced by the United States government to rally to his support when the Reagan administration threatened military action against him as a gesture of Arab solidarity.

Qaddafi's *Green Book*

The Reagan administration publicly attempted to justify its overall goal of deposing Colonel Qaddafi by also claiming that he was a fanatical revolutionary leader preaching values that were contrary to the interests of the United States of America. They cited in particular Qaddafi's *Green Book*, which consists of three slim volumes giving his viewpoints on a variety of international and domestic issues. While in Libya, I had the opportunity to publicly debate the meaning of the *Green Book* with some Libyan professors and in particular whether or not the teachings of the *Green Book* could be applied to the United States of America. So I submit that I have some familiarity with its contents both in theory and in practice as applied in Libya.

It is certainly true that Qaddafi was attempting to carry out the philosophy that he articulated in the *Green Book* for Libya. What enabled him to do this was the incredible revenue that Libya had derived from its oil income. Without those oil resources, however, the dreams which Qaddafi set forth for Libya in the *Green Book* would have been completely impossible to attain. Thus, the prescriptions of the *Green Book* could only have been carried out, if at all, in an oil-based economy of substantial wealth that existed perhaps within a very few Arab states in the Middle East--viz., Saudi Arabia, Kuwait, the Gulf Sheikhdoms, etc. Feasible only because of its unusual combination of economic (oil), cultural (North African), religious (moderate Sunni Muslim), and ethnic (Arab Bedouin) elements, Qaddafi's *Green Book* would have (and has had) quite limited appeal to other states and peoples around the world.

Even then, the argument that somehow Qaddafi was a fanatic revolutionary is simply misconceived and distorted. There is nothing at all revolutionary about the teachings of the *Green Book*. Essentially, the *Green Book* is a modernized and relatively simplified rendition of Jean-Jacques Rousseau's *The Social Contract*. I will not bother to go through a comparison and contrast of the two works here. Suffice it to say that although Rousseau's *Social Contract* was revolutionary when it was published in 1762 and generally is considered to be the harbinger for the French Revolution of 1789, the basic principles set forth in that book lie at the very heart of West European civilization today. In particular, many of Rousseau's ideas can be found in the constitutions of advanced democratic-socialist nation states currently existing throughout Europe.

From that perspective, therefore, there is nothing at all revolutionary about Qaddafi trying to model Libya on Rousseau's *Social*

Contract. This endeavor only became revolutionary when one considers that under King Idris Libyans basically lived in a feudal society that was somewhat akin to the European middle ages. It would certainly be true that to apply Rousseau's *Social Contract* to a feudalistic society is indeed a revolutionary act. But it was a revolution whose time was long overdue and most of us schooled in a Rousseauian tradition could only applaud such a progressive development.

It is for this reason then that the teachings of the *Green Book* represented a definite threat in the eyes of several elite groups that governed the other Arab oil states. Some Arab oil states are controlled by dynastic regimes who still conduct themselves on feudalistic principles reminiscent of the Western middle ages. If Qaddafi's ideas were to be generally accepted by their respective peoples, then of course that would lead to their depositions. For this reason, they saw Qaddafi as a threat to their existence in power, and in this sense they were certainly correct in their perceptions.

In my opinion, however, the United States government had no interest in seeing the preservation of feudal or reactionary regimes throughout the Middle East and Persian Gulf in order to maintain their continuance in power in return for the free flow of expensive oil to the United States, Western Europe, or Japan. At some point in time these regimes will either have to reform themselves (which seems to be most unlikely) or will be overthrown by their own people. The latter might in turn institute an Islamic fundamentalist government *à la* Iran that is far more "radical" (from a Western perspective) than anything Qaddafi had ever envisioned.

Qaddafi's Relations with the Soviet Union

The Reagan administration's irresistible impulse to overthrow Qaddafi at all costs also put into proper perspective Libya's connection with the Soviet Union. As far as I could tell from three trips to Libya as their guest in 1985, 1987, and 1988, as well as three trips to the Soviet Union/Russia as their guest in 1986, 1989, and 1993, this was purely an alliance of convenience on both sides that in the opinion of most Libyans was dictated by considerations of military necessity. The Libyans were not overly enthusiastic about being driven to a point by the Reagan administration where they would become even more dependent on the Soviets than they already were for their military subsistence and thus political survival.

The Libyans had to buy military equipment from the Soviet Union because the Soviets proved to be one of the few major suppliers of arms willing to give them what they believed was necessary for their legitimate defense. The United States government made it exceedingly difficult for the Libyans to purchase military weapons, equipment, and supplies from countries in Europe. In particular the Reagan administration used whatever influence it had over its NATO allies to reduce or terminate their provision of any form of military assistance to Qaddafi. The Libyans definitely would have liked to multilateralize their sources for arms supplies. But the U.S. government left Qaddafi with no alternative but to turn to the Soviets in order to acquire those weapons he believed were necessary to defend himself from aggression by the United States or Egypt or both.

I could not accept at face value Qaddafi's claim that Libya would go communist if the Reagan administration continued to threaten it with aggression. When I was in Libya I was struck by the fact that, overall, it seemed to be a moderately devout Sunni Muslim society. I could not really imagine Libya becoming Marxist-Leninist precisely because that would be completely inconsistent with the tenets of Islam. In his *Green Book* Qaddafi made it quite clear that Third World countries such as Libya needed to develop and implement an ideology that provided a third pathway that was separate and distinct from capitalism, on the one hand, and communism, on the other, but which was nevertheless compatible with Islam.

With the U.S. Sixth Fleet operating in the Gulf of Sidra, the Egyptian army to the East, a government in Chad that had been installed by the C.I.A. and bolstered by the French army, a pro-U.S. government in Tunisia, and a history of governments in the Sudan that had been complacent to the wishes of the United States and Egypt, the Libyans felt surrounded on all sides by overtly hostile military forces under the direct or indirect control of the United States government. If Qaddafi believed it would be necessary to preserve himself in power, he would have been prepared to give the Soviet Union a naval base on the Gulf of Sidra, or an air base in the nearby desert, or both. Qaddafi would have done anything that was necessary to defend himself and his country and his people and his Revolution against military aggression by the United States government. To be sure, however, the Soviets were quite reluctant to accept such overtures because, in their opinion, Qaddafi was unpredictable and uncontrollable.

Hence the primary reason for the substantial Soviet presence in Libya had more to do with the aggressive policies pursued by the Reagan administration and its predecessors and its successors, than with the natural predilections of the Libyans. We can see this phenomenon in operation with respect to Qaddafi's reaction to the 1981 Gulf of Sidra incident. This and other events eventually led him to request Soviet SAM-5 missiles that were then installed along the Gulf of Sidra from Benghazi down through the oil facilities and up to Sirte and Tripoli. These missiles were under the supervision of Soviet troops. It was clear that the purpose and presence of the Soviet installation of SAM-5s commencing in the late fall of 1985 was to protect Libyan airspace from any further hostile intrusion by United States jet fighters as occurred in 1981. And in the 1986 crisis the Soviets dispatched several combat ships to the Gulf of Sidra and placed numerous radar and intelligence ships strung out along the Mediterranean coast from the Gulf of Sidra to Israel in order to provide the Libyans with early warning intelligence of a U.S., Egyptian, or Israeli military attack.

Qaddafi's Relations with Egypt

The Reagan canard that Qaddafi was some great threat to the vital national security interests of the United States was complete nonsense. At the time Libya was a very small country with approximately 3.5 million people, 1 million of whom lived in Tripoli the capital, 500,000 in Benghazi, and the rest were scattered throughout towns that are basically oases in the midst of the desert wasteland. Libya's major security threat was of course from the Egyptian army, a good deal of which was deployed on the Libyan border. As mentioned above, Egypt had invaded Libya once before in 1977 with the approval of the neoliberal Carter administration.[65]

As reported in the *New York Times*, former Egyptian President Anwar Sadat and former French President Valery Giscard d'Estaing once plotted an attempt to assassinate Qaddafi.[66] In addition, the late President Sadat repeatedly offered to the United States government to remove Qaddafi from power by means of an Egyptian invasion. Obviously, an Egyptian invasion of Libya to overthrow Qaddafi could very well have led to the further destabilization of what was already a volatile internal situation in Egypt. Nevertheless undaunted, the Reagan administration made repeated overtures to Egyptian President Hosni Mubarak to take joint military action against Qaddafi.[67]

If it were ever seen that Mubarak had invaded a fellow Arab state at the behest of the United States government, there could have occurred very serious internal disturbances in Egypt that could have precipitated his overthrow. As demonstrated by the 1986 riots by the Egyptian paramilitary police, Mubarak already confronted an incredibly precarious internal situation to begin with. An invasion of a fellow Arab state by Mubarak could have resulted in the installation of a more radical regime that not only would completely disassociate itself from the United States government but perhaps also repudiate the Israel-Egyptian Peace Treaty of 1979.[68] Mubarak would eventually fall to his own people as part of the "Arab Spring" in 2011, to be replaced by an elected President from the Muslim Brotherhood in 2012. Yet in their mindless rush to destroy Qaddafi, the Reagan administration was prepared to jeopardize Mubarak and consequently to undermine this monumental accomplishment by the Carter administration.

For one reason or another, Mubarak did not overtly associate himself with Reagan's obsessive compulsion to destroy Qaddafi. Reportedly, Egyptian Defense Minister Abu-Ghazala would have been more than happy to go along with an American plan for joint military action against Qaddafi. Aware of this problem, in April of 1988 Qaddafi wisely decided to ease tensions with Egypt by announcing the withdrawal of Libyan troops from the Egyptian border.

The European Attitude toward Qaddafi and Reagan

In light of the above analysis, it now becomes quite clear and eminently understandable why European governments were reluctant to support the Reagan administration's demand to impose political and economic sanctions against Qaddafi. From the European perspective the U.S. foreign policy with respect to Libya was completely misconceived and thoroughly counterproductive. They would take only minimal gestures in support of the U.S. position primarily because of the great pressure brought to bear by the United States government and their fear that if they did not do something the Reagan administration would cynically manipulate their cautious hesitations in order to justify U.S. resort to the further threat and use of military force. As Prime Minister Margaret Thatcher of the United Kingdom quite rightly pointed out the first time, retaliatory military measures taken against Libya clearly violated international law.[69] I submit the other European governments viewed the matter in precisely the same way.

The European powers were essentially bludgeoned by the Reagan administration into taking action against Libya despite their better judgment and instincts to the contrary. The Reagan administration argued to the Europeans that if they did not take decisive measures against Qaddafi, then the United States government would have to give serious consideration to taking further military action against him. A constant refrain of U.S. foreign policy! Yet, while their Foreign Ministers were meeting at The Hague to discuss taking such further diplomatic, political, and economic steps, the United States government had already put into operation the plan for the bombing of Libya which took place on April 14.[70] This sequence of events made a mockery of the Reagan administration's claim that it was the European governments' failure to support them vigorously that led the United States into taking unilateral military action against Qaddafi. Conversely, even if the European governments were to fully support the Reagan administration by imposing extensive diplomatic and economic sanctions on Libya, the Reagan neoconservatives would have only cynically transmogrified these half-hearted measures into a European imprimatur for an escalation of tensions for yet another round of U.S. military action against Libya specifically designed for the purpose of destroying Qaddafi.

Thus, U.S.-based criticism of European governments to the effect that they would not actively support America in its "war against international terrorism" primarily because of economic motivations was simply unwarranted. To be sure, oil was one among many factors. But the main reason they did not support Reagan with respect to Qaddafi or on U.S. Middle East foreign policy in general was simply because of their good faith belief that America's approach was fatally flawed.

This raised a much broader point with respect to European attitudes toward the Reagan administration's overall foreign policy toward the Middle East. Quite frankly, none of the countries of Europe agreed with the Reagan administration's policy toward the Middle East because it essentially gave Israel a blank check to do whatever it wanted in the region. As far as the Europeans were concerned, this policy was foolish, counterproductive, and would only lead to more bloodshed and violence in that volatile area of the world.

In particular, from the European perspective the United States government must be willing to take some tangible gestures in recognition of the international legal right of the Palestinian people to self-determination and an independent state of their own. As far as the Europeans were concerned, until this occurred American foreign policy toward the Middle East would prove to be an abysmal failure and, in their opinion, they wanted little to do with it. After all, Europeans live on the other side of the Med. Hence, Americans cannot expect the Europeans to support America on its overall Middle East foreign policy unless America becomes more fair, even-handed, and balanced with respect to the international legal rights of Arab states and Muslim peoples, and especially the Palestinians.

Qaddafi as Reagan's Bête Noire

Shortly after the bombings of Tripoli and Benghazi the Reagan administration began making the patently bogus claim that their savagery had somehow diminished the number of terrorist attacks against United States targets, thus proclaiming the existence of some direct cause-and-effect relationship in an effort to justify the raids on an ex post facto basis. This argument--based on the unsupported and fallacious assumption that Qaddafi and Libya were somehow behind the major terrorist attacks against Americans during the preceding four years--was also proved wrong by the facts.[71] The administration's argument was particularly reprehensible because it simply encouraged and incited further terrorist attacks against American interests to prove that their boasts were incorrect. Interviewed four months after the raid, Rand Corporation terrorism expert Brian Jenkins reported that the figures lent no support to the administration's hypothesis that the Libyan bombing had reduced the frequency of terrorist attacks around the world.[72]

In essence, Qaddafi had very little to do with all of this. Most of these anti-American terrorist attacks originated out of Lebanon and the Bekaa Valley with the patronage, support, or tacit approval of the Syrian government. Qaddafi perhaps provided funding to some of these groups; he undoubtedly provided some ideological and propaganda support. But Qaddafi was a very minor actor in terms of the amount and extent of terrorism that had been inflicted upon the United States since the 1982 Israeli invasion of Lebanon with the proverbial "green light" by the neoconservative Reagan administration.

It was a cheap shot for the Reagan administration to take military action against Qaddafi. Libya was somewhat akin to the Grenada of the Middle East. As a direct result of the Tripoli and Benghazi bombings, the rank hypocrisy and pernicious consequences of the neoconservative Reagan administration's so-called war against international terrorism became glaringly obvious to the vast majority of states and peoples in the world community. Yet the American people, Congress, and media continued to work themselves into a rage of self-righteous indignation whenever the victims of the Reagan administration's belligerent foreign policies toward the Middle East responded by engaging in acts of retail terrorism against wholesale purveyors such as the United States and Israel.

In my opinion, the main reason why the neoconservative Reagan administration placed Qaddafi at the very top of its hit list from the start of its term in office was because of Qaddafi's viewpoints on the Israel-Arab dispute, though to be sure there were other sources of genuine contention that did indeed exist between our two countries. As of 1981 Qaddafi was the only leader in the entire Arab world who still publicly supported the demise of the state of Israel. Even Iraq gave up this demand in light of its attempt to normalize relations with the United States government because of the pressures of its war with Iran. The so-called "Steadfastness Front" in opposition to the Camp David Accords and the Egyptian-Israeli Peace Treaty was no longer effectively operating.[73] Together with Iran (which is not an Arab state) Qaddafi stood alone among Middle East leaders publicly pining for the end of Israel. In fairness to Qaddafi, however, I should point out that after the

1986 bombings of Tripoli and Benghazi, he quite wisely no longer uttered public pronouncements to that effect.

Yet whatever disputes or disagreements the United States government had with Qaddafi over Israel or other matters, there was no justification under international law and no rationale in terms of *realpolitik* for America undertaking measures to overthrow him or indeed to precipitate a war with Libya pretextually over the Gulf of Sidra or over his alleged support for international terrorism. Based upon my three visits to Libya, I believed that about 85% of America's outstanding disputes with the Libyan Jamahiriya could have been negotiated satisfactorily with a modicum of good faith on both sides. Even with respect to Israel, if the United States government would have been prepared to formally recognize the international legal right of the Palestinian people to self-determination and an independent state of their own, I knew for a fact that there were many responsible people in Libya who would have been fully prepared to recognize the right of Israel to exist as a state. Of course, there was no guarantee that our viewpoints on this matter would have been able to prevail with Qaddafi. But then again the only way to have found out would have been for the United States government to live up to the legal commitments it had already given to the Palestinian people as far back as the United Nations Partition Plan of 1947. I submit that Qaddafi would have given serious consideration to simply ignoring Israel provided the Palestinians were given the opportunity to live in an independent state of their own.

The Syrian Factor in the Middle East Equation

Even assuming for the sake of argument that with sufficient historical hindsight it were to be proved that there was in fact a statistically significant diminution of terrorists attacks upon Americans around the Mediterranean basin starting in the spring of 1986, this phenomenon would still have little to do with Reagan's terror bombings of Tripoli and Benghazi. Rather it would have been because the Syrians finally decided to exercise some degree of restraint over the numerous terrorist groups operating out of Lebanon and Damascus. Moreover, such a change in Syrian policy would not be attributable to the Libyan bombings, but rather to the fact that the Peres-Shamir coalition government of Israel was then preparing for and publicly threatening to launch a "preemptive" military strike upon Syria—in other words, aggression. By the spring of 1986, it appeared that Syria had finally built up its military establishment to a level equivalent to that which it occupied in relation to Israel prior to the Israeli attack on Syrian forces during the course of the former's 1982 invasion of Lebanon. Hence, the Peres-Shamir government argued it must strike Syria first in order to preserve Israeli military superiority.

Pursuant thereto, the Peres-Shamir government commenced a campaign of building up war hysteria in Israel in order to prepare the public for the supposed need to attack Syria. This propaganda was then dutifully conveyed by pro-Israeli U.S. news media in order to acclimate U.S. elite groups to the inevitable "necessity" for such Israeli military action. Thus, when Israeli Defense Minister Rabin went to Washington in May of 1986, the *Christian Science Monitor* reported that he probably was going to get permission from the United States government for a preemptive military strike upon Syria, i.e., aggression.[74] As best as can be figured out, the response he received from the Reagan administration was that any such attack should not occur under the turbulent circumstances then prevailing after the bombings of Libyan cities. But presumably this decision would not necessarily preclude an attack later on. Previously, for example, the Reagan administration had imposed the same type of operational delay upon the Begin government for the one year preceding the 1982 Israeli invasion of Lebanon despite repeated requests for permission to invade by then Minister of Defense Ariel Sharon.

This U.S.-Israeli orchestrated war scare was definitely responsible for the flurry of diplomatic activity subsequently occurring in the Middle East during the summer of 1986. Fear of an Israeli attack upon Syria with the sponsorship of the United States led President Hafez al-Assad to try to shore up his external relations with Jordan, Iraq, and Greece, among others. It was also responsible for the futile attempt by Jordan's King Hussein to try to bridge the longstanding chasm between Iraq and Syria. And, as stated above, this threat might have influenced the Syrians to exercise a greater degree of control over groups operating out of Lebanon and Damascus for the purpose of undertaking terrorist attacks against American and Israeli interests.

Another Middle East War?

Nevertheless, even lukewarm support by the Reagan administration for the idea of an Israeli offensive strike on Syria could easily have proved to be a cosmic blunder for U.S. foreign policy in the Middle East. For example, in the unfortunate event of an Israeli attack on Syrian territory it was questionable whether the Israeli-Egyptian Peace Treaty could have survived at the time. A Minute to article VI, paragraph 5 of the Israeli-Egyptian Peace Treaty provided that it is agreed by the parties that there is no assertion that the Peace Treaty prevails over other treaties or agreements or that other treaties or agreements prevail over the Peace Treaty.[75] This Minute makes it clear that the Peace Treaty does not prevail over the defense treaties that Egypt had concluded with Syria, pursuant to their mutual right of collective self-defense recognized by article 51 of the United Nations Charter.[76] In the event Israel were to perpetrate an "armed attack" upon Syrian territory, the Egyptian defense treaties would enter into operation, and nothing in the Peace Treaty would stand in the way of Egypt coming to the defense of Syria in accordance with the formers' respective terms.

I strongly suspect that the Egyptian government interpreted its legal obligations in the manner indicated above. Shortly after the Peace Treaty was signed, then Egyptian Prime Minister Khalil stated that he would regard any attempt by Syria to recover the Golan Heights as a defensive war that would bring into play the Egyptian-Syrian defense treaty despite the provisions of the Israeli-Egyptian Peace Treaty. According to reports received at the time, Prime Minister Begin immediately called up President Sadat on the so-called "hot line" between Jerusalem and Cairo that was established in the aftermath of the signing of the Peace Treaty in order to complain. Khalil then issued a clarification of his statement to the effect that Syria would not be entitled to use force to regain the Golan Heights so long as Israel was willing to negotiate in good faith.[77] A fortiori, however, this episode tended to indicate that if Israel were to have invaded Syrian territory itself, the Egyptian government would not have viewed the Peace Treaty as negating its legal right and duty to come to the assistance of Syria under the terms of their mutual defense treaty and U.N. Charter article 51.

As of 2013 the political situation seems to have altered somewhat when Egyptian President Morsi has supported the U.S./NATO war of so-far indirect aggression against Syria. But it is still not clear what revolutionary Egypt would do if Israel were to attack let alone invade Syria. It would behoove Israel not to test the patience of the revolutionary Egyptian people, parliament and president by attacking let alone invading Syria or Jordan.

The same line of analysis would likewise be applicable to Egyptian international legal obligations toward Jordan in the event of an Israeli military attack upon the latter country. Ariel Sharon and the Likhud Party had long suggested that the best solution to the right of self-determination for the Palestinian people would be for Israel to depose King Hussein and then turn Jordan over to the P.L.O. Whereupon Israel would annex the West Bank and expel the native Palestinians to Jordan.

By relying upon Israel as its regional "policeman" for the Middle East, the United States government seems to have forgotten the primary lesson that historians have drawn from the First World War: Namely, it was the very dynamics and rigidities of the European great power spheres-of-influence system that, to a great extent, were responsible for the outbreak of that conflagration over the Balkans under the impetus of an act of international terrorism at Sarajevo. As Miles Kahler so astutely observed in his now classic article, *Rumors of War: The 1914 Analogy*,[78] it is a repetition of this "systemic breakdown" scenario responsible for the eruption of the First World War, not necessarily the "madman" explanation for the outbreak of the Second World War, which today's thermonuclear decision-makers should most scrupulously guard against. Only the passage of time can tell whether the United States government would foolishly permit the Israeli government to attack Syria or Jordan or Iran, thus preparing the way for the development of yet another general war in the Middle East that would immediately put the two thermonuclear superpowers at loggerheads and threaten to engulf the rest of the world in a nuclear cataclysm. Peace in the Middle East, if not the world at large, demands that the United States government disengage from its unholy but only de facto and not de jure alliance with Israel.

Tripoli Revisited

Most of what one could read about Libya in the American news media and academic literature was (and indeed, post 2011 R2P remains) total nonsense. For a variety of reasons, I was unable to return to Tripoli until mid-August of 1987. What I found at that time shocked my sensitivities as a human being and my conscience as an American citizen and lawyer.

I spent the better part of one morning touring the formerly devastated section of the Libyan metropolitan area that was still undergoing reconstruction. That afternoon I visited the bombed-out home of Colonel Qaddafi and his family. I was greatly moved to see the little bed where his adopted daughter Hana was crushed to death by a beam from the ceiling. Her autopsy picture is grisly. Hana was a Palestinian rendered an orphan by the Israeli invasion of Lebanon whom Mr. and Mrs. Qaddafi had adopted. Now murdered by a U.S. bomb while sleeping in her crib in Tripoli.

I then had the opportunity to discuss the events of that fateful evening with Qaddafi himself. He received me in a tent pitched in an open field a bit down the road from his destroyed home that had been preserved as a museum. At the end of our conversation, Qaddafi turned to me and said (in Arabic): "Who would have thought that a superpower like the United States would come over to a small country like Libya and bomb innocent people sleeping in their homes during the middle of the night?" When you think about it, Reagan's savagery really was extraordinary and incomprehensible. But most do not, nor likely did Reagan realize how truly bizarre the action was, when seen from the viewpoint of those on the receiving end in its actuality.

It was obvious that the destruction inflicted upon Tripoli

and Benghazi was clearly intended by the neoconservative Reagan administration to constitute terror bombings designed to send a message to the people of Libya that such is the price they paid for the leadership of Colonel Qaddafi. But as my international relations teacher Robert Jervis pointed out in his classic *Perception and Misperception in International Politics* (1976), it is usually the case in international politics that the message you intend to send is very different from the message that is received by the intended recipients and third parties. Throughout the two weeks that I spent in Libya in August 1987, everyone I met was appalled, shocked, and outraged over this barbarous attempt by the Reagan administration to murder the entire Qaddafi family by killing innocent people sleeping in their beds at night. Any residual feelings of good will towards the United States of America had drastically diminished.

The fact that Qaddafi survived was deemed to be a miraculous event. After touring Qaddafi's home, one could only conclude that Allah must have been on Qaddafi's side. Otherwise, he would not have survived the direct bombs hitting his house and tent.

Somewhat paradoxically, therefore, and despite their best intentions, the Reagan administration had elevated Colonel Qaddafi into the realm of epic myth. His internal position became more unassailable than ever before because it was perceived to be ordained by divine providence itself. Henceforth, whatever has happened to Qaddafi the man, the legend of Qaddafi will live on in Arab folklore long after Reagan is gone.

Two years to the day after the bombings of Tripoli and Benghazi, former U.S. Attorney General Ramsey Clark filed a lawsuit in U.S. Federal District Court in Washington, D.C. seeking compensation on behalf of the victims against all the U.S./U.K. mad dog bombers and the two governments involved. Pursuant to my personal promise to Colonel Qaddafi, I served as Legal Advisor to Ramsey from the beginning to the end of these legal proceedings, including two trips all the way up to the United States Supreme Court and down again. I also submitted a 107-page Affidavit sworn under oath backing up everything in Clark's lawsuits under International Law, U.S. Constitutional Law, and the Laws of War that was twice filed in all three courts in order to make a record for history that we had at least tried to hold them all accountable. Sometimes that is all lawyers can do.

U.K. Prime Minister Margaret Thatcher was so irate at my claims that she was a war criminal that she had her lawyers request the presiding U.S. Federal District Judge to strike my Affidavit from the record on the grounds that it was "scurrilous." This he declined to do. He also rejected the requests by the lawyers for both sets of U.S. and U.K. defendants that Clark be sanctioned for filing a "frivolous" lawsuit. Nevertheless, on appeal, two Reaganite Judges sanctioned Clark for filing a "frivolous" appeal and "frivolous" lawsuits.[79] In other words, as far as this Panel of the United States Court of Appeals for the District of Columbia was concerned, filing lawsuits that were thoroughly grounded in the Nuremberg Charter of 1945 and the Nuremberg Judgment of 1946 had become "frivolous" and indeed sanctionable. Citing Nuremberg has now become a sanctionable offense in United States Federal Courts when it is applied to U.S. government officials and their great noble allies. Notorious Nazi Law Professor Carl Schmitt must feel proud and vindicated. At the end of the day, Clark had to pay "sanctions" to the British government out of his own retirement funds.

Reagan's Parting Blow Against Libya

Just before the Reagan administration was to cede power to Bush Senior, on January 4, 1989 U.S. Navy F-14 Tomcat jet fighters maneuvering off the coast of Libya with a Sixth Fleet aircraft carrier task force organized around the *John F. Kennedy* shot down two Libyan airplanes within fifty miles or so north of Tobruk. Unlike as allegedly occurred in the summer of 1981, however, the Tomcats did not even bother to wait to be fired upon first before they destroyed the Libyan aircraft. The Reagan administration attempted to justify this wanton aggression under the doctrine of self-defense as recognized by article 51 of the United Nations Charter. Suffice it to say that if the shoe were on the other foot, there is no way the United States government would have tolerated Libyan jet fighters engaging in highly provocative aerial maneuvers right off the U.S. coast, let alone in conjunction with a Libyan aircraft carrier task force.

This incident had been immediately preceded by and contemporaneously accompanied with public intimations by various members of the Reagan administration--including one by the President himself--that they were then contemplating a Sixth Fleet military operation to destroy an alleged chemical weapons plant at the Libyan town of Rabta, which is approximately 40 miles southwest of Tripoli. Launching provocative naval and air exercises off the coast of Libya in order to produce some type of Libyan response for the express purpose of escalating an incident into an outright conflict had been the standard operating procedure of the Reagan administration since the summer of 1981. This January 1989 incident readily fit into the pattern of belligerent conduct previously established by the Reagan administration whenever it sought to create a pretext for engaging in major military operations against Libya for the purpose of either overthrowing or murdering Muammar Qaddafi.

No point would be served here by discussing whether or not the Rabta chemical factory was actually designed for the production of pharmaceuticals as maintained by Libya. It is important to note, however, that Libya formally offered to allow the United States government to inspect this plant but the Reagan administration peremptorily rejected this forthcoming overture. Next, Libya made an offer to allow the United Nations to inspect the Rabta plant. Moreover, Colonel Qaddafi publicly offered to settle this dispute with the incoming Bush Senior administration by means of direct negotiations. Furthermore, Libya attempted to work through third countries such as Italy and Saudi Arabia in order to produce a peaceful settlement of this dispute with the United States government.

Yet, consistent with its longstanding pattern of aggressive behavior toward Libya, the Reagan administration brusquely rejected all offers of third party intermediation as well as of direct bilateral negotiations despite the clear-cut requirements of United Nations Charter articles 2(3) and 33 mandating the peaceful resolution of this dispute. Under these circumstances, there was no valid justification under international law for the latest and last example of the Reagan administration's threat and use of military force against Libya. Nevertheless, a second U.S. aircraft carrier task force organized around the *Theodore Roosevelt* was ordered to arrive on station in the Mediterranean off the coast of Libya for precisely this purpose. The United States government had previously determined that two aircraft carrier task forces constituted the minimum amount of military deployment required for mounting major military operations against Libya.

Reagan's Hypocrisy and Double-standards on Chemical and Biological Weapons (W.M.D)

Even assuming that the Libyan plant at Rabta was indeed a chemical weapons production facility, there would have been no violation of international law for Libya to have pursued such a capability. The Geneva (Gas) Protocol of 1925 only prohibits *"the use in war* of asphyxiating, poisonous or other gases, and of all analogous liquids materials or devices" as well as "bacteriological methods of warfare." (Emphasis added.) Whereas, by contrast, the Biological Weapons Convention of 1972 expressly requires state parties "never in any circumstances to develop, produce, stockpile or otherwise acquire or retain" biological agents or toxins except for "prophylactic, protective or other peaceful purposes." At the time, there was nothing illegal for a state to develop, possess, and stockpile chemical weapons.

Thus, for example, no matter how regrettable it might have been, many other states in the Middle East already possessed chemical weapons--viz., Israel, Iraq, Syria, and Egypt, among others. Moreover, the Reagan administration had just recently looked the other way when Iraq used chemical weapons against Iran during the course of the Iraq-Iran war in gross and obvious violation of the Geneva Protocol of 1925. The Reagan administration's righteous indignation over chemical weapons was nowhere in evidence when Iraq was gassing thousands of Iranian soldiers and civilians, as well as several hundred of its own Kurdish citizens at the Iraqi town of Halabja, precisely because the United States government had been "tilting" quite strenuously in favor of Iraq against Iran throughout the course of that conflagration.

Furthermore, the one state in the Middle East that right then was illegally using chemical weapons in warfare was Israel, America's de facto ally. During the first year of the first Palestinian Intifadah starting in December 1987, approximately 66 Palestinian civilians were tear-gassed to death by the Israeli army in occupied Palestine. The use of tear-gas in warfare or international armed conflict clearly violated the terms of the Geneva (Gas) Protocol of 1925 despite the U.S. government's self-exonerating protestations to the contrary during the Vietnam War. Moreover, the lethal Israeli tear-gas had been obtained from two manufacturing companies located in the United States of America. As far as a good deal of the world was concerned, the United States government became an accomplice to Israeli violations of the Geneva (Gas) Protocol against innocent civilians in occupied Palestine.

While all this was going on, the Reagan administration's co-convocation with France--Iraq's other de facto ally during the Gulf War--of the Conference on the Prohibition of Chemical Weapons at Paris from January 7-11, 1989 constituted an act of incredible duplicity. Prior thereto, the Reagan administration had successfully bludgeoned the U.S. Congress into funding the production of a new generation of so-called binary nerve gases that would replace and modernize the U.S. government's aging stockpile of less-efficient and less-lethal chemical weapons left over from the First World War. This decision represented a significant ratcheting-up of the worldwide chemical arms race. In contrast, the offer by the Soviet government at the 1989 Paris conference to proceed unilaterally to dismantle its chemical weapons establishment created a glimmer of hope for humankind to put the genie of chemical warfare released by Iraq back into the bottle of the Geneva Protocol.

As mentioned above, the Geneva Protocol of 1925 also prohibits the use of "bacteriological methods of warfare." Nonetheless, in addition to the production of a new generation of chemical weapons and their attendant delivery systems, the Reagan administration proceeded apace to undermine the terms of the Biological Weapons Convention of 1972. In the several years before the Paris Conference, the Reagan administration launched an enormous research campaign into the development of biological weapons under the guise of allegedly "defensive" or "peaceful" purposes.[80]

The Serendipities of International Law

On January 11, 1989, a resolution deploring the destruction of the two Libyan planes by American jet fighters over the Mediterranean the preceding week and requesting the U.S. Navy to suspend its maneuvers off Libya was vetoed in the United Nations Security Council by the United States, Britain, and France. Canada also voted against the resolution, while Finland and Brazil abstained. Nevertheless, had it not been for the triple-veto, the resolution would have been adopted because it received the required nine favorable votes: viz., the Soviet Union, China, Algeria, Colombia, Ethiopia, Malaysia, Nepal, Senegal, and Yugoslavia. In other words, the Libyan legal position was effectively vindicated by this, the highest court of international public opinion. At the end of the vote, the Libyan Permanent Representative, Dr. Ali Treiki, expressed the hope that the end of the Reagan administration and the beginning of the Bush Senior administration would create "a new era of understanding and dialogue" between the United States and Libya.

This 1989 U.N. Security Council debate over the destruction of the two Libyan planes also produced a major diplomatic victory on behalf of the Palestinian people. The new "*Palestine* Observer Mission to the United Nations" was granted permission to intervene directly into the debate without the need for the sponsorship of a U.N. member state. In other words, the Palestine Observer Mission was allowed to participate in the Security Council debate as if it represented a full-fledged member state of the United Nations Organization. The United States was the only member of the fifteen-member Security Council to oppose this procedure, though Britain, France and Canada abstained.

When the Alternate Palestinian Observer, Dr. Nasser al-Kidwa, took his chair to speak before the Security Council, he stated that he was "proud to be sitting for the first time behind the sign which bears the name Palestine." Afterward, in remarks made to reporters outside the Security Council chamber, both the U.S. representative and the Soviet representative agreed that the successful Palestinian procedural maneuver would enhance the concept of Palestinian statehood.[81] This novel precedent served as a prelude to the newly proclaimed state of Palestine in 1988 being accorded many of the rights, privileges and immunities of a member state throughout the entire United Nations Organization on a de facto basis. By means of its own wanton aggression against Libya, the Reagan administration had inadvertently further promoted the just cause of the Palestinian people. International law certainly works in strange, mysterious, paradoxical, and sometimes wondrous ways!

ENDNOTES

1   *See* Schaap, *The Endless Campaign: Disinforming the World on Libya*, **Covert Action Info. Bull.**, Summer 1988 at 76, 69-70.

2   *See* N.Y. Times, Jan. 22, 1986, at A4, col. 1 (Germany); N.Y. Times, Jan. 23, 1986, at A6, col. 1 (Greece).

3   *Reagan's Raiders*, **Newsweek**, Apr. 28, 1986, at 26.

4   Wash. Post, Dec. 29, 1985, at A1, col. 6.

5   *See generally* **F. Boyle, World Politics and International Law** 230-249 (1985) (Israeli invasion of Lebanon).

6   *Id.*

7   N.Y. Times, May 21, 1986, at A1.

8   In 1977 Libya dissolved its then existing government to become the Socialist People's Libyan Arab Jamahiriya (i.e., state of the masses), where the people govern themselves. Therefore, as a matter of both international and domestic law it would have been incorrect to refer to any entity known as the "government" of Libya. In deference to the Libyans' sensitivity on this distinction, I will eschew the use of such a term despite the somewhat awkward constructions that must be substituted for it.

9   *See generally* **B. Weston, R. Falk, & A. D'Amato, International Law and World Order** 738 (1980).

10   *See Pentagon Reports Dozen Encounters With Libyan Jets Over Mediter- ranean*, Wash. Post, Feb. 13, 1986, at A28; *see also U.S. Naval Forces to Cross Qaddafi's 'Line of Death' Soon*, Wash. Post, Mar. 21, 1986, at A1, *reprinted in* **Current News Early Bird Edition**, Mar. 21, 1986, at 1.

11   *See U.S. Naval Forces to Cross Qaddafi's 'Line of Death' Soon*, Wash. Post, Mar. 21, 1986, at A1, *reprinted in* **Current News Early Bird Edition**, Mar. 21, 1986, at 1.

12   *See, e.g., A Warning to Libya*, **Newsweek**, Jan. 13, 1986, at 20, 22; *State Dept. Official Warns Libyans*, N.Y. Times, Jan. 28, 1986, at A8, col. 4.

13   *Get Tough: The Reagan Plan*, **Newsweek**, Jan. 20, 1986, at 16.

14   *Reagan Based Mission Approval on Reports of Danger to Envoys*, N.Y. Times, Mar. 26, 1986, at A1, col. 4.

15   Blundy, *Britons Worked on Gadaffi's Missiles*, Sunday Times (London), Apr. 6, 1986, at 12, col. 1.

16   *See* Parks, *Crossing the Line*, **U.S. Naval Instit. Proceedings**, Nov., 1986, at 40, 45.

17   *The Raid on Libya*, **Middle East Pol'y Surv.**, Apr. 18, 1986, at 1.

18   *Bomb Kills Four on T.W.A. Jet Nearing Athens*, 46 **Facts on File** 217 (Apr. 4, 1986).

19   Gelb, *Libyan Link: Sorting It Out*, N.Y. Times, Apr. 12, 1986, at A1, col. 5.

20   N.Y. Times, May 7, 1986, at A1.

21   *U.S. Data Said to Conclude Soviet Mistook Korean Plane*, N.Y. Times, Aug. 24, 1986, at A1, col. 3.

22   *See* **Current News Special Edition: Terrorism**, May 14, 1986.

23   Defense Secretary Weinberger, who had earlier opposed military re- taliation against Libya, was reported to have "reservations" about some aspects of the plans to bomb Libya. *President Based His Decision on 'Incontrovertible' Evidence*, Wash. Post, Apr. 15, 1986, at A1, *reprinted in* **Current News Early Bird Edition,** Apr. 15, 1986, at 15. According to one report, some State Department officials suspected that the Pentagon insisted on using British-based planes in the hope that Prime Minister Thatcher would refuse permission and thereby thwart the bombing plans. *See The Raid on Libya*, **Middle East Pol'y Surv.**, Apr. 18, 1986, at 1. *But*

cf. Kennedy, *Why Were F-111s 'Misused' in the Raid on Libya?*, Chicago Trib., Aug. 19, 1986, at 11, col. 3 (reflecting Pentagon resentment because the long-range flights unnecessarily risked pilots' lives and implying that the Pentagon would not have suggested using British-based planes).

24   *Investigator Comments*, (GPA radio broadcast, Apr. 8, 1986) (English transcript published in **Current News Special Edition: Terrorism**, May 15, 1986, at 47).

25   *Id.*

26   *Id.* A report suggested that the two Palestinians later charged in connection with the bombing may actually have been double agents working for Israel. *Report Suggests Israeli Role in Berlin Attack*, Wash. Post, Dec. 2, 1986, at 25.

27   *Investigator Comments*, (GPA radio broadcast, Apr. 8, 1986) (English transcript published in **Current News Special Edition: Terrorism**, May 15, 1986, at 47).

28   *U.S. Urges Sanctions*, (GPA radio broadcast, Apr. 8, 1986) (English transcript published in **Current News Special Edition: Terrorism**, May 15, 1986, at 49-50).

29   *Kohl Warned of New Attacks*, (Agence France Press radio broadcast in English, Apr. 8, 1986) (transcript published in **Current News Special Edition: Terrorism**, May 15, 1986, at 50).

30   *Antiterrorist Police Chief*, (GPA radio broadcast, Apr. 11, 1986) (English transcript published in **Current News Special Edition: Terrorism**, May 15, 1986, at 52).

31   *FDP Concerned About U.S. Strike Against Libya*, (GPA radio broadcast, Apr. 12, 1986) (English transcript published in **Current News Special Edition: Terrorism**, May 15, 1986, at 53).

32   *Cables Cited as Proof of Libyan Terror Role*, L.A. Times, Apr. 15, 1986, at A1, *reprinted in* **Current News Special Edition: Terrorism**, May 14, 1986, at 41.

33   Finan. Times (London), Apr. 17, 1986, at 4, *reprinted in* **Current News Special Edition: Terrorism**, May 15, 1986, at 58.

34   *Id.*

35   N.Y. Daily News, May 23, 1986, at 8, *reprinted in* **Current News Special Edition: Terrorism**, Aug. 14, 1986, at 42.

36   *See The "Phantom Battle" That Led to War: Can It Happen Again?*, **U.S. News & World Rep.**, July 23, 1984, at 56.

37   **D. Martin & J. Walcott, Best Laid Plans: The Inside Story of America's War Against Terrorism** 292 (1988).

38   Text of the President's Address to the Nation of Apr. 14, 1986, *reprinted in* **Dept. of State Bull.**, June, 1986, at 2.

39   *See* **Dept. of State Bull.**, June, 1986, at 3 (joint news conference held by Secretary Shultz and Secretary Weinberger on April 14, 1986).

40   *See, e.g.,* Jost, *Self Defense Seen as Key to Legality of Attack on Libya*, L.A. Daily Journal, Apr. 16, 1986, at 1, col. 6.

41   For example, in an article published the next year, Vice President George Bush wrote:
> On the night of 14 April 1986 U.S. Navy and Air Force planes struck selected targets in Libya. As all the world knows, this action was taken in retaliation against Libyan-sponsored attacks on Americans, particularly the Libyan-organized bombing of a Berlin nightclub several days earlier . . . .

Bush, *Prelude to Retaliation: Building a Governmental Consensus Against Terrorism*, **SAIS Rev.**, Winter-Spring 1987, at 1, *reprinted in* **Current News Special Edition,** May 20, 1987, at 1.

42   [T]he negotiations focused on finding a rationalization for the planned raid in international law. It was at British insistence that Mr. Reagan, in his speech Monday night, justified the attack as an exercise of the right of self-defense under Article 51 of the United Nations Charter.
N.Y. Times, Apr. 16, 1986, at A14, col. 1. *See also, Reagan's Raiders*, **Newsweek**, Apr. 28, 1986, at 26: Thatcher demanded, and got, the right to approve Washington's target list. She also insisted that, in line with Article 51 of the United Nations Charter, the raid had to be "defensive" rather than retaliatory. This piece of hairsplitting was necessitated by her own pronouncement earlier this year that bombing in retaliation for terrorism is illegal.

43   N.Y. Times, Apr. 16, 1986, at A14, col. 1.

44   *Id.*

45   *See* **Senate Comm. on Foreign Relations, Supplementary Extradition Treaty with the United Kingdom, S. Exec. Rep. No.** 17, 99th Cong., 2d Sess. (1986). *See also* Lelyveld, *Thatcher Faults U.S. Terror Policy*, N.Y. Times, Apr. 28, 1986, at 6, col. 6 (Thatcher contrasts her help in Libyan bombing to U.S. inaction in passing extradition treaty changes).

46   The Senate approved the treaty by a vote of 87-10 on July 17, three months after the bombing of Libya. Kennedy, *supra* note 23.

47   *See generally,* **J. Sweeney, C. Oliver & N. Leech, The International Legal System** 774-75 (1988) (reprinting excerpt from **Starke, Introduction to International Law** 499 (1984)).

48   In a Mutual Defense Assistance Agreement of July 23, 1952, Israel agreed that American-supplied weapons "will be used solely to maintain its internal security, its legitimate self-defense or to permit it to participate in the defense of the area of which it is a part, or in United Nations collective security arrangements and measures, and that it will not undertake any act of aggression against any other state." *Israeli Use of U.S. Arms An Old Dispute*, 1981 **Cong. Q. Weekly Rep.** 1036 (June 13, 1981).

49   22 **U.S.C.** § 2754 (1982).

50   *See* U.S. Dept. of State, File No. P74 0071-1935, *reprinted in* 1974 **Digest of U.S. Practice in International Law** 700 (response to Rostow). *See also* Dept. of State File No. P79 0058-1597, *reprinted in* 1979 **Digest of U.S. Practice in International Law** 1749-52 (review of U.S. position on reprisals and self-defense).

51   Reagan administration officials reported that they had turned down half a dozen diplomatic initiatives by Qaddafi in the first four months of 1986. Wash. Post, Apr. 2, 1986, at A1, col. 5.

52   *See, e.g., Italy, Fearing U.S. Attack on Libya, Asks West European Meeting*, N.Y. Times, Apr. 12, 1986, at A4, col. 2; *Qaddafi Overtures Rejected by U.S.*, Wash. Post, Apr. 2, 1986, at A1, col. 5; N.Y. Times, Mar. 27, 1986, at A8, col. 1; DiScala, *Malta's Bid for Peacemaking*, Christian Sci. Monitor, Mar. 10, 1986, at 20, col. 1; *Libya Requested Help on Truce, Belgian Says*, N.Y. Times, Apr. 15, 1986, at A15, col. 6.

53   Wash. Post, Apr. 2, 1986, at A1, col. 5.

54   "No person employed by or acting on behalf of the United States Government shall engage in, or conspire to engage in, assassination." Exec. Order No. 12,333, § 2-305, 3 **C.F.R.** 571, 584 (1961-1985), *reprinted in* 50 **U.S.C.** § 401 app. at 44, 50 (1982).

55   **U.S. Army, The Law of Land Warfare** (1956) (Department of the Army Field Manual 27-10).

56   Paragraph 501 is based upon the famous case of General Yamashita, *In re Yamashita*, 327 U.S. 1 (1946).

57   War Powers Resolution, Pub. L. No. 93-148, 87 Stat. 555 (effective 1973).

58   Note, *The Legality of Assassination as an Aspect of Foreign Policy*, 27 **Va. J. Int'l Law** 655, 686 n.196 (1987); *see also* 132 **Cong. Rec.** S4425 (Apr. 17, 1986).

59   **B. Tuchman, The Guns of August** 91-92 (1964).

60   The Allied and Associated Governments affirm and Germany accepts the responsibility of Germany and her allies for causing all the loss and damage to which the Allied and Associated Governments and their nationals have been subjected as a consequence of the war imposed upon them by the aggression of Germany and her allies.
Treaty of Peace with Germany (Treaty of Versailles), June 28, 1919, art. 231, 225 Parry's T.S. 188, 286.

61   1 **G. Santayana, The Life of Reason** 284 (1905).

62   The resolution passed on November 20, 1986. G.A. Res. 41/38, 41 GAOR Supp. (No. 53) at 34, U.N. Doc. A/41/53 (1987).

63   *U.S. Said Planning to Stir Irrational Act by Gadhafi*, Wash. Post, Aug. 27, 1986, at A1.

64   Oberdorfer, *How U.S. Decided to Pressure Gadhafi*, Wash. Post, Aug. 29, 1986, at A18.

65   **D. Blundy & A. Lycett, Qaddafi and the Libyan Revolution** 105 (1987).

66   Shipler, *Trail of Mideast Terror: Seeking a Link to Libya*, N.Y. Times, Jan. 5, 1986, at A1, col. 2.

67   *See Egypt Rebuffs 3 U.S. Offers to Fight Libya*, Wash. Times, Apr. 1, 1986, at 1; Woodward, *U.S. Unable to Persuade Egypt to Back Plan for Joint Anti-Qaddafi Move*, Wash. Post, Apr. 2, 1986, at 1.

68   Treaty of Peace, Mar. 26, 1979, Egypt-Israel, 18 **I.L.M.** 362.

69   *Reagan's Raiders*, **Newsweek**, Apr. 28, 1986, at 26.

70   Sir Geoffrey Howe, the British Foreign Minister, said he had no confirmation that Reagan had even made a decision, let alone already authorized bombing raids that night, until he returned from the EEC conference and talked with Prime Minister Thatcher. *See Reagan's Laser-beam Blitz*, **Africa Events**, May-June 1986, at 13, 36.

71   *See Keeping Count of Terror*, **Economist**, July 26, 1986, at 32.

72   *See* Kidder, *The Libyan Raid, Four Months Later*, Christian Sci. Monitor, Aug. 11, 1986, at 21, *reprinted in* **Current News Special Edition: Terrorism**, Sept. 25, 1986, at 7.

73   *See* **R. Freedman, The Middle East Since Camp David** 39-40 (1984). Syria, Libya, Algeria, and South Yemen formed the Steadfastness Front in 1977. *Id.* at 175-76.

74   *Spotlight on Terrorism Shifts to Syria*, Christian Sci. Monitor, May 16, 1986, at 9.

75   Treaty of Peace, Mar. 26, 1979, Egypt-Israel, Minute to art. VI(5), 18 **I.L.M.** 362, 392.

76   Joint Defense Agreement Between Syria and Egypt, Oct. 20, 1955, 227 U.N.T.S. 126.

77   *See Egypt Bars Apology to Israel for Private Speculation on Aiding Syria*, N.Y. Times, April 11, 1979, at A3, col. 1.

78   Kahler, *Rumors of War: The 1914 Analogy*, 58 **For. Aff.** 374 (1979-1980).

79   *See* Anthony D'Amato, *The Imposition of Attorney Sanctions for Claims Arising from the U.S. Air Raid on Libya*, 84 **Am. J. Int'l L.** 705 (1990). Federal Rules of Civil Procedure Rule 11 under which Clark was sanctioned for filing a "frivolous" lawsuit was later revised to provide for a "safe-haven" procedural defense.

80   *See* **Francis A. Boyle, Biowarfare and Terrorism** (2005).

81   *See* Blair, *U.S., in U.N., Vetoes Resolution on Libyan Planes*, N.Y. Times, Jan. 11, 1989.

27 February 1992 Letter of Instruction

27th FEBRUARY 1992

PROFESSOR FRANCIS A. BOYLE
PROFESSOR OF INTERNATIONAL LOW
UNIVERSITY OF ILLINOIS
AT URBANA - CHAMPAIGN

Dear friend,

Please be informed that i recieved notice from my Government confirming
your suggestions , Instructions has been issued to the ambassador Mr.
Hedairie to cooperate with you to prepare Memorandum to the World Court
in Lahai .
Our prime Minister orderd me to ask you to be present personaly in Lahai
to help our mission there.
Iam waiting for your urgent cooperation,i remain under your disposal
regarding the mater.
Kindly contact me as soon as possible in the following numbers:-
office : 00356- 697202 - 6
Res.   371313
Fax   697207

Yours truly,

MUKHTAR AZIZ

CHAPTER 4[1]

RESOLVING THE LOCKERBIE DISPUTE BY MEANS OF INTERNATIONAL LAW[2]

I. THE FACTUAL NATURE OF THE DISPUTE OVER THE LOCKERBIE BOMBING

Factual Allegations

I predicted to Libya that they would be set-up as a scapegoat for the Lockerbie bombing by the United States. So when the Lockerbie bombing allegations first emerged in the U.S. and the French news media sources trying to implicate Libya back in June of 1991,[3] Libya immediately contacted me to serve as Counsel to them on the matter. It was certainly clear to me at the time that Libya was being scapegoated by the C.I.A. and French "intelligence." All the evidence on the incident pointed in directions other than Libya.[4]

The story first broke here in the *Wall Street Journal*, which is very close to the C.I.A.[5] If you read the convoluted story, it was completely preposterous. All of a sudden, some C.I.A. agent completely out of nowhere reviewed, discredited, and reversed all the evidence that they had previously used to blame Iran, Syria and a renegade Palestinian group whose headquarters were under the control of Syria.[6] I am not saying that they did it. I do not know, but the C.I.A. had been blaming these others all along.[7] But then, when it became geopolitically convenient for the Bush Senior administration not to blame Iran and Syria, they immediately switched the blame to Libya. Bush Senior needed Iranian and Syrian cooperation in order to wage his war against Iraq.[8] So Bush

Senior decided not to blame Iran and Syria.[9] Once again I am not saying they did it, but all of sudden there was a remarkable turn-around in the U.S. party line, and the accounts for it were completely incredible.

These new-found intelligence sources went back to two countries: Senegal and Malta. You will note that when all these allegations began to emerge out of Senegal, that exact same week the *Financial Times* of London reported that Senegal's public debts had been miraculously rescheduled by the Paris Club at a highly preferential rate that Senegal was not entitled to.[10] I thought it was pretty clear that someone in Senegal was bought off.[11]

As for Malta, all the alleged evidence of Libya's involvement went back to two Libyan nationals who were working for Libyan airlines over in Malta.[12] But the Maltese government had undertaken a very extensive investigation, and their conclusion was that there was no unaccompanied baggage on the flight from Malta to Frankfurt (and from there allegedly to the Pan Am jet in London), and that they had been able to account for all the baggage.[13] Those sources of new "intelligence" took care of what flimsy evidence there was against Libya.

Remember that the burden of proof here was upon the United States and the United Kingdom, not Libya; and that the international law standard of proof required proof beyond a reasonable doubt. What little evidence they claimed to have would not stand up in any fair, impartial, and independent court of law. That is why Libya was more than happy to turn over the Lockerbie matter to a fair, impartial, and independent tribunal. Conversely, that was also why the United States and the United Kingdom were adamantly opposed to turning over the Lockerbie dispute to any fair, impartial, and independent court of law.[14]

The Montreal Sabotage Convention[15]

When the public accusations were made in late 1991, around the third anniversary of the Lockerbie bombing, the United States and the United Kingdom publicly and officially implicated Libya. Immediately after this, acting on my advice, Libya offered to submit the entire dispute to the International Court of Justice, to an international tribunal, to an impartial international commission of investigation, or to any other type of impartial international proceeding, in order to resolve it.[16] All those offers were immediately rejected out of hand by the United States and the United Kingdom. Obviously these two imperial states had no interest or desire to establish the real truth behind the Lockerbie bombing.

There matters stood until after the first of the new year, when the two governments indicated that they were going to move for a resolution against Libya at the U.N. Security Council. At that point, acting on my advice, Libya proceeded to draft and to send two diplomatic notes to U.S. Secretary of State James Baker and to U.K. Foreign Minister Douglas Hurd, invoking Article 14 of the Montreal Sabotage Convention of 1971.[17] The United States, the United Kingdom, and Libya were all parties to this Convention.[18] The destruction of the plane over Lockerbie clearly constituted an act of sabotage directed against civil aviation that fell directly within the meaning of the Montreal Sabotage Convention. Article 14 said that in the event that a dispute over the interpretation or application of the Montreal Sabotage Convention cannot be resolved by negotiations, then either party can demand international arbitration, and if that does not transpire, they can unilaterally go to the International Court of Justice, the World Court of the United Nations System, despite the wishes of the other side. [19]

Around January 18, Libya sent these notes to the United States and the United Kingdom, formally demanding arbitration of the dispute before an international arbitration tribunal, as was Libya's right. Libya's position was that the United States and the United Kingdom refused to negotiate as required by the Montreal Sabotage Convention, which said quite clearly that negotiations were required. The United States and the United Kingdom refused to negotiate, as for years they had refused to negotiate in good faith with Libya. So the notes were sent. The United States and the United Kingdom ignored them, but instead convened a session of the U.N. Security Council to obtain the adoption of what became Resolution 731. [20]

Security Council Resolution 731[21]

Originally, the United States and the United Kingdom wanted Resolution 731 to demand that Libya turn over the two accused Libyan citizens to the U.S. and U.K. They did not get that demand in Resolution 731. Indeed, the Western mainstream news media, true to its history, thoroughly distorted--and I submit on purpose[22]--the true meaning of Resolution 731.[23] If you read Resolution 731, it did not demand anyone's extradition.[24] It urged Libya to cooperate with the U.N. Secretary General in resolving this dispute,[25] which Libya had done from the get-go when the allegations were first publicly uttered toward the end of 1991. The U.S. and the U.K. wanted to have a demand for extradition in there, but the Third World states would not go along with it,[26] taking the position, and quite rightly so, that extradition is a matter that is determined in accordance with extradition treaties. The Security Council had no jurisdiction to demand anyone's extradition, [27] and there was no extradition treaty between the United States or the United Kingdom, on the one hand, and Libya, on the other.

Nevertheless, Bush Senior had the votes to ram the resolution through the Security Council. The key vote was that of China. To get the Chinese vote, Bush Senior agreed to have his infamous meeting in New York with Premier Li Peng, the Butcher of Beijing, the official in charge of the Tiananmen Square massacre.[28] That was the quid pro quo for the Chinese vote.[29]

So Resolution 731 was adopted.[30] Everyone at the Security Council knew it was wrong. Everyone knew that Libya had nothing to do with the Lockerbie bombing, and that Libya had once again been made a scapegoat by the United States, just as it had throughout the 1980s by the Reagan administration. Whenever the U.S. government wanted some fairly defenseless Third World country to beat up on, it would attack Libya--the Grenada of the Middle East that could barely defend itself. By now Colonel Qaddafi and Libya had become America's imperial punching bag.

In the debate at the Security Council, both the United States and the United Kingdom rejected the applicability of the Montreal Sabotage Convention. The United States and Britain were flaunting the illegality of the proceeding, obviously to assert their imperial power over international law. For example, U.S. Ambassador Thomas Pickering, after the passage of Resolution 731, stated that no longer will countries fostering terrorism be able to hide behind international law.[31] Truly Orwellian! Acting on my advice, Libya took that statement and cited it against the United States in the World Court, and successfully so. There were other statements that Pickering and the British Ambassador David Hannay made that were just as reprehensible and outrageous. Acting on my advice, Libya cited them all to establish Libya's claims before the World Court. They were ambassadors plenipotentiary, and their statements legally bound their governments. The arrogance of power! But you can always count on that.

At that point, it was pretty clear to me that the U.S. and the U.K. were going to move for a second Security Council resolution in order to sanction Libya.[32] So, acting on my advice, Libya proceeded to prepare to file lawsuits at the International Court of Justice under that same Article 14 against the United States and the United Kingdom. When it was obvious that arbitration was rejected, then the third sequential procedural step under the Montreal Sabotage Convention was to go to the World Court and to sue the United States and the United Kingdom involuntarily. The World Court lawsuits were filed on March 3, the day before Libya was originally scheduled to be sanctioned by the Security Council.

Indeed, immediately prior thereto, pursuant to instructions I had received from the Prime Minister of Libya set forth above, I proceeded to New York in order to co-ordinate the World Court lawsuits with Libyan Ambassador to the United Nations El Houderi. According to the Ambassador, U.S./U.N. Ambassador Pickering had just told him: "We know what Boyle is going to do!" Obviously, our phones were tapped. I figured an attempt would be made somehow to take me out of the picture. So I consulted with Ramsey Clark while in New York City, who advised me to look out for intelligence agents. Sure enough, that is exactly what happened!

When I arrived in Europe to file the World Court lawsuits against the United States and the United Kingdom, Libya had sent a team of their own Libyan lawyers to assist me. One of those Libyan lawyers did everything humanly possible to sabotage, stall, and delay the filing of those lawsuits: Mr. Kamal Maghour. I concluded that he was the Western intelligence agent that Ramsey had warned me about.

As the clock was ticking down on the Security Council adopting the sanctions resolution against Libya and as the Sixth Fleet and its jet fighter aircraft were bearing down on Libya and the Libyans for another military attack, I told this Mr. Maghour in front of the entire Libyan legal team that if those two World Court lawsuits were not filed immediately and Libya were to be sanctioned by the Security Council, I would be on the next flight to Tripoli where I would meet personally with Colonel Qaddafi, tell him what had happened, blame Mr. Maghour personally for not filing the lawsuits on time, and tell the Colonel that Mr. Maghour should be held personally responsible for the consequences. Those two World Court lawsuits were filed the very next day. I would later cross paths again with this Mr. Maghour whom I presumed to be a Western intelligence agent as related below. Mr. Maghour has since gone on to his "reward"--whatever that might be.

Libya's filing of the lawsuits against the U.S. and the U.K. at the World Court postponed the sanctions resolution meeting by the Security Council *sine die*. Even more importantly, the filing of the lawsuits aborted an imminent U.S. military attack upon Libya. At the time the Sixth Fleet was on hostile military maneuvers right off the coast of Libya, and U.S. jet fighters were repeatedly penetrating Tripoli Flight Information Center.[33] This was exactly the same type of hostile, provocative, and aggressive military maneuvers that the Reagan administration had engaged in throughout the decade of the 1980s prior to an outright military attack and aggression upon Libya.

Upon the filing of the lawsuits against the U.S. and the U.K. with their accompanying requests for the international equivalents of temporary restraining orders against both states that were coupled with a demand for an Emergency Hearing by the World Court to hear our requests for the T.R.O.'s immediately, Bush Senior ordered the Sixth Fleet to stand down. There was no military conflict. This time no one died on either side. A tribute to the "hard power" of international law and the World Court.

When the war clouds had dissipated, an American artist friend of mine whom I had met in Libya spontaneously called to congratulate me excitedly: "It looks like you just prevented a war!" I responded, "Yeah, I guess I did."

Towards the end of his life, I told this story to my teacher, mentor, and friend the late, great Louis B. Sohn, Bemis Professor of International Law at Harvard Law School and co-author with Grenville Clark of their monumental *World Peace Through World Law* (3d ed. 1966). Sensing I would not be seeing Louis again, as I then walked out of his home in Arlington Virginia, I gave him a big hug and said: "It works Louis!" Louis knowingly smiled. R.I.P.

The World Court Lawsuits[34]

Briefly put, Libya's Applications against the United States and the United Kingdom at the World Court made the following basic points:

(1) Libya had fully complied with all the terms of the Montreal Sabotage Convention in the handling of this dispute.[35]

(2) There was no requirement to extradite per se under the Montreal Sabotage Convention. The requirement was to extradite or prosecute, and Libya had decided to institute criminal proceedings against its two citizens and to prosecute them.[36]

(3) The United States and the United Kingdom had themselves violated the Montreal Sabotage Convention; and in particular Article 11, which required them to turn over whatever evidence they had to Libya, and to cooperate with Libya on the prosecution. Both states refused to do that. How could Libya mount a prosecution of anyone if the two states involved refused to turn over the evidence?[37]

The reason why they never turned over the evidence to Libya was that the evidence against Libya was not there. It had all been concocted by the C.I.A., F.B.I., and Scotland Yard. Air Malta and the Maltese government had already issued an official statement that, based on their investigation, there was no unaccompanied baggage from Malta to Frankfurt, and that they had been able to account for all the baggage from Malta to Frankfurt.

(4) The fourth point that Libya raised in the Applications to the World Court was that the United States and the United Kingdom were going to go ahead and try to sanction Libya at the U.N. Security Council as well as to engage in a military attack against Libya over this dispute, which ultimately was a legal dispute, a question of international extradition law

and the interpretation of a treaty; and that therefore the Court should act immediately to prevent this from happening by issuing temporary restraining orders against the U.S. and the U.K.[38]

I remember quite vividly at the time that Bush Senior had sent the Sixth Fleet on hostile military maneuvers off the coast of Libya and that U.S. jet fighters had repeatedly penetrated the Tripoli Flight Information Center. The Sixth Fleet was preparing to attack Libya and deliberately trying to provoke a conflict. I recall this distinctly because I traveled right into the midst of it all in order to get Colonel Qaddafi's personal authorization to file the World Court lawsuits against the United States and the United Kingdom. Just before taking off from Champaign, I called up a lawyer friend of mine and asked him to look after my wife and then two sons if anything should happen to me, which he kindly agreed to do.

I flew as far as Malta and was about to take the ferry boat to Tripoli the next day because of the dangerous Sixth Fleet jet fighter air traffic interference over Tripoli Flight Information Center. Then the Libyan Prime Minister informed me that my World Court proposal had been approved and that I should immediately return to the Libyan Mission to the United Nations in New York in order to assist Ambassador El Houderi there. I had a nice seafood dinner in Malta that night, then flew back to New York first thing the next day. So I missed my second rendezvous with the Sixth Fleet then maneuvering off the coast of Tripoli prior to attacking Libya. It never did so then or again until 2011. Another tribute to the "hard power" of international law and the World Court.

I will devote the next two chapters of this book to analyzing the 2011 war against Libya by the neoliberal Obama administration and the NATO Alliance under the pretext and rubric of the Responsibility to Protect (R2P) doctrine. Maybe if Jesus Christ himself had walked back and forth across and on top of the southern Mediterranean throughout 2011, he could have saved Libya from Obama and NATO. I am a lawyer--not a miracle-worker!

The Requests for Provisional Measures of Protection[39]

Tied into the Applications were what are called Requests for the indication of provisional measures of protection by the World Court. This is the international equivalent of a temporary restraining order. Libya asked for the temporary restraining orders against the United States and the United Kingdom to prevent them from taking measures of unilateral coercion or sanctions at the Security Council or a military attack against Libya, pending the decision of all these legal issues by the Court.

When the Applications were filed, of course, there was no guarantee that the matter would be set for an emergency hearing by the Court on the Requests for the temporary restraining orders. Yet the Applications and Requests were accepted by the Court. So they were receivable and admissible, and the Court concluded that there were good grounds to schedule an Emergency Hearing on Libya's request for the T.R.O. provisional measures. A preliminary victory and a good omen to be sure.

The hearing date was set to open for March 26. The World Court hearings on March 26-28 were only on the temporary restraining orders. They were not on the merits of the dispute one way or the other.

Once that date had been set, the Bush Senior strategy then became to try to ram the sanctions resolution through the Security Council before the World Court could decide on the temporary restraining orders against the U.S. and the U.K. They had come out with the sanctions Resolution 748. [40] This sanctions resolution first surfaced during the last week of February, and they wanted sanctions adopted in the first week of March. The filing of the World Court lawsuits postponed that schedule *sine die*.

When the World Court set the hearing for March 26, it became very clear to Bush Senior that he had to ram the sanctions resolution through the Security Council before the Court could prevent it. Enormous pressure was put on the members of the Security Council to go along with this illegal strategy. This time China was threatened by the U.S. government overtly, by telling them that if they vetoed this resolution they would lose their Most Favored Nation (M.F.N.) trading status with the United States. With that threat, and other votes in his pocket, Bush Senior convened the Security Council shortly after the Court had heard the arguments over the temporary restraining orders, and it adopted Resolution 748 by a vote of 10 in favor, none against, and five abstentions. [41]

Clearly, this procedure violated the basic canon of Anglo-American law and international legal practice and procedure, that pending resolution of a dispute by a court, the litigants are not to take any action that would interfere with, prejudice, or prejudge the legal proceedings while they are *sub judice*. Yet that is exactly what Bush Senior did on purpose. He deliberately moved for the sanctions resolution at the Security Council before the Court could render its decision on the T.R.O.s. The five states that abstained on Resolution 748 at the Security Council all pointed that out--that the matter was before the World Court and that the Council should wait for a Court ruling. [42] That fundamental legal objection did not bother Bush Senior. He had his 10 votes, which was only one more than he needed. But it was a severe embarrassment to Bush Senior, in my opinion; he barely scraped through the Security Council. And there were five abstentions, basically in agreement with Libya's position. But Resolution 748 was passed anyway. Might is "right" at the Security Council. But not always at the World Court, as we shall see below.

Security Council Resolution 748[43]

Another technical legal defect with Resolution 748 was the Chinese abstention on it. If you read U.N. Charter article 27(3), it clearly says that decisions of the Security Council on non-procedural matters require the concurring votes of all five Permanent Members, which would include China, which abstained. So there was a very serious legal challenge as to the validity of Resolution 748 in the first place, which was premised upon the previous Security Council Resolution 731 being valid, which was also defective.

Once Resolution 748 was passed, and with its mandated sanctions coming into effect on April 15, the World Court--in an effort at least to assert its independence from Bush Senior and the Security Council--said it would render its decision on April 14. I knew some of the Judges were quite displeased by what Bush Senior had done here. Their decisions on the 14th were only on the Requests for the temporary restraining orders. They did not get into the merits of the cases at all. What they said in the key provisions, found paragraphs 39 and 40, was that since the Security Council had already adopted Resolution 748, there was nothing the Court could do about it at this time. However, Libya remained free to contest the legal validity of Resolution 748 when the Court got into the next stages of the proceedings, which Libya did, acting pursuant to my advice. So the Court refused to give any legal validity to Resolution 748.

The World Court Orders of 14 April 1992[44]

So the World Court Orders of 14 April 1992 were very narrow, technical, limited rulings, which basically said Bush Senior had beaten Libya and the World Court to the punch on the sanctions resolution at the Security Council. Bush Senior got his sanctions resolution rammed through the Security Council before the World Court could act, and there was nothing the World Court could do about it at that point in time, while certainly leaving it open in the future that the Court would be prepared to consider the legal validity of Resolution 748. The vote at the World Court was 11 to 5. Five Judges agreed with Libya, that the Court should have issued the temporary restraining orders against the U.S. and the U.K.

Five votes in the Security Council and five Judges on the World Court basically agreed with Libya. I think that this already indicated there was substantial merit to Libya's claims.[45] Otherwise, Libya would not have gotten those five votes on the World Court and those five votes in the Security Council. Even two of the World Court Judges who voted with the majority expressed severe reservations about the procedure used here--that the Security Council acted while the very issue was before the Court itself, and in essence preempted the ability of the Court to rule on the temporary restraining orders, thus disrespecting the Court.

All this meant, then, was that Libya lost the temporary restraining order requests. It did not mean Libya lost the case, and the case was still going forward toward the merits of the dispute under the Montreal Sabotage Convention. Also, Libya remained free under the Rules of the Court to go back into the Court in the event the U.S. government threatened more military force against Libya--say, put Libya under a naval blockade, or threatened another bombing, or imposing an oil embargo, etc. The Rules of the Court provide that a state can always go back in again for new provisional measures in the event that there is a fundamental change in circumstances. So, again, the western news media thoroughly distorted what had happened. But there was nothing new about that, since this is what they have always done on everything concerning Libya. The mainstream western news media were not much better than conveyor belts for Bush Senior's New World Order, especially when it came to Libya.

A World Court Decision on the Merits

At the time, there was an unidentified diplomat quoted by *Reuters* who said that the decisions of the Security Council were international law, and therefore that the vote of the Security Council superseded international treaty obligations or any other law. But this matter would be decided by the World Court itself when Libya got to the proceedings on the merits. The Court would look into that theory: Is Resolution 748 a law unto itself or isn't it? I did not believe so for reasons explained in the next sections of this paper. And that is how I so advised Libya. The World Court would later agree with me in their 1998 Judgments overwhelmingly in favor of Libya and against the United States and the United Kingdom as explained below.

There had been a prior history of the World Court looking into Security Council resolutions and their validity. If you read the terms of the U.N. Charter, it makes it very clear that the Security Council, when it acts, is bound by Article 1 and Article 2 of the U.N. Charter,[46] the Purpose and Principles of the U.N. Charter. That certainly allows for the doctrine of *ultra vires*, that there are certain matters beyond the powers of the Security Council.[47]

Also, one of the Judges pointed out that Resolution 748 arguably violated the most basic tenet of all legal systems, that no man shall serve as his own judge.[48] Clearly, this was a legal dispute; yet the United States and the United Kingdom went right ahead and rammed this sanctions resolution through the Security Council in order to benefit themselves and to pre-empt the World Court from acting against them. But it is simply not true that the Security Council can do whatever it wants to do and by so doing, create valid, binding international law.

For example, the U.N. Security Council cannot authorize violations of international humanitarian law, the Geneva Conventions, the Hague Regulations, the Genocide Convention, or *jus cogens*. The Security Council cannot authorize the commission of war crimes, crimes against humanity, or genocide. The World Court made it very clear in paragraph 40 of the Orders that Libya was free to attack the validity of the Security Council Sanctions Resolution 748 in the proceedings towards the merits of the dispute, which Libya would then successfully do acting pursuant to my advice.

It was also true that the Bush Senior diktat would be illegal under U.S. law, not just the Montreal Convention. Since there was no extradition treaty between the United States or the United Kingdom, on the one hand, and Libya, there could be no legal basis for extradition. That is why the Third World states never went along with including any demand for extradition in Resolution 731. U.S. law was the same here as Libyan law. Under the U.S. Supreme Court case of *Valentine v. Neidecker*, the Supreme Court held that it is a fundamental requirement of due process of law that no one can be extradited to another country in the absence of an extradition treaty.[49] Libyan law was the same. There was a double-standard being applied here by the United States. But there's nothing new about that at all!

The Iran Airbus Precedent

Indeed, let us look at the destruction of the Iran Airbus by the *U.S.S. Vincennes* during the summer of 1988 about six months before the Lockerbie bombing.[50] There it was clear that the U.S. Navy Captain who shot down that plane knew it was a civilian airliner when he destroyed it.[51] If you read the transcript of the interchange on the bridge, his radar person clearly identified it as a civilian airliner, but he shot it down anyway, and killed about 290 innocent people. [52] What did the neoconservative Reagan administration do with that Captain? They gave him a medal![53]

The United States did not extradite him to Iran, or even prosecute him for his crimes. When the Iranians protested, the U.S. government eventually agreed to go to the World Court, and the whole matter was presented there, but finally the United States "settled" this dispute on terms barely minimally acceptable to Iran.[54] So notice that when the U.S. government blew up a civilian airplane--and everyone agreed America did it, no one denied it--it was perfectly fine for the United States to go to the World Court and not to turn over its Captain to Iran, or even to prosecute him for his crimes, but rather give him a medal. But when someone else blows up a U.S. airliner--and it was a flimsy, concocted case against Libya--the United States went for sanctions at the Security Council. Total hypocrisy! But again, nothing new about that either.

If the Reagan administration had not obstinately stonewalled Iran on the U.S. destruction of the Iranian Airbus, had court-martialed its Captain, had officially apologized to Iran, and had quickly paid Iran substantial reparations for the victims and the plane, there was a good chance we could have avoided the destruction of the Pan Am Jetliner just a few months later. Hobbesian American political scientists approvingly call this latter type of reprehensible behavior "tit-for-tat": We lost our airplane. You lost your airplane. Hopefully you have now learned your lesson and will not do it again. Or else we will have to do it again too.

Whoever did it, America and Scotland paid a very high price in innocent human lives because of the Reagan administration's wanton destruction of completely innocent Iranian lives six months beforehand in gross violation of the most rudimentary principles of international law, and then refused to take international legal responsibility for it. It was the neoconservative Reagan administration that had reduced its adversaries into operating in accordance with the Biblical Law of the Talon: "Eye for eye, tooth for tooth, hand for hand, foot for foot, burning for burning, wound for wound, stripe for stripe." (*Exodus 21:24*). The Law of the Jungle is the standard alternative default strategy to International Law.

No Due Process of Law for the Two Accused Libyan Nationals

The other point that needs to be kept in mind is that of course the two accused Libyan citizens could not get a fair trial in the United States or the United Kingdom.[55] Look at what happened to General Manuel Noriega in U.S. courts under Bush Senior. The whole trial was a show trial, a kangaroo court proceeding all the way up and down. It was a set-up, a political trial.

And these two Libyans, if they were ever sent over to the United States or the United Kingdom for trial, the same thing would happen to them. They would never get a fair trial in the United Kingdom either. Look at all the Irish people who had been repeatedly railroaded by British courts and spent years in prison on trumped-up terrorism charges and concocted evidence manufactured by Scotland Yard. That is why Libya had offered to have their citizens tried in some neutral country, because they had nothing to hide. You do not go into court, especially the World Court, if you have anything to hide.

Libya was willing to have a trial in some country that was neutral. The United States and the United Kingdom were free to bring in their evidence there. Well, it was clear why the United States and the United Kingdom rejected that option, because they had no evidence that would stand up in a neutral court of law. Indeed, the United States and the United Kingdom could have brought their evidence to the World Court if they had had valid evidence. But they never did that either for obvious reasons, let alone in the far more favorable politicized environment of the U.N. Security Council.

There was no real evidence for the Lockerbie bombing against Libya and its two citizens that would have held up in any neutral court of law. Indeed, I had advised Libya to offer to the United States and the United Kingdom to have their two citizens tried by the International Court of Justice itself under article 38(2) of the Statute of the International Court of Justice. That good–faith proposal was also rejected by the two imperial powers. The United States and the United Kingdom were never interested in obtaining justice or truth when it came to the Lockerbie bombing and its victims.

II. THE LEGAL NATURE OF THE DISPUTE
OVER THE LOCKERBIE BOMBING

This Section II was originally printed by Libya as a bound pamphlet and then circulated by them to all member states of the United Nations Organization at U.N. Headquarters in New York with the title page on it: "Memorandum of Law on the Dispute Between Libya and the United States and the United Kingdom over the Lockerbie Bombing Allegations, by Francis A. Boyle, Professor of International Law, February 21, 1992." The Libyan Ambassador circulated my Memorandum to the U.N. member states in an effort to prevent the Security Council from adopting a sanctions resolution against Libya. My Memorandum of Law then also served as the basis for drafting Libya's Applications against the United States and the United Kingdom that were filed at the World Court on March 3, 1992 together with the requests for the T.R.O. provisional measures and the emergency hearing to consider them.

This theory of the case that I articulated below was ultimately accepted, approved, and vindicated by the International Court of Justice itself in its two Judgments on Preliminary Objections of 27 February 1998 that were overwhelmingly in favor of Libya against the United States and the United Kingdom, which will be analyzed below. My Memorandum of

Law paved the way for the peaceful resolution of the Lockerbie dispute among the United States, the United Kingdom, and Libya. Another tribute to the "hard power" of international law and the World Court.

Introduction

Libya and most Members of the Security Council are parties to the 1971 Convention for the Suppression of Unlawful Acts Against the Safety of Civil Aviation, the so-called Montreal Sabotage Convention. The United States, the United Kingdom, and Libya are all parties to the Montreal Convention without any reservations, whereas France has reserved its position as to the compulsory dispute settlement procedures set forth in article 14. It is clear that the Montreal Convention applies to the Lockerbie bombing allegations.

The Montreal Sabotage Convention

The two Libyan citizens accused by the United States and the United Kingdom for the Lockerbie bombing are alleged to have committed what would amount to offenses as defined by article 1, paragraphs (a),[56] (b)[57] or (c)[58] of the Montreal Convention. Article 5, paragraph 2 states quite clearly that a contracting state such as Libya must take measures as may be necessary to establish its jurisdiction over such offenses mentioned in article 1 "in the case where the alleged offender is present in its territory and it does not extradite him pursuant to article 8 to any of the states mentioned in paragraph 1 of this article."[59] In other words, it is made quite clear by article 5, paragraph 2 that a contracting state such as Libya must either extradite an alleged offender, or else prosecute the alleged offender itself.

Concerning the Lockerbie allegations, it is quite clear that Libya has fully discharged its obligations under article 5 by instituting criminal proceedings against the two Libyan citizens that have been accused by the United States and the United Kingdom. Under these circumstances, there is no obligation whatsoever for Libya to extradite its two citizens to either the United States or the United Kingdom.

Article 6 of the Montreal Convention then provides that a contracting state such as Libya must take such subjects into custody or take other measures to ensure their presence "as provided in the law of that state."[60] In other words, it is the domestic law of Libya that clearly applies here, and Libya is already applying its domestic law by taking its two citizens into custody and prosecuting them. Thus, Libya has discharged these obligations under article 6 of the Montreal Convention.

Article 6, paragraph 1 then continues by stating that the suspects shall be detained "for such time as is necessary to enable any criminal or extradition proceedings to be instituted." Notice the use of the disjunctive word "or." It expressly did not use the conjunctive word "and."[61] Rather, the obligation of a contracting state such as Libya is either to prosecute the suspects, or, in the event Libya chooses not to prosecute them, to extradite them. In this case, Libya has chosen to prosecute them. Under the terms of the Montreal Convention, that is Libya's sovereign treaty right.

Article 6, paragraph 2 then requires that a contracting state such as Libya "shall immediately make a preliminary enquiry into the facts."[62] Libya is currently doing this.

Article 6, paragraph 4 of the Montreal Convention then requires Libya to notify the concerned states that it has taken these people into custody and the relevant circumstances surrounding their detention.[63] Libya has done this.

Article 6, paragraph 4 concludes: "The State which makes the preliminary enquiry contemplated in paragraph 2 of this Article shall promptly report its findings to the said States and shall indicate whether it intends to exercise jurisdiction."[64] In other words, article 6, paragraph 4 makes it quite clear that the detaining state has the option to prosecute or to extradite. In this case, Libya has indicated to the United States and to the United Kingdom that it intends to exercise its jurisdiction by prosecuting the two Libyan citizens. Hence, Libya has so far fulfilled all of its obligations under article 6 of the Montreal Convention.

Libya's Obligation to Prosecute OR Extradite

If there were any doubt about this analysis, article 7 of the Montreal Convention makes it quite clear that a contracting state such as Libya has the option either to extradite or to prosecute these alleged offenders:[65]

ARTICLE 7

The Contracting State in the territory of which the alleged offender is found shall, if it does not extradite him, be obliged, without exception whatsoever and whether or not the offence was committed in its territory, to submit the case to its competent authorities for the purpose of prosecution. Those authorities shall take their decision in the same manner as in the case of any ordinary offence of a serious nature under the law of that State.[66]

Once again, nothing could be clearer as a matter of international law that Libya has discharged all of its obligations under article 7 of the

Montreal Convention by instituting criminal proceedings against the two Libyan nationals who have been accused of committing the Lockerbie bombing by the United States and the United Kingdom. Hence, Libya has no obligation to extradite its two nationals to either the United States or the United Kingdom.

United States Extradition Law

In regard to this point, the Libyan law on extradition is similar to the extradition laws of the United States of America. The United States Extradition Statute confers the power to extradite "only during the existence of any treaty of extradition with such foreign government."[67] There is no extradition treaty between the United States and Libya.

Indeed, the United States Supreme Court "has gone so far as to hold that if a treaty does not require extradition in a particular case ... a provision in the treaty giving the requested state the option to extradite does not suffice to authorize the United States government to seize an accused and surrender him to a foreign power."[68] In *Valentine v. United States ex. rel. Neidecker*, the Supreme Court said; "[The President's] power, in the absence of a statute conferring an independent power, must be found in the terms of the treaty ..."[69] Once again, there is no extradition treaty between Libya, on the one hand, and the United States, or the United Kingdom, on the other.

The Requirement of International Cooperation

Article 11, paragraph 1 of the Montreal Convention provides that contracting states shall afford one another the greatest measure of assistance in connection with criminal proceedings brought in respect of the offenses charged. In other words, both the United States and the United Kingdom have a treaty obligation to cooperate with Libya when it comes to the prosecution of these two Libyan citizens. So far, both the United States and the United Kingdom have refused to so cooperate in violation of article 11(1).

Article 13 of the Montreal Convention requires a contracting state such as Libya to report "as promptly as possible" to the Council of the International Civil Aviation Organization any relevant information in its possession concerning the alleged offense and any legal proceedings related thereto. As best as can be told, Libya has done this.

Compulsory Dispute Settlement Procedures

The Montreal Convention concludes its operative provisions

by including in article 14 on the compulsory settlement of disputes a compromissory clause as follows:

ARTICLE 14

1. Any dispute between two or more Contracting States concerning the interpretation or application of this Convention which cannot be settled through negotiation, shall, at the request of one of them, be submitted to arbitration. If within six months from the date of the request for arbitration the Parties are unable to agree on the organization of the arbitration, any one of those Parties may refer the dispute to the International Court of Justice by request in conformity with the Statute of the Court.[70]

2. Each State may at the time of signature or ratification of this Convention or accession thereto, declare that it does not consider itself bound by the preceding paragraph. The other Contracting States shall not be bound by the preceding paragraph with respect to any Contracting State having made such a reservation.[71]

3. Any Contracting State having made a reservation in accordance with the preceding paragraph may at any time withdraw this reservation by notification to the Depositary Governments.[72]

Therefore, it is clear from article 14 that in the event the United States and the United Kingdom have any objections to the manner in which Libya is handling the allegations over the Lockerbie bombing, then it is incumbent upon these two states to demand international arbitration over this dispute with Libya, as is their unilateral right to do so under article 14. So far, both the U.S. and the U.K. have refused to do this.

By contrast, Libya has repeatedly offered to submit this dispute to international arbitration, to the International Court of Justice, to an international commission of investigation, or to some other type of ad hoc international institutional arrangement for the impartial investigation and adjudication of these allegations. So far, both the United States and the United Kingdom have rejected all of these good faith efforts by Libya to resolve this dispute in a peaceful manner. Hence, both the United States and the United Kingdom have effectively violated most of the provisions of the Montreal Convention when it comes to the handling of this dispute with Libya.

The United Nations Charter Obligation for the Peaceful Settlement of International Disputes

Thus, both the United States and the United Kingdom have also violated their solemn obligation mandating the peaceful resolution of international disputes found in article 2, paragraph 3 of the United Nations Charter:

> All Members shall settle their international disputes by peaceful means in such a manner that international peace and security, and justice, are not endangered.[73]

This obligation is reiterated and specified in Chapter VI, article 33, paragraph 1 of the Charter:

CHAPTER VI

PACIFIC SETTLEMENT OF DISPUTES

Article 33

> 1. The parties to any dispute, the continuance of which is likely to endanger the maintenance of international peace and security, shall, first of all, seek a solution by negotiation, enquiry, mediation, conciliation, arbitration, judicial settlement, resort to regional agencies or arrangements, or other peaceful means of their own choice.[74]

The conclusion is inescapable that the reason why the United States and the United Kingdom have illegally rejected all means for the peaceful resolution of this dispute with Libya is that both States know full well that Libya was not responsible for the Lockerbie bombing.

Libya Has Invoked Article 14 of the Montreal Convention

In its letter to the Security Council that was dated 18 January 1992, Libya indicated that it had formally invoked article 14 of the Montreal Sabotage Convention against the United States and the United Kingdom in order to resolve the dispute concerning these allegations. Pending the completion of the international arbitration or adjudication mandated by article 14, both the United States and the United Kingdom were and still are obliged to abstain from any type of action that would interfere with or prejudge the arbitration or adjudication processes. Indeed, since almost all Member States of the Security Council are also parties to the Montreal Convention, they had and still have an absolute international legal obligation to do nothing that would interfere with or prejudice the arbitration or adjudication processes mandated by article 14 in any way. Most regrettably, this is exactly what happened when the Security Council adopted Resolution 731 on 21 January 1992.

The Illegality of Resolution 731 (1992)

Pursuant to article 33, paragraph 2 of the U.N. Charter, the Members of the Security Council had and still have an obligation to call upon the United States and the United Kingdom to settle their dispute with Libya by the pacific means specified in article 33, paragraph 1,[75] especially the arbitration and adjudication processes mandated by article 14 of the Montreal Convention.[76] This they failed to do in adopting Resolution 731 (1992).[77] Nevertheless, the Members of the Security Council are still obliged to take no further action that would interfere with or prejudice the arbitration or adjudication processes mandated by article 14 in any way. The United States and the United Kingdom must pursue peaceful means for the settlement of this dispute with Libya--especially arbitration and adjudication under article 14--before the Members of the Security Council can have the lawful authority under the Charter to adopt any type of sanctions against Libya under Chapter VII.

In this regard, U.N. Charter article 36, paragraph 2 states quite clearly:

> The Security Council should take into consideration any procedures for the settlement of the dispute which have already been adopted by the parties.[78]

Since all the parties to this dispute had already agreed to article 14 of the Montreal Convention, the Security Council had no lawful authority to adopt any resolution that failed to call for the arbitration or adjudication of this dispute pursuant thereto. For this reason, Resolution 731 (1992) violated Charter article 36(2).

Furthermore, article 36, paragraph 3 makes it quite clear that the Security Council should ordinarily encourage the parties to a legal dispute of this nature to refer the dispute to the International Court of Justice:

> In making recommendations under this Article the Security Council should also take into consideration that legal disputes should as a general rule be referred

by the parties to the International Court of Justice in accordance with the provisions of the Statute of the Court.[79]

Article 14 of the Montreal Convention makes it quite clear that if the parties to a dispute thereunder are unable to agree upon the organization of the arbitration tribunal, then within six months from the date of the request for arbitration, any party can take the dispute to the International Court of Justice.

For this reason, both the Security Council itself, and all the Member States constituent thereof, were obligated under Charter articles 2(3), 33(1) and (2), and 36(2) and (3), inter alia, to respect and to encourage respect for the compulsory dispute settlement procedures mandated by article 14 of the Montreal Convention. This solemn treaty obligation still applies today. For the Member States of the Security Council to adopt sanctions against Libya would constitute a gross violation of their obligations under the aforementioned terms of the United Nations Charter and the Montreal Convention to respect, encourage, and require the pacific settlement of this international dispute in accordance with the required arbitration or adjudication.

The United States and the United Kingdom
Illegally Rejected Libya's Demand for Arbitration

During the course of the debate on the adoption of Resolution 731 (1992) by the Security Council, the representatives of the United States and the United Kingdom expressed their opinion that the Montreal Convention did not apply to this situation. To the contrary, article 14 states quite clearly that "any dispute" concerning the "interpretation or application of this Convention" shall be submitted to arbitration. It is for the international arbitration tribunal or the International Court of Justice to decide whether or not the Montreal Convention applies to the circumstances of this case, not the United States and the United Kingdom by themselves. Otherwise, the entire Montreal Convention itself could be negated, defeated, and violated by a contracting state unilaterally proclaiming that the Convention does not apply--according to its own self-interested judgment. Such a conclusion would be the exact antithesis of the Rule of International Law and its basic principle that *pacta sunt servanda*.

The Violent Settlement of International Disputes

In rejecting the applicability of the Montreal Convention, U.S.

Ambassador Thomas Pickering stated: "The issue at hand is not some difference of opinion or approach that can be mediated or negotiated." In other words, the United States government has admitted that it will pay no attention whatsoever to its obligations mandating the peaceful resolution of international disputes as required by U.N. Charter articles 2(3)[80] and 33(1).[81] In particular, article 33(1) clearly requires "negotiation," "mediation," "arbitration," and "judicial settlement" among the many means mandated for the pacific resolution of international disputes. But the United States government has specifically rejected all these measures.

Pickering's high-handed statements should shock the conscience of the civilized world. His illegal rejection of negotiations also expressly violated the terms of Montreal Convention article 14 that specifically requires negotiations between the parties to any dispute that might arise thereunder before resort to international arbitration or adjudication. The United States government has purposefully and illegally made it impossible for there to be a pacific settlement of this dispute precisely because it has rejected negotiations, let alone arbitration or adjudication. It should be clear to the entire world community, therefore, that the United States government is manipulating the Lockerbie bombing allegations for the purpose of preparing the way for aggressive measures against the people and State of Libya and, ultimately, for an armed attack upon them.

The United States government has already threatened the use of military force against Libya over this legal dispute in violation of article 2, paragraph 4 of the United Nations Charter:

> All Members shall refrain in their international relations from the threat or use of force against the territorial integrity or political independence of any state, or in any other manner inconsistent with the Purposes of the United Nations.[82]

The Members of the Security Council must not permit the United States and the United Kingdom to proceed any further down the path of lawless violence against the people and State of Libya. The very Purposes and Principles of the United Nations Organization itself that are found in Charter articles 1 and 2 demand that this dispute be resolved by any of the pacific means that have so far been proposed by Libya.

Resolution 731 (1992) Is Ultra Vires of the Security Council

For these reasons, the Security Council acted beyond its powers (*ultra vires*) when it adopted Resolution 731 (1992). Charter article 24, paragraph 2 makes this point quite clear:

> In discharging these duties the Security Council shall
> act in accordance with the Purposes and Principles of
> the United Nations. The specific powers granted to the
> Security Council for the discharge of these duties are
> laid down in Chapters VI, VII, VIII, and XII.[83]

The Security Council did not and still does not have any lawful authority or power to adopt a resolution that ignores, abrogates, or circumvents the basic principle of international law mandating the peaceful resolution of international disputes.

This sacrosanct principle of international law and politics goes all the way back to the Treaty Providing for the Renunciation of War as an Instrument of National Policy of August 27, 1928, the so-called Paris Peace Pact.[84] The United States, Great Britain, and France are all parties to the Paris Peace Pact. Its operative provisions can be found in articles I and II as follows:

> Article I. The High Contracting Parties solemnly
> declare in the names of their respective peoples that
> they condemn recourse to war for the solution of
> international controversies, and renounce it as an
> instrument of national policy in their relations with
> one another.[85]

> Article II. The High Contracting Parties agree that the
> settlement or solution of all disputes or conflicts of
> whatever nature or of whatever origin they may be,
> which may arise among them, shall never be sought
> except by pacific means.[86]

These requirements of the Paris Peace Pact constitute peremptory norms of international law (*jus cogens*) that are binding upon all states of the world community whether they like it or not. Resolution 731 (1992) violates article II of the Paris Peace Pact as well as the peremptory norm of international law mandating the pacific settlement of international disputes.

The United States, the United Kingdom, and France
Illegally Voted for Resolution 731 (1992)

Finally, the Security Council adopted Resolution 731 (1992) pursuant to its powers under Chapter VI of the U.N. Charter, which governs the pacific settlement of international disputes.[87] But in this regard, Charter article 27, paragraph 3 states quite clearly:

Decisions of the Security Council on all other matters shall be made by an affirmative vote of nine members including the concurring votes of the permanent members; provided that, in decisions under Chapter VI, and under paragraph 3 of Article 52, a party to a dispute shall abstain from voting.[88]

In other words, the United States, the United Kingdom, and France were obliged to abstain from the vote on Resolution 731 (1992) because they are parties to this dispute with Libya over allegations surrounding the Lockerbie bombing and the U.T.A. bombing that were the very subject matter of this resolution.

These three Permanent Members refused to abstain from the vote and thus violated Charter article 27(3). This flagrant and gross procedural violation of the Charter by the three most powerful members of the Security Council calls into question the validity of the votes cast in favor of Resolution 731 (1992) by the other Members of the Security Council. The world's one self-proclaimed superpower and two of the world's greatest military powers illegally used their overwhelming power and influence to induce and coerce the other Member States of the Security Council to unfairly blame Libya for the Lockerbie bombing.

It seems that the so-called "New World Order" is to be governed by the sophistic principle that "might is right": The strong do what they will, and the weak suffer what they must. But how long will it be before the Permanent Members of the Security Council apply this same principle of realpolitik against the rest of the world, including the Non-Permanent Members of the Security Council? For the good of themselves and their own peoples, the other Member States of the Security Council must not permit the United States and the United Kingdom to set themselves up as self-deputized judges, juries, and executioners of the people and State of Libya.

III. THE TWO WORLD COURT JUDGMENTS OF 27 FEBRUARY 1998 OVERWHELMINGLY FAVORED LIBYA

The wheels of international justice turn slowly, but eventually they do turn--and sometimes with astounding consequences. Section III sets forth a 28 February 1998 Memorandum I prepared at the request of the Libyan Ambassador to the United Nations in New York on an expedited and emergency basis analyzing the two World Court Judgments of 27 February 1998 to be used for the purpose of explaining their meaning and significance to the member states of the United Nations Organization as well as in and by Tripoli. These two World Court Judgments paved the way for the peaceful resolution of the Lockerbie dispute among the United States, the United Kingdom, and Libya. No one else died. Another tribute to the "hard power" of international law and the World Court.

On 27 February 1998 the International Court of Justice issued two Judgments on Preliminary Objections raised by the United States and the United Kingdom in the cases concerning *Questions of Interpretation and Application of the 1971 Montreal Convention Arising from the Aerial Incident at Lockerbie (Libyan Arab Jamahiriya v. United Kingdom)*[89] *and (Libyan Arab Jamahiriya v. United States of America)*,[90] General List Nos. 88 and 89, respectively. These two Judgments by the World Court constitute great victories for Libya, for the rule of international law, and for the sacred principle of the peaceful settlement of international disputes as enshrined in the United Nations Charter. The holdings of these two Judgments by the International Court of Justice pave the way for a definitive settlement of the Lockerbie dispute between Libya and the United Kingdom and the United States. As a result of these two Judgments, there is no reason for the Security Council to renew the imposition of the terrible sanctions upon Libya and its people. This is true for the following reasons:

First, the World Court by overwhelming votes rejected the contentions by the United States and the United Kingdom that the Montreal Sabotage Convention did not govern the Lockerbie dispute. In the precise words of the World Court itself: "Such a dispute, in the view of the Court, concerns the interpretation and application of the Montreal Convention and, in accordance with Article 14, paragraph 1, of the Convention, falls to be decided by the Court."[91] Since the World Court has now definitively and overwhelmingly ruled that the Montreal Sabotage Convention governs the Lockerbie dispute, whatever the purported legal basis for the imposition of sanctions against Libya might have been has now been rendered inoperative and nugatory by the International Court of Justice itself.

Second, despite the contrary contentions by the United States and the United Kingdom, the World Court has ruled by overwhelming votes that there currently exists a legal dispute between these two states and Libya over the Lockerbie incident that must be decided by the International Court of Justice itself. In this regard, I call to your attention Article 36(3) of the United Nations Charter, which clearly provides: "In making recommendations under this Article the Security Council should also take into consideration that legal disputes should as a general rule be referred by the parties to the International Court of Justice in accordance with the provisions of the Statute of the Court."[92] Since the International Court of Justice has now decided by overwhelming votes to formally exercise jurisdiction over the Lockerbie dispute despite the objections of the United States and the United Kingdom, there is no longer any purported basis for the Security Council to renew the imposition of sanctions against Libya and its people.

I believe that Libya fully intends to honor and obey whatever final Judgments on the merits are rendered by the International Court of Justice in these two Lockerbie cases. Libya has an excellent track record of compliance with decisions by the International Court of Justice. By comparison, I recall to your attention the sorry history of outright defiance by the United States government of the decisions by the International Court of Justice in the *Nicaragua* Case.

Third, the World Court overwhelmingly rejected the contentions by the United States and the United Kingdom that Libya's claims against these two states under Articles 1, 5, 6, 7 and 8, inter alia, of the Montreal Sabotage Convention were invalid and should be rejected and dismissed.[93] The International Court of Justice itself will now rule upon the validity of Libya's claims under Articles 1, 5, 6, 7, and 8, inter alia, of the Montreal Sabotage Convention. In particular and especially, the World Court itself will decide the dispute between Libya, on the one hand, and the United States and the United Kingdom, on the other, that Libyan domestic law precludes the extradition of its two citizens to the United States and the United Kingdom. For this reason as well, therefore, the purported basis for the continuation of sanctions against Libya and its people has now been rendered inoperative and nugatory by the International Court of Justice itself.

Fourth, rejecting contrary contentions by the United States and the United Kingdom, the World Court overwhelmingly ruled that there currently exists a genuine dispute between Libya and these two states over Article 11 of the Montreal Sabotage Convention, inter alia, which provides in relevant part as follows: "1. Contracting States shall afford one another the greatest measure of assistance in connection with criminal proceedings brought in respect of the offenses. The law of the State requested shall apply in all cases..."[94] The International Court of Justice ruled that this dispute "falls to be decided by the Court."[95] For this reason as well, the purported legal basis for continuing the imposition of sanctions against Libya and its people has now been rendered inoperative and nugatory by the International Court of Justice itself in these two Judgments of 27 February 1998.

Fifth, the International Court of Justice expressly rejected contentions by the United States and the United Kingdom that it was not for the Court to decide upon the lawfulness of actions taken by these two states to secure the surrender of Libya's two accused citizens. In the precise words of the World Court: "The Court cannot uphold the line of argument thus formulated. Indeed, it is for the Court to decide, on the basis of Article 14, paragraph 1, of the Montreal Convention, on the lawfulness of the actions criticized by Libya, in so far as those actions would be at variance with the provisions of the Montreal Convention."[96] Therefore, the World Court has expressly ruled that it will exercise jurisdiction over Libya's claims that both the United States and the United Kingdom have blatantly violated the Montreal Sabotage Convention by means of their deliberate exploitation of the Lockerbie incident as a pretext in order to inflict grave harm upon the people and State of Libya pursuant to their longstanding and well-known plans to that effect. In this regard, I recall to your attention the criminal attacks by the United States and the United Kingdom on Tripoli and Benghazi in 1986; their mass killing and grievous injury of its people at that time; their attempt to assassinate the Leader of Libya's Revolution Muammer Qaddafi, his wife and his children; and their murder of his adopted Palestinian daughter, Hanah. Libya's claims have merit and will be resolved in Libya's favor by the International Court of Justice in its decisions on the merits. Since these claims will now be definitively adjudicated by the International Court of Justice itself during the next phases of these cases, there is no longer any purported basis for the continuation of sanctions against Libya and its people.

Sixth, the International Court of Justice overwhelmingly rejected the contentions by the United States and the United Kingdom[97] that Libya's rights under the Montreal Sabotage Convention were somehow superseded by Security Council Resolution 748(1992) and 883(1993)[98]--which imposed the sanctions against Libya--by means of Articles 25 and 103 of the United Nations Charter.[99] According to these two Judgments by the International Court of Justice on 27 February 1998, Libya's rights under the Montreal Sabotage Convention remain in full force and legal effect irrespective of Security Council Resolutions 748(1992) and 883(1993). Once again, therefore, the purported legal basis for the continued imposition of sanctions against Libya and its people has been rendered inoperative and nugatory by the World Court itself.

Seventh, the World Court expressly rejected the contentions by the United States and the United Kingdom that Resolutions 731(1992), 748(1992) and 883(1993) require Libya to surrender its two citizens to the United States and the United Kingdom for trial irrespective of Libya's rights under the Montreal Sabotage Convention.[100] To the contrary, according to the World Court, these rights of Libya under the Montreal Sabotage Convention still remain in full force and legal effect irrespective of Resolutions 748(1992) and 883(1993).[101] Once again, therefore, the purported legal basis for the continuation of economic sanctions against Libya and its people has been rendered inoperative and nugatory by the International Court of Justice itself.

Eighth, the International Court of Justice expressly rejected the contention by the United Kingdom and the United States that these legal proceedings should be immediately terminated on the ridiculous grounds that decisions of the Security Council could not form the subject of any contentious proceedings before the Court. Furthermore, the International Court of Justice expressly rejected the bogus contention[102] by the United Kingdom that the Court should not proceed to the merits of the case because they were "likely to be lengthy and costly" and also because "the handling of evidentiary material ... might raise serious problems."[103] In these two Judgments the World Court clearly deemed the issues at stake in the Lockerbie dispute to be justiciable and therefore subject to the mandatory jurisdiction of the Court, and that they can be properly presented to the Court by Libya. For this reason as well, the purported legal basis for the continuation of sanctions against Libya and its people has been rendered inoperative and nugatory by the International Court of Justice itself.

Ninth, in their Joint Declarations appended to the Court's Judgments in Libya's cases against the United States and the United Kingdom, Judges Bedjaoui, Ranjeva, and Koroma point out that it is not sufficient to invoke the provisions of Chapter VII of the Charter so as to bring to an end ipso facto and with immediate effect all argument on the Security Council's decisions mentioned above.[104] As Judge Kooijmans phrased the issue in his Separate Opinions in these cases: "5. Whether the eventual finding of the Court on the merits is compatible with binding decisions of other United Nations organs, in particular the Security Council, is quite another matter and in the Court's view must be considered at a later stage."[105] As already stated above, the International Court of Justice expressly rejected the contention by the United Kingdom and the United States that these legal proceedings should be immediately terminated on the spurious grounds that decisions of the Security Council could not form the subject of contentious proceedings before the Court.

Consequently, in the event the Security Council were to renew the imposition of sanctions against Libya, Libya will have no alternative but to contest the validity of Resolutions 748(1992) and 883(1993), and in particular will have to argue that these two Resolutions are beyond the powers of the Security Council (i.e., *ultra vires*) under the terms of the United Nations Charter. In light of these two resounding and overwhelming World Court Judgments in its favor, I am fully confident that Libya's position on this matter will be upheld on the merits by the International Court of Justice. In order to avoid that result, it would be best for the Security Council not to renew the sanctions against Libya.

In conclusion, Libya most emphatically repeats before the Security Council and to the entire world that it was not responsible for the tragic destruction of the Pan Am jet at Lockerbie and the horrendous loss of innocent human beings resulting therefrom. If the United States and the United Kingdom really believe in good faith that they actually have some circumstantial evidence that might somehow implicate Libya, then these two states are obligated to bring their so-called evidence to the International Court of Justice at The Hague in accordance with the binding rules of international law and with the normal practice for resolving serious legal disputes between sovereign nation states. Libya has nothing to hide. That is precisely why Libya brought the United States and the United Kingdom before the Bar of the World Court on 3 March 1992 by instituting these legal proceedings. The Security Council must not permit the United States and the United Kingdom to set themselves up as some sort of self-deputized judges, juries and executioners of the people and State of Libya. Libya hereby repeats and renews all of its outstanding offers for a peaceful resolution of the Lockerbie dispute for the trial of its two nationals. In particular, Libya hereby repeats and renews its outstanding offer to have its two nationals tried by the International Court of Justice itself during subsequent proceedings in our Lockerbie cases against the United States and the United Kingdom that are now currently pending before the World Court.

IV. THE WORLD COURT VERSUS THE SECURITY COUNCIL

Section IV sets forth a 6 March 1998 Memorandum that I prepared at the request of the Libyan Ambassador to the United Nations to be used for the purpose of explaining to the U.N. member states as well as in and by Tripoli the overlapping dual-competences of the Security Council and the International Court of Justice to deal with Libya's Lockerbie bombing dispute with the United States and the United Kingdom; and why Security Council Resolution 748 did not trump Libya's legal rights under the Montreal Sabotage Convention and other sources of international law.

Normally it is the case that both the Security Council and the International Court of Justice can exercise dual competence over an international dispute. The Security Council is supposed to deal with the political aspects of the dispute provided it constitutes a threat to the maintenance of international peace and security. Whereas the International Court of Justice is supposed to deal with the legal aspects of the dispute. However, the Lockerbie dispute is different.

In the Lockerbie dispute, Libya filed papers at the International Court of Justice asking the Court to deal with all the legal aspects of this dispute, including and especially the extradition of the two Libyan citizens, well before the Security Council had adopted any Resolution pursuant to Chapter VII of the United Nations Charter. In particular, Libya had asked the International Court of Justice to resolve the legal dispute over the extradition of the two Libyan citizens before the Security Council had acted on this matter pursuant to Chapter VII of the United Nations Charter. Despite the fact that Libya had submitted all of the legal aspects of the Lockerbie dispute to the International Court of Justice pursuant to the Montreal Sabotage Convention, the Governments of the United States and the United Kingdom abused their powers as Permanent Members of the Security Council to ram Sanctions Resolutions through the Security Council while these very legal issues themselves were pending before the International Court of Justice. In other words, the United States and the United Kingdom deliberately set out to usurp, thwart, and render nugatory the powers, competence, and authority of the International Court of Justice as established by the Charter of the United Nations, the Statute of the International Court of Justice, and the Montreal Sabotage Convention. Never before in the history of the United Nations Organization have two Permanent Members of the Security Council so thoroughly and completely abused, misused, and perverted their powers under the terms of the United Nations Charter.

Article 24 of the Charter obligates the Security Council to act in accordance with the "Purposes and Principles of the United Nations."[106] This terminology refers back to Article 1, Paragraph 1 of the Charter, which makes it clear that the action of the Security Council must be pursued "in conformity with the principles of justice and international law."[107] Pursuant to Article 92 of the Charter, the International Court of Justice--not the Security Council--is "the principal judicial organ of the United Nations."[108] It is clear that by acting in this high-handed manner, the Security Council Resolutions imposing sanctions upon Libya over Libya's failure to extradite its two citizens are *ultra vires* the powers of the Security Council under the terms of the United Nations Charter, which incorporates the Statute of the International Court of Justice. The extradition of citizens is clearly a legal matter for the World Court to decide, not the Security Council, let alone the United States and the United Kingdom by themselves.

In his book *The New World Order and the Security Council: Testing the Legality of its Acts*,[109] Judge Mohammed Bedjaoui of the International Court of Justice, and formerly the President of the World Court, agrees with this analysis:

> ...But the difficulty that arose lay in the fact that the Security Council had not only taken a number of political measures against Libya, but had also required it to extradite two of its nationals. *It was this specific political demand made by the Council that resulted*

> *in overlapping with the very substance of the legal*
> *dispute with which the Court was bound to deal in legal*
> *terms on the basis of the 1971 Montreal Convention*
> *and international law in general.*[110] [Emphasis added.]

In his book, Judge Bedjaoui makes it quite clear that normally the Security Council deals with the political aspects of a dispute, whereas the World Court deals with the legal aspects of the dispute. But in the Lockerbie dispute, the Security Council improperly intruded upon the legal dispute that had already been submitted by Libya to the International Court of Justice under the terms of the Montreal Sabotage Convention. Once again, the Security Council had never attempted to do something like that before. As Judge Bedjaoui said with respect to the Provisional Measures phase of Libya's World Court proceedings:

> ...For it was manifestly incompatible with the Charter
> that a political organ of the United Nations should
> prevent the Court from fulfilling its vocation or place
> it de facto in a state of subordination which is contrary
> to the principle of the separation and independence of
> the judicial power in relation to the executive power
> within the United Nations.[111]

Judge Bedjaoui concludes his analysis by pointing out that in fact it was the Security Council that violated the separation of powers established under the Charter of the United Nations, and that failed and refused to cooperate and coordinate with the other organs of the United Nations Organization, including and in particular the International Court of Justice itself:

> ...The fact remains that in the radical exercise of its
> power without absolute necessity and, above all,
> without taking into account the impact on the exercise
> of the powers of another organ, like the Court, the
> Council betrays an "isolationist" and "imperial"
> conception of its role which pays scant attention to the
> virtues of co-operation and the duty of coordination
> between organs.[112]

By abusing their powers as Permanent Members of the Security Council, the United States and the United Kingdom attempted to impose on the question of extraditing the two Libyan citizens a mandatory solution in the hope and expectation of rendering the Judgments on the

Merits that the World Court still has to give in these cases meaningless in advance. Of course, that maneuver was rejected by the World Court in its Judgments of 27 February 1998. Therein the World Court overwhelmingly repudiated this blatant attempt by the United States and the United Kingdom to deprive the Court of its acknowledged right to determine all of the legal issues in dispute with Libya over the Lockerbie incident, including and especially their demand for extradition of the two Libyan citizens.

Since this *ultra vires* demand is at the very heart of the two Sanctions Resolutions, there are no longer any legal grounds for the imposition of sanctions against Libya. The World Court itself will rule on this matter of extradition as well as upon all other legal aspects of the Lockerbie dispute arising under the Montreal Sabotage Convention. Now that the World Court overwhelmingly ruled in its Judgments of 27 February 1998 that the Court will exercise its jurisdiction over the Lockerbie dispute, the legal basis for the sanctions against Libya has been nullified and rendered inoperative by the World Court itself. The conclusion is inexorable that Libya is entitled to have these sanctions lifted or at least suspended at this time pending the World Court's final Judgments on the merits of Libya's Lockerbie cases against the United States and the United Kingdom.

V. THE SCOTTISH KANGAROO COURT AT THE U.S. MILITARY BASE IN THE NETHERLANDS

The two World Court Judgments of 27 February 1998 constituted massive and overwhelming victories for Libya against the United States and the United Kingdom. A careful reading of these two Judgments indicated to any astute lawyer that at the end of the day the United States and the United Kingdom would lose the entirety of the Lockerbie cases when the World Court came to the final Judgments on the merits. That was because Libya filed the lawsuits before it was illegally and unjustly sanctioned by the Security Council. The filing of the lawsuits the day before Libya was originally scheduled to be sanctioned perfected and froze into perpetuity all of Libya's legal rights under the Montreal Sabotage Convention, the United Nations Charter, the Statute of the International Court of Justice, and all other sources of applicable international law. The World Court had made this point very clear in its Judgments of 27 February 1998.

It was obvious that the World Court would ultimately agree with Libya on the merits of the Lockerbie cases because the lawsuits were filed before Libya was sanctioned by the Security Council. If the Five Permanent Members of the Security Council insisted upon renewing or extending sanctions against Libya, then eventually they would get two World Court final Judgments on the merits against their Lockerbie Chapter VII Sanctions Resolutions. *Not only this disaster, but they would get two World Court Judgments that would undercut and undermine the significance of **all** Resolutions that the Security Council had adopted or ever will adopt under Chapter VII of the U.N. Charter.* I doubted very seriously that this eventual catastrophe was something that the Permanent Five Members of the Security Council would like to see happen, especially the United States.

It seemed to me that the Permanent 5 would not want the World Court to be examining the validity of their Resolutions adopted under Chapter VII of the Charter. But that was exactly what the World Court would be doing in the Lockerbie cases from then on. *In other words, creating a precedent for the International Judicial Review of Chapter VII Security Council Resolutions.* Of course, the establishment of some system for the international judicial review of Chapter VII Security Council Resolutions by the World Court was a dire necessity and long overdue. That was precisely why Judge Bedjaoui wrote his book on this subject in 1994. I was certain that Judge Bedjaoui, Judge Weeramantry and the other World Court Judges from Third World Countries would love to have the opportunity to begin examining the legal validity of Chapter VII Security Council Resolutions.

With such absolute and total and existential defeat staring them straight in the face, the United States and the United Kingdom proceeded to cobble together a plan for a kangaroo court proceeding and Stalinist show-trial of the two accused Libyan citizens by three Scottish judges sitting at a former United States air force base in The Netherlands in a desperate effort to head off this inevitable train wreck for the Security Council at the World Court courtesy of my original 1991-1992 advice to Libya. The U.S. and the U.K. then rammed this Scottish kangaroo court plan through the Security Council and attempted to impose their new diktat upon Libya by means of Resolution 1192 (1998). Both governments publicly threatened yet another round of economic sanctions if Libya did not succumb to their latest ukase despite Libya's crushing victory over them in the World Court.

But even another Chapter VII Sanctions Resolution would not prejudice Libya's rights in the World Court under the Montreal Sabotage Convention and other sources of international law. Rather, it would only increase the amount of damages that Libya would obtain from the United States and the United Kingdom during the final Reparations phase of the Lockerbie bombing World Court proceedings. Consequently, my advice to Libya was to reject the Scottish kangaroo court and Stalinist show-trial in The Netherlands for their two citizens.

VI. THE BASIC HUMAN RIGHTS OF THE TWO ACCUSED LIBYAN NATIONALS

From the very outset of the World Court proceedings on the Lockerbie bombing cases, I had been in communication with and attempted to provide assistance to the Libyan attorney of record for the two unjustly accused Libyan nationals: Mr. Ibrahim Legwell of Tripoli. Having met with him personally, it was my professional opinion that Mr. Legwell was doing the very best he could to defend his clients under extremely difficult circumstances. For obvious reasons, Mr. Legwell was adamantly against turning over his two clients to the not-so-tender mercies of the Scottish kangaroo court sitting at the U.S. military base in The Netherlands for a Stalinist show-trial. I did the best I could to support Mr. Legwell in Tripoli with my own contacts over there. Section VI is based upon a 27 August 1998 Memorandum I sent to Mr. Legwell to be used as ammunition on behalf of his clients in Tripoli.

Libya's two citizens have a basic human right under customary international law and treaties to a fair trial before an independent and impartial tribunal established by law, not by means of a diktat. Article 10 of the Universal Declaration of Human Rights (U.D.H.R.) says quite clearly; "Everyone is entitled in full equality to a fair and public hearing by an independent and impartial tribunal, in the determination of his rights and obligations and of any criminal charge against him."[113] Clearly, a trial before three Scottish judges would not be fair, or independent, or impartial. Thus, the U.S. and U.K. diktat was calling upon Libya to violate the Universal Declaration of Human Rights, which must not be done. And Article 10 clearly enunciates the rules of customary international law on this matter, if not *jus cogens* as well. Moreover, the United States government had taken the position that such a basic provision of the U.D.H.R. is customary international law.

The obligation of Article 10 of the Universal Declaration of Human Rights has been codified into Article 14(1) of the 1966 International Covenant on Civil and Political Rights, which provides in relevant part as follows; "All persons shall be equal before the courts and tribunals. In the determination of any criminal charge against him, or of his rights and obligations in a suit at law, everyone shall be entitled to a fair and public hearing by a competent, independent and impartial tribunal established by law..."[114] The U.S. and U.K. demand that Libya's citizens be tried by three Scottish Judges violates Article 14(1) of this Covenant. Both the United States and the United Kingdom are parties to this Covenant, as well as Libya. Therefore, all three states have an obligation to make sure that Libya's nationals received a "fair" trial by an "independent and impartial tribunal established by law," not by means of a diktat. A trial by three Scottish Judges would not be either fair, or independent, or impartial.

In addition, most Members of the Security Council and most Members of the U.N. General Assembly are also parties to this Covenant. Therefore, Libya has the perfect right and indeed the obligation to demand that its citizens be given (1) a "fair" trial by a tribunal that is both (2) independent, and (3) impartial, and (4) established by law, instead of by diktat. Libya would have a very strong, compelling, and conclusive argument to that effect in the Security Council, the General Assembly, and the International Court of Justice, as well as before the court of world public opinion....

For the above reasons, inter alia, I must conclude that the U.S. and U.K. diktat was never made in good faith and should be rejected by Libya because it violates the most basic human rights of Libya's two citizens.

VII . THE FIX IS IN

During the last conversation I ever had with Mr. Legwell, he informed me that he was being replaced as the Libyan attorney of record for the two unjustly accused Libyan nationals by Mr. Maghour, the presumptive Western intelligence agent who had previously tried to sabotage my filing of the World Court cases for Libya against the United States and the United Kingdom in early March of 1992. Having grown up on the Irish Southside of Chicago under the auspices of the Dick Daley Machine, I knew then that the proverbial "fix" had been put in against the two Libyan nationals.

But there was nothing more I could do to stop it. They were not my clients. Nevertheless, thereafter I would give some occasional interviews to inquiring news media sources condemning the Scottish kangaroo court *cum* Stalinist show-trial and their fake appellate proceedings in no uncertain terms.

The reader does not have to take my word alone for it. These are also the conclusions of Professor Hans Koechler, President of the International Progress Organization, whom the U.N. Secretary-General appointed to serve as an International Observer of the Lockerbie Trial at The Netherlands pursuant to Security Council Resolution 1192 (1998). In this capacity Professor Koechler issued two official reports, first on the Scottish trial proceedings and then on the Scottish appellate proceedings in The Netherlands. In addition, Professor Koechler also made numerous statements to the world news media condemning the entirety of these Scottish "legal" proceedings. This author agrees with everything Professor Koechler had to say about the Lockerbie Scottish kangaroo court proceedings and their related sham appeals.[115]

True to form, and following in the footsteps of his previously unethical, reprehensible, and destructive behavior, the presumptive Western Intelligence agent Mr. Maghour proceeded to sabotage the defense of his clients before the Scottish kangaroo court in The Netherlands. As Professor Koechler correctly pointed out in his report:[116]

> 9.   In the analysis of the undersigned, the strategy of the defense team by suddenly dropping its "special defense" and cancelling the appearance of almost all defense witnesses (in spite of the defense's ambitious announcements made earlier during the trial) is totally incomprehensible; it puts into question the credibility of the defense's actions and motives. In spite of repeated requests of the undersigned, the defense lawyers were not available for comment on this particular matter.

Having followed the proceedings myself, I concur with the conclusions by Professor Koechler. Mr. Maghour had a mountain of evidence and a stable of witnesses that he could have used to exculpate his clients. Instead, Mr. Maghour abandoned and betrayed his clients to the not-so-tender mercies of the Scottish kangaroo court—exactly as I had feared and anticipated and discussed in my last conversation with his good-faith predecessor, the Libyan attorney Mr. Legwell.

After this Stalinist show-trial at the U.S. air force base in The Netherlands was concluded, the Scottish kangaroo court issued a split-verdict finding Mr. Fhima "not guilty," whereas Mr. Megrahi was found to be "guilty." Of course this split-verdict defied belief and was logically inconsistent. From the very outset of the allegations made by the United States government against the two of them, both were alleged to have been the "masterminds" and co-conspirators behind the Lockerbie bombing. Either they both should have been found "not guilty"; or they both should have been found "guilty"; and in the event of one of them having been found "not guilty", they both should have been found "not guilty" and acquitted. As Professor Koechler described the bizarre split-verdict in his report:[117]

> 12.   Furthermore, the Opinion of the Court seems to be inconsistent in a basic respect: while the first accused was found "guilty," the second accused was found "not guilty." It is to be noted that the judgment, in the latter's case, was *not* "not proven," but "not

guilty." This is totally incomprehensible for any rational observer when one considers that the indictment in its very essence was based on the joint action of the two accused in Malta.

This nonsensical split-verdict incontestably proved that the Scottish kangaroo court proceedings at the U.S. military base in The Netherlands were a travesty of justice. The same can be said for the Scottish kangaroo appellate courts that rubber-stamped the irrational split-verdict. Mr. Megrahi was an innocent man who had been railroaded by "Scottish justice"—an oxymoron to be sure—into spending the rest of his cancer-free life behind bars.

On August 20, 2009 the Scottish government announced that it would release Mr. Megrahi from prison on "compassionate grounds." Of course that was not true either. In order to procure Mr. Megrahi's return home, the Libyan government had deliberately dangled the prospect of access to the lucrative Libyan oil fields by British oil companies before the beady and greedy little eyes of U.K. Prime Minister Tony Blair et al.[118] The Libyans knew their men.

Besides, everyone involved in the process knew that Mr. Megrahi was innocent. The hysterical demands emanating from the United States and the United Kingdom for the extraction of the last ounce of flesh out of Mr. Megrahi while he lay dying from prostate cancer in Libya were truly revolting. At least Mr. Megrahi died a free man. R.I.P.

VIII. DENOUEMENT

On May 31, 2006, the neoconservative Bush Junior administration resumed full diplomatic relations with Libya. This was an objective I had set for myself way back in 1981 when I first came to the defense of Libya after the neoconservative Reagan administration commenced a series of illegal and unjustified military attacks against that country. I had always believed that there were no grounds for severing diplomatic relations by the United States against Libya and for the subsequent hostile relations between the two countries. I had always been of the opinion that the United States and Libya should be able to negotiate over and resolve most of the outstanding sources of disagreement that existed between our two countries. Now my original assessment had been proven to be correct and vindicated by the re-establishment of normal diplomatic relations between Libya and the United States by the neoconservative Bush Junior administration itself. *Mirabile dictu!* To be sure, the hydrocarbon-laden Bush Junior administration had also been salivating at the prospect of getting access to all that Libyan oil and gas. Qaddafi had to pay close to $3 billion in extortion funds to the families of the Lockerbie bombing victims and their rapacious lawyers in order to put this matter behind him. A mere drop in Libya's sea of oil.

I felt very happy for Libya, for the Libyans, and for Colonel Qaddafi and his Revolution. The two countries seemed to have just opened a new chapter in their relationship that looked constructive and could become quite promising. So I decided to close my *Libya File* with the proverbial self-congratulatory pat on the back and move on to more urgent matters. Case closed!

Five years later, all hell would break loose. Libya had always been sitting on those vast pools of oil and gas; and the Libyans could hardly defend themselves against great-power predators. The American neoconservatives had called this phenomenon "low-hanging fruit." In 2011 the neoliberals of the Obama administration decided to pluck Libya. As far as U.S. imperialism was concerned, plucking Libya was only a question of timing—when, not if.

Indeed, on December 13, 2004 I had basically predicted America's rape of Libya in a speech I delivered in Dubai before the *Arab Strategy Forum* on "Political Systems in the Arab World in 2020: Moving Towards Reform and Development" that was convened by the Crown Prince of Dubai:

> The demand by the Bush Jr. administration and its Zionist neoconservative operatives for democratization in the Arab world is a joke and a fraud that is designed to pressure, undermine, and destabilize Arab governments and states at the behest of the genocidal Israeli apartheid regime, and to pursue America's continuing campaign for outright military control and domination of the Gulf oil and gas resources that the United States government launched in direct reaction to the Arab oil embargo of the West in 1973. For over the past three decades American foreign policy toward the entire Middle East has been determined by oil and Israel, in that order.
>
> The United States government will seek direct military control and domination of the hydrocarbon resources of the Arab and Muslim world until there is no oil and gas left for them to steal, using Israel as its regional "policeman" towards that end. Oil and Israel were behind both the Bush Sr. and Bush Jr. wars against Iraq. And now Bush Jr. is threatening to attack Syria, Lebanon, and Iran in conjunction with the genocidal apartheid regime in Israel. As the oil and gas in the

Arab and Muslim world proceed to run out, the United States and Israel will become even more predatory, aggressive, destructive, and genocidal toward Arab and Muslim states and peoples.

The Bush Jr. administration and its Zionist neoconservative operatives could not care less about democracy in the Arab world. In fact, Bush Jr. and his Neo-Cons are all trying very hard to build a Police State in the United States of America that we lawyers are vigorously opposing. What the Bush Jr. administration and its Zionist neoconservative operatives really want in the Arab world are quisling dictators who will do their dirty work for them and the genocidal Israeli apartheid regime against the wishes and prayers of the Arab people for democracy, human rights, the rule of law, constitutionalism, as well as for the liberation of Palestine and Al Quds....

Obama was the Black velvet glove covering the white racist iron fist of U.S. imperialism and capitalism. Bush Junior was the iron fist. Ditto for Romney. That is why Obama won and Romney lost in 2012.

ENDNOTES

1   The viewpoints expressed here are solely those of the author and cannot be attributed to Libya for any reason.

2   A preliminary version of this chapter was originally delivered as a paper before a Conference on *Post-cold War International Security Threats: Terrorism, Drugs, and Organized Crime*, held at the University of Michigan Law School in Ann Arbor on February 19-20, 1999.

3   Michael Wines, *French Suspect Top Libyans in Pan Am Blast*, N.Y. Times, Jun. 27, 1991 (*L'Express*, a French news outlet, reported that Libya was the sole mastermind of the bombing).

4   The accusation of Libya as behind the Pan Am bombing raised doubts from quite a few news reporters: *E.g.*, Andrew I. Killgore, *Did Libya Really Destroy Pan Am 103? Or Is There a Cover-Up?*, The Washington Report on Middle East Affairs, Dec. 31, 2001, Vol. XX, Issue 9, at 17 (noting that in the decision at the Scottish Court in The Hague for the Lockerbie bombing the "three judges' unanimous 75-page opinion all but demanded a 'not proven' rather than the 'guilty' verdict" and that there is widespread doubt about the conviction for Mr. Megrahi who was accused of the bombing); Roy Rowan, *Pan Am 103: Why Did They Die?*, Time, Apr. 27, 1992, Vol. 139, Issue 17, at 27.

5   Walter S. Mossberg, *Pan Am Bombing Investigators Believe They Can Identify Those Responsible*, Wall Street Journal, June 14, 1991, at A5C.

6   Roy Rowan, *supra* note 4, at 27 (indicating that the allegation against Libya was developed "suddenly" by the U.S. Justice Department).

7   At least until early 1991, Syria and Iran were touted as masterminds of the bombing of Pan Am 103. *See* George de Lama, *U.S.: Syria Still Backs Terrorists*, Chicago Tribune, May 1, 1991, at 4 (suggesting that a renegade Palestinian terrorist group operating in Syrian territory had been long believed to have played a role in bombing of Pan Am 103. It added that this group was closely allied, supported, and directed by Syria).

8   Christopher Hitchens, *Minority Report*, The Nation, Mar. 30, 1992, Vol. 251, No. 12 (Magazine), at 402 (indicating that the fact that Syria had been a U.S. partner in the Gulf War led Bush Senior administration to publicly drop all charges against Syria and instead indict Libya on the Lockerbie bombing). *See also* Walter S. Mossberg, *supra* note 5 (stating that there is controversy likely to erupt over whether Syria was spared blame because it helped the U.S. in the Persian Gulf War).

9   Walter S. Mossberg, *supra* note 5 (reporting that "the investigation has pointed away from Syria and Iran" and established that Libya planted the bomb).

10   George Graham, *Senegal Wins Improved Deal on Its Debts*, Financial Times, London, Sec. 1, June 25, 1991, at 4.

11   Walter S. Mossberg, *supra* note 5 (reporting that police found a part of the bombing device that was discovered in the possession of Libyan agents in Senegal in February of 1988); Khalil I. Martar et al., *Lockerbie and Libya*, 9 McFarland & Company (2004) (explaining that "the F.B.I. lab investigating the evidence suddenly 'discovered' a link between remnants of timers found on the scene in Lockerbie and similar timers discovered in *Africa*.") (emphasis added).

12   Andrew Rosenthal, *U.S. Accuses Libya as 2 are Charged in Pan Am Bombing*, N.Y. Times, Nov. 15, 1991, at A1.

13   *See generally* Roy Rowan, *supra* note 4 (records showed that no unaccompanied suitcases were put aboard).

14   Gerald P. McGinley, *The I.C.J. Decision in the Lockerbie Cases*, 22 **Ga. J. Int'l & Comp. L**. 577, 584 *quoting* Kevin Toolis, *When British Justice Failed*, N.Y. Times, Feb. 25, 1990 (noting it is ironic that the United Kingdom does not have a particularly good record in handling terrorism, but it accused Libyan judicial officials of being incapable of dealing with terrorism).

15   Convention for the Suppression of Unlawful Acts Against the Safety of Civil Aviation, *opened for signature* Sept.23, 1971, 24 U.S.T. 565 [hereinafter Montreal Convention].

16   *See* Questions of Interpretation and Application of the 1971 Montreal Convention Arising from the Aerial Incident at Lockerbie (Libya v. U.K.), 1992 I.C.J. 3, 31 (Order of Apr. 14, 1992) [hereinafter Libya v. U.K.] (separate opinion of Judge Shahabuddeen noted that the demand of the United Kingdom appearing in documents S/23306, S/23308, and S/23309 constituted a public and widely publicized announcement and prior determination that the two Libyan accused were in fact guilty of the offences charged).

17   Letter from Ibrahim Bishari, Libyan Foreign Minister, to James Baker, U.S. Sec'y of State, & Douglas Hurd, British Foreign Minister (*Letter Dated 18 January 1992 from the Permanent Representative of the Libyan Arab Jamahiriya to the United Nations Addressed to the President of the Security Council*, U.N. Doc. S/23441, Annex 2, Jan. 18, 1992).

18   As of 2011, 188 parties have ratified the Montreal Convention including the U.S. (Nov. 11, 1972), the U.K (Oct. 25, 1973), and Libya (Feb. 19, 1974).

19   Article 14 provides for three sequential steps for the peaceful resolution of disputes thereunder (negotiation, arbitration, adjudication) in the following language:

> Any dispute between two or more Contracting States concerning the interpretation or application of this Convention which cannot be settled through negotiation, shall, at the request of one of them, be submitted to arbitration. If within six months from the date of the request for arbitration the Parties are unable to agree on the organization of the arbitration, any one of those Parties may refer the dispute to the International Court of Justice by request in conformity with the Statute of the Court.

Id., art. 14, para. 1.

20   S.C. Res. 731, U.N. SCOR, 47th Sess., 3033rd meeting, U.N. Doc. S/RES/731 (Jan. 21, 1992) [hereinafter S.C. Rec. 731].

21   *Id.*

22   *Libya Accused of Hiding Chemical Arms - U.N. Demands Cooperation in Jet -Bombing Probe,* Seattle Post-Intelligencer, Jan 22, 1992, at A1 (suggesting that Resolution 731 intended to require "extradition" even though it does not include the word "extradition" in its text).

23   Extradition of the two Libyan nationals was not even requested by the U.S. and the U.K. to Libya because they were aware of the legal impossibility of demanding extradition of Libyan nationals. Professor Graefrath noted that:

> The term surrender is obviously chosen because the United States and the United Kingdom were well aware that under international law there is no obligation for Libya to extradite her own nationals and there is no extradition treaty.... As Professor Bassiouni has put it: 'the U.S. and British government certainly know that Libya legally cannot extradite its nationals. These government[s]...would prefer the propaganda benefits of condemning Libya for not extraditing.'

Bernhard Graefrath, *Leave to the Court What Belongs to the Court: the Libyan Case,* 4 **Eur. J. Int'l L.** 184, 188 (1993) (quoting Bassiouni, *The Need for an International Criminal Tribunal in the New International Order, in* An International Criminal Court 9, 22 (Parliamentarians for Global Action, 1992)).

24   *See* Christopher C. Joyner, *Libya and the Aerial Incident at Lockerbie: What Lessons for International Extradition,* 14 **Mich. J. Int'l L** 222, 223 (noting that the 1992 resolution of Security Council first urged Libya to cooperate with the international investigation of the bombing).

25   The operative part of Security Council Resolution 731 demanding action by Libya was:

> ....
>
> 3. *Urges* the Libyan Government immediately to provide a full and effective response to those requests so as to contribute to the elimination of international terrorism;
> 4. *Requests* the Secretary-General to seek the cooperation of the Libyan Government to provide a full and effective response to those requests, ...

S.C. Res. 731, *supra* note 21, arts. 3 & 4.

26   Paul Lewis, *U.S. and Allies to Seek U.N. Support Against Libya,* N.Y.Times,

Jan. 4, 1992, at sec. 1. (reporting that "President Hosni Mubarak of Egypt has already expressed unhappiness" about plans by three countries, the U.K., the U.S. and France, to ask the Security Council to approve sanctions, and a resolution supporting extradition, against Libya for refusing to turn over suspects designated by the three countries).

27   *Id.* (reporting an interview with a high-ranking official in the Bush Senior administration who said that it would be "an unprecedented action" to ask the Security Council to adopt a resolution supporting extradition and sanctions and bringing the Libyan matter to the Council was "going to be very difficult").

28   *U.N. at its Peak World Leaders Gather for Summit: World Leaders Seek a Stronger U.N.*, Philadelphia Daily News, Feb. 1, 1992, at A3.

29   Leo Rennert Bee, *Bush to Put Spotlight on Yeltsin - He Plans Elaborate Welcome for Russian, Short Talk with Chinese Premier*, Sacramento Bee, Jan. 31, 1992, at A10 (reporting that President Bush arranged diplomatic meeting so that Chinese Prime Minister Li Peng could gain a measure of international respect).

30   S.C. Res. 731, *supra* (Resolution 731 of Security Council was adopted with ten votes against Libya including the votes of the U.S. and the U.K., and five abstentions. It was only one more vote than the nine required for adopting a resolution by Security Council).

31   Lee Michael Katz, *U.N. to Libya : Turn over Pan Am Suspects*, USA Today, Jan. 22, 1992, at 1A *quoting* Ambassador Thomas Pickering ("The resolution makes it clear neither **Libya** nor any other state can seek to **hide** support for **international** terrorism behind traditional principles of **international law.**").

32   John J. Goldman, *U.N. Council Demands Libya Hand over Pan Am Suspects*, The Dallas Morning News, Jan. 22, 1992, at 1A *quoting* Ambassador Pickering ("The council will be acting in a *step-by-step measure* to ensure its commitment to international peace and security") (emphasis added).

33   *See, e.g.*, Executive Intelligence Review News Service (EIRNS),*Libyan Response to Anglo-American Pressure Tactics Becoming More Shrill*, Jan. 9, 1992.

34   Questions of Interpretation and Application of the 1971 Montreal Convention Arising from the Aerial Incident at Lockerbie (Libya v. U.K.), Application, I.C.J., http://www.icj-cij.org/docket/files/88/7207.pdf [hereinafter Libya v. U.K., Application]; Questions of Interpretation and Application of the 1971 Montreal Convention Arising from the Aerial Incident at Lockerbie (Libya v. U.S.), Application, I.C.J., http://www.icj-cij.org/docket/files/89/7209.pdf (both Applications were filed in the Registry of the Court on Mar. 3, 1992) [hereinafter Libya v. U.S., Application].

35   Libya v. U.K., Application, *supra*, IV(a); Libya v. U.S., Application, *supra*, IV(a).

36   Libya v. U.K., Application, *supra*, III(c), (e); Libya v. U.S., Application, *supra*, III(c), (e).

37   Libya v. U.K., Application, *supra*, III(f), IV(b); Libya v. U.S., Application, *supra*, III (f), IV(b).

38   Libya v. U.K., Application, *supra*, IV(c); Libya v. U.S., Application, *supra*, IV(c).

39   Request for the Indication of Provisional Measures of Protection Submitted by the Government of the Socialist People's Libyan Arab Jamahiriya (Libya v. U.K..), Incidental Proceedings, Mar. 3, 1992, http://www.icj-cij.org/docket/files/88/13251.pdf; Request for the Indication of Provisional

Measures of Protection Submitted by the Government of the Socialist People's Libyan Arab Jamahiriya (Libya v. U.S.), Incidental Proceedings, Mar. 3, 1992, http://www.icj-cij.org/docket/files/89/13253.pdf.

40   S.C. Res. 748, U.N. SCOR, 47th Sess., 3063rd meeting, U.N. Doc. S/RES/748 (Mar. 31, 1992).

41   Trevor Rowe, *U.N. Votes Embargo on Libya - Security Council Sanctions Will Take Effect April 15 If Two Suspects in the Pan Am Bombing Are Not Handed Over*, Fort Worth Star-Telegram, Apr. 1, 1992, at 1 (The United States and Britain failed to get the support of all 15 members: Cape Verde, China, India, Morocco and Zimbabwe abstained, reflecting concerns that negotiations and Libya's appeal to the World Court had not been given enough time to work.).

42   *Id.*

43   S.C. Res. 748, *supra*.

44   Questions of Interpretation and Application of the 1971 Montreal Convention Arising from the Aerial Incident at Lockerbie (Libya v. United Kingdom) (Libya v. U.S.), 1992 I.C.J. at 3 & 114 (Orders of Apr. 14, 1992), 31 **Int'l Mats.** 662 (1991).

45   Christopher C. Joyner, *supra* note 24, at 250-51 (supporting the view that Libyan claims before I.C.J. had legal merit because Libya's refusal to extradite its nationals had considerable support in contemporary international law). *See also* **Kenneth Manusama, The United Nations Security Council in the Post-Cold War Era: Applying the Principle of Legality** 175 (Martinus Nijhoff: 2006).

46   U.N. Charter, Chapter I, Purposes and Principles, arts. 1 & 2.

47   Manusama, *supra* note 45, at 175 (explaining that "resolution 731 (1992) recommended terms of settlement contrary to those permitted under international law, which the Council was obliged to respect." It concluded that "it can be plausibly be claimed that the I.C.J. would have judged the resolution to be *ultra vires*....").

48   Judge Ajibola made this point in his dissenting opinion that "[a]rguably, certain intrinsic defects may invalidate the two resolutions.... For example, there is the issue of *[n]emo iudex in causa sua*...." *See* Libya v. U.K., *supra*, at 88; *See also* Libya v. U.S., *supra*, at 193.

49   Chief Justice Hughes made this clear in the majority opinion:

> It rests upon the fundamental consideration that the Constitution creates no executive prerogative to dispose of the liberty of the individual. Proceedings against him must be authorized by law. There is no executive discretion to surrender him to a foreign government, unless that discretion is granted by law.... It must be found that statute or treaty confers the power.

Valentine v. United States *ex rel.* Neidecker, 299 U. S. 5 (1936).

50   George C. Wilson, *Navy Missile Downs Iranian Jetliner*, Washington Post, July 4, 1988, at A01.

51   Stephen Engelberg, *Downing of Flight 655: Questions Keep Coming*, N.Y. Times, July 11, 1988, at A1.

52   *Id.*

53   *The Navy: Commending The Vincennes*, Time, Vol. 135, Issue 19, May 7, 1990, at 37.

54   Robert Pear, *U.S. Offers Money in Iran Air Case*, N.Y. Times, July 18, 1989, at A6 (reporting that Iran sued the United States in the International Court of Justice to obtain compensation for the deaths of the Iranian passengers); **Farhan Rajaee, The Iran-Iraq War: the Politics of Aggression**

143 (University Press of Florida: 1993) (noting that the United States first refused to pay compensation to the Iranian government); *Iran, U.S. Settle Claims for $131.8 Million*, **Chicago Tribune, Feb. 23, 1996, at 8 (reporting the U.S. and Iran reached settlement for the 1988 shooting down of Iranian airliner).**

55   Jonathan B. Schwartz, *Dealing with a "Rogue State": the Libya Precedent*, 101 **Am. J. Int'l L.** 553, 558 (2007) (suggesting that, as a result of the statements made by the U.S. and U.K. governments, the two states would not be able to give the Libyans a fair trial).

56   Montreal Convention, *supra,* art. 1(a) (violence against a person on board an aircraft in flight).

57   Montreal Convention, *supra,* art. 1(b) (to destroy an aircraft in service).

58   Montreal Convention, *supra,* art. 1(c) (to place a device likely to destroy an aircraft).

59   Montreal Convention, *supra,* art. 5(2).

60   Montreal Convention, *supra,* art. 6(1) ("[t]he custody and other measures shall be as provided in the law of that State...").

61   The whole sentence in the article is "[t]he custody and other measures shall be as provided in the law of that State but may only be continued for such time as is necessary to enable any criminal or extradition proceedings to be instituted." *Id.*

62   Montreal Convention, *supra,* art. 6(2).

63   Montreal Convention, *supra,* art. 6(4).

64   *Id.*

65   Manusama, *supra,* at 175 (explaining the U.K. or U.S. could not demand the extradition under Article 7 of the Montreal Convention. He also added that Article 8 in the treaty provides that domestic law determines whether a person can be extradited.).

66   Montreal Convention, *supra,* art. 7.

67   18 U.S.C. §3181.

68   **A. Lowenfeld, Aviation Law** §3.2, at 8-64 (2d ed. 1981).

69   299 U.S. 5, 18 (1936).

70   Montreal Convention, *supra,* art. 14(1).

71   Montreal Convention, *supra,* art. 14(2).

72   Montreal Convention, *supra,* art. 14(3).

73   U.N. Charter, art. 2(3).

74   U.N. Charter, art. 33(1).

75   U.N. Charter, art. 33(1); Manusama, *supra,* at 175 ("the resolution 731 recommended terms of settlement contrary to those permitted under international law, which the Council was obliged to respect.").

76   U.N. Charter, art. 33(2) ("The Security Council shall, when it deems necessary, call upon the parties to settle their dispute by such means.").

77   Professor Manusama at the University of Amsterdam made the following observation on the passage of Resolution 731:

> [b]y demanding extradition of the suspects..., the Security Council chose to ignore the systematic preference of the Charter for settling disputes peacefully and the general rule laid down in the Article 36(3) concerning legal disputes and the I.C.J. Thus resolution 731 (1992) already seems to have been inappropriate, as it undermined the sovereignty and free choice of means afforded to states... that lies at the heart of Chapter VI.

Manusama, *supra,* at 175.

78   U.N. Charter, art. 36(2).

79   U.N. Charter, art. 36(3).
80   U.N. Charter, art. 2(3) (obligation for the peaceful settlement of interna-
      tional disputes).
81   U.N. Charter, art. 33(1) (pacific settlement of disputes).
82   U.N. Charter, art. 2(4).
83   U.N. Charter, art. 24(2).
84   Treaty Between the United States and Other Powers Providing for the
      Renunciation of War as an Instrument of National Policy, *opened for
      signature* Aug. 27, 1928, 46 Stat. 2343, 94 L.N.T.S. 57 [hereinafter Paris
      Peace Pact].
85   *Id.,* art. I.
86   *Id.,* art. II.
87   U.N. Charter, Ch. VI. (pacific settlement of disputes).
88   U.N. Charter, art. 27(3).
89   Questions of Interpretation and Application of the 1971 Montreal Conven-
      tion arising from the Aerial Incident at Lockerbie (Libya v. U.K.), Prelimi-
      nary Objections, Judgment, 1998 I.C.J. 9, Gen. No. 88 (Feb. 27, 1998)
      [hereinafter Libya v. U.K, Judgment of 1998].
90   Questions of Interpretation and Application of the 1971 Montreal Conven-
      tion arising from the Aerial Incident at Lockerbie (Libya v. U.S.), Prelimi-
      nary Objections, Judgment, 1998 I.C.J. 115, Gen No.89 (Feb. 27, 1998)
      [hereinafter Libya v. U.S., Judgment of 1998].
91   Libya v. U.K, Judgment of 1998, *supra,* para. 25, at 18; Libya v. U.S.,
      Judgment of 1998, *supra,* para. 24, at 123.
92   U.N. Charter, art. 36(3).
93   The Court decided that a specific dispute exists between the U.K/U.S
      and Libya as follows:
          In view of the positions put forward by the Parties, the
          Court finds that there exists between them not only a
          dispute of a general nature, as defined in paragraph 24
          above, but also a specific dispute which concerns the
          interpretation and application of Article 7—read in con-
          junction with Article 1, Article 5, Article 6 and Article 8—of
          the Montreal Convention, and which, in accordance with
          Article 14, paragraph 1, of the Convention, *falls to be
          decided by the Court.*
      Libya v. U.K, Judgment of 1998, *supra,* para. 29, at 21-22; Libya v. U.S.
      Judgment of 1998, *supra,* para. 28, at 127 (emphasis added).
94   Montreal Convention, *supra,* art. 11(1).
95   Libya v. U.K, Judgment of 1998, *supra,* para. 29, at 21-22; Libya v. U.S.
      Judgment of 1998, *supra,* para. 28, at 127 (emphasis added).
96   Libya v. U.K., Judgment of 1998, *supra,* para. 36, at 23; Libya v. U.S.,
      Judgment of 1998, *supra,* para. 35, at 128.
97   The Court found that the U.K and the U.S. claimed the following:
          In the present case, the United Kingdom has contended,
          however, that *even if the Montreal Convention did confer
          on Libya the rights it claims, they could not be exercised
          in this case because they were superseded by Security
          Council resolutions 748 (1992) and 883 (1993)* which, by
          virtue of Articles 25 and 103 of the United Nations Charter,
          have priority over all rights and obligations arising out of
          the Montreal Convention.
      See Libya v. U.K., Judgment of 1998, *supra,* para. 37, at 23; See Libya
      v. U.S., Judgment of 1998, *supra,* para. 36, at 128 (emphasis added).

The Court rejected the above argument because the jurisdiction once established by the Libyan Application was still valid:

> The Court cannot uphold this line of argument. Security Council resolutions 748 (1992) and 883 (1993) were in fact adopted after the filing of the Application on 3 March 1992....In the light of the foregoing, the Court concludes that the objection to jurisdiction raised by the United Kingdom on the basis of the alleged absence of a dispute between the Parties concerning the interpretation or application of the Montreal Convention must be rejected....

Libya v. U.K., Judgment of 1998, *supra*, para. 38-9, at 23-4; *See* Libya v. U.S., Judgment of 1998, *supra*, para. 37-8, at 129.

98   The U.K. claimed that the Security Council's resolutions override any rights of Libya under the Montreal Convention and therefore there is no dispute under the Montreal Convention that the jurisdiction of I.C.J. could reach:

> With regard to Security Council resolutions 748 and 883, the position is more complex. If those resolutions have created obligations for Libya which *prevail over any rights* which Libya claims to have under the Montreal Convention, the United Kingdom, as the respondent in this case, must be able to rely upon the inherent jurisdiction of the Court to establish this....

Questions of Interpretation and Application of the 1971 Montreal Convention arising from the Aerial Incident at Lockerbie (Libya v. U.K.), Preliminary Objection of U.K., para. 3.12, at 49 (Jun. 20, 1995), http://www.icj-cij.org/docket/files/88/11257.pdf [hereinafter Libya v. U.K., Preliminary Objection of U.K.] (emphasis added).

U.S. also made the same line of the argument with U.K.:

> ...[T]he obligation of States to accept and carry out decisions of the Security Council under Article 25 *prevail over* the obligations of such States under any other international agreement, including the Montreal Convention.

Questions of Interpretation and Application of the 1971 Montreal Convention arising from the Aerial Incident at Lockerbie (Libya v. U.S.), Preliminary Objection of U.S., at 78 (Jun. 20, 1995), http://www.icj-cij.org/docket/files/89/11249.pdf [hereinafter Libya v. U.S., Preliminary Objection of U.S.] (emphasis added).

99   S. C. Res. 883, U.N. Doc. S/RES/883 (Nov. 11, 1993); *See* Libya v. U.K., Preliminary Objection of U.K., *supra*, para. 37, at 23; *See* Libya v. U.S., Preliminary Objection of U.S., *supra*, para. 36, at 128.

100   The United States argued that "even if the court has jurisdiction, it should decline to exercise jurisdiction" because "the Security Council has full authority to require Libya to surrender the two accused." Libya v. U.S., Preliminary Objection of U.S., *supra*, at 92, 101.

It presented the following argument in its counter-memorial:

> In any event, the decision to require the surrender of these two individuals was made by the Council in the exercise of its duties under the charter for the maintenance of international peace and security. *Any complaint that Libya may have against the Security Council should be taken up with the Security Council* and not with the United States (and the United Kingdom) by reference to the Montreal Convention.

Libya v. U.S., Preliminary Objection of U.S., *supra*, at 106.
The Court rejected that view:

> The Respondent has also argued that because of the adoption of those resolutions, *the only dispute which existed...was between Libya and the Security Council*; this clearly would be a dispute falling within the terms of Article 14 ... of the Montreal Convention and *thus not one which the Court could entertain.*
>
> The Court cannot uphold this line of argument. Security Council resolutions 748 (1992) and 883 (1993) were in fact adopted after the filing of the Application on 3 March 1992. In accordance with its established jurisprudence, if the Court had jurisdiction on that date, it continues to do so; *the subsequent coming into existence of the above-mentioned resolutions cannot affect its jurisdiction once established.*

Libya v. U.K., Judgment of 1998, *supra*, para. 38, at 23-4. *See* Libya v. U.S., Judgment of 1998, *supra*, para. 36-7, at 128-9 (*quoting* Nottebohm, Preliminary Objection, 1953 I.C.J. 122 (Judgment of Nov. 18, 1953); Right of Passage over Indian Territory, Preliminary Objections, 1957 I.C.J. 14 (Judgment of Jul. 6, 1957)).

101   The Court rejected the argument of absence of disputes and said it will hear the existing disputes between parties concerning the Montreal Convention. Libya v. U.K., Preliminary Objection of U.K., *supra*, para. 39, at 24; *See also* Libya v. U.S., Preliminary Objection of U.S., *supra*, para. 38, at 130.

102   The Court rejected the U.K.'s contention that it does not need to proceed to the merits: "[t]hus it is on the question of the "exclusively" or "non-exclusively" preliminary character of the objection here considered that the Parties are divided and on which *the Court must now make a determination.*" *See* Libya v. U.K., Judgment of 1988, *supra*, para. 48, at 27 (emphasis added).

103   Questions of Interpretation and Application of the 1971 Montreal Convention arising from the Aerial Incident at Lockerbie (Libya v. U.K.), Preliminary Objection, Public Sitting, Oct. 20, 1997, at 12, http://www.icj-cij.org/docket/files/88/5237.pdf (presented by Franklin Berman, Agent of U.K, Legal Advisor to the Foreign and Commonwealth Office); Libya v. U.K., Judgment of 1998, *supra*, para. 48, at 27.

104   The three Judges added additional reasons and judgment about the argument by the U.K. and U.S. that the case was without merit:

> To characterize as *not exclusively preliminary* the United Kingdom objection that the Security Council resolutions rendered the Libyan claims without object, and to postpone consideration of it to the merits stage, mean in Our view that it is not sufficient to invoke the provisions of Chapter VII of the Charter so as to bring to an end *ipso facto* and with immediate effect all judicial argument on the Security Council's decisions. The Court will have to decide that point when it reaches the merits of the case.

Joint Declaration of Judges Bedjaoui, Ranjeva and Koroma, Questions of Interpretation and Application of the 1971 Montreal Convention arising from the Aerial Incident at Lockerbie, Preliminary Objection, 1998 I.C.J. 46 (Libya v. U.K.), 1998 I.C.J. 138 (Libya v. U.S.).

105   Libya v. U.K., Judgment of 1998, at 54 (in the separate opinion of Judge

Kooijmans); Libya v. U.S. Judgment of 1998, at 145 (in the separate opinion of Judge Kooijmans).

106   U.N. Charter, art. 24.

107   U.N. Charter, art. 1, para. 1.

108   U.N. Charter, art. 92.

109   **Mohammed Bedjaoui, The New World Order and the Security Council: Testing the Legality of Its Acts** (Martinus Nijhoff: 1994).

110   *Id.* at 46.

111   *Id.* at 73.

112   *Id.* at 75.

113   Universal Declaration of Human Rights, art. 10, G.A. Res. 217A, U.N. GAOR, 3d Sess., 1st plen. mtg., U.N. Doc A/810 at 73 (Dec. 12, 1948).

114   International Covenant on Civil and Political Rights, art. 14(1), GA res. 2200A (XXI), U.N. GAOR, 21st Sess., Supp. No. 1, U.N. Doc. A/6316, at 53, 6 **I.L.M.** 368 (Dec. 16, 1966).

115   **Hans Koechler & Jason Suber, The Lockerbie Trial: Documents Related to the I.P.O. Observer Mission (**International Progress Organization: 27 Studies in International Relations) (Vienna: 2002).

116   *Id.* at 19.

117   *Id.* at 20.

118   Patrick Wintour, *Libya Oil Deals Were Factor in Megrahi Talks, Says Straw*, The Guardian, Sept. 4, 2009.

CHAPTER 5

RESPONSIBILITY TO PROTECT (R2P) VERSUS INTERNATIONAL LAW

In 2011 the neoliberal Obama administration and the NATO states waged war against Libya under the pretext of the "responsibility to protect" (R2P) doctrine. R2P is a repackaged and sanitized version of the hoary and archaic doctrine of "humanitarian intervention" that the neoliberal Clinton administration and NATO had previously resurrected in a vain attempt to justify their illegal war against Serbia over Kosovo in 1999. Indeed, the script for the 2011 neoliberal Obama/NATO war against Libya seems to have been plagiarized from the script for the 1999 neoliberal Clinton/NATO war against Serbia. Both U.S./NATO neoliberal wars were alleged to have been for "humanitarian" reasons using the rubrics of humanitarian intervention against Serbia and its avatar R2P against Libya.

In both neoliberal wars, U.S./NATO deployed their cobbled-together indigenous proxy land forces that they then combined with their hand-picked foreign mercenaries—all of whom were armed, equipped, supplied, and directed by U.S./NATO. In both neoliberal wars, U.S./NATO served as the Air Force for their concocted surrogate ground armies. In both neoliberal wars, the U.S./NATO Air Force working with their proxy mercenary armies succeeded in ousting the legitimate government of Serbia from Kosovo and Qaddafi from Libya. Both neoliberal wars were originally designed by U.S./NATO to establish puppet regimes that would rule those countries on their behalf. Both neoliberal U.S./NATO wars set off humanitarian catastrophes for the innocent people living in those two countries.

Many of the Obama administration's personnel had already worked for President Clinton, including Obama's Secretary of State, Mrs. Clinton. So they were intimately familiar with the Clinton/NATO war plan to oust Serbia from Kosovo. It appears that Pentagon/NATO simply took their Kosovo war plan off the shelf and applied it to Libya *mutatis mutandis*. Having resisted both of these U.S./NATO neoliberal wars, I find the similarities between them uncanny!

Whether or not U.S./NATO will establish an effective puppet regime in Libya as it has successfully done in Kosovo remains undetermined as this book goes to press, but it seems most unlikely. For reasons previously explained, there is significant residual support for Qaddafi and his Green Revolution in Libya today. As demonstrated by the September 2012 killing of the U.S. Ambassador in Benghazi, the political and military situation is extremely volatile and thus unpredictable throughout all of Libya. Things could quickly get out of anyone's control and the state of Libya itself could readily disintegrate into its constituent tribal units—if it has not done so already. Besides, all the U.S./NATO really care about in Libya is its continued free flow of oil from eastern Libya organized around Benghazi. The rest of Libya could disintegrate into the Sahara as far as U.S./NATO are concerned.

Nevertheless undaunted by its experience in Libya, the Obama administration is now using the R2P doctrine in order to destabilize Syria and overthrow the Assad Family regime there—Israel's long-time nemesis. America's Zionist neoconservatives have always referred to Syria as the archetypal "low-hanging fruit." U.S. imperialism appears to have decided that the time is now ripe to pluck Syria for itself and for its adjunct Israel—exactly as I had predicted in my 2004 Dubai speech quoted at the end of the previous chapter. Since U.S. imperialism's neoliberal Democratic establishment under President Clinton and then under President Obama/Clinton have now twice successfully manipulated the doctrines of humanitarian intervention and then R2P to oust governments in Kosovo and Libya, respectively, they figured they could get away with it for yet a third time in Syria. The jury is still out on the "success" of their latest imperialist venture against Syria in the name of "humanity." But tens of thousands of Syrians are now unmistakably dead and injured—and it is still rising. We must never forget that both President and Mrs. Obama *et alia* are the sons and the daughters of Harvard's *The Best and the Brightest* (1972) who gave us the genocidal Vietnam war. Genocide looms on the horizon for Syria.

The next chapter of this book will examine in detail the 2011 neoliberal Obama/Clinton/NATO/R2P war against Libya. But before doing so, this chapter will describe the antithesis between international law and the doctrines of R2P/ humanitarian intervention—which are the exact same thing despite the deceptively shifting imperialist rhetoric. Both doctrines are sheer propaganda manufactured by the government officials, the media, sycophantic academics, prostituted intellectuals and self-styled but either naïve or misanthropic "do-gooders" in the U.S. and the NATO states to justify wars of aggression against Third World Countries such as Libya in order to plunder and steal their natural resources and/or to remove such stalwart obstacles to their imperial agenda of worldwide domination as Serbia, Saddam Hussein, Qaddafi, the Assad Family regime, and perhaps someday soon the Islamic Republic of Iran. Could World War III be far behind?

R2P/Humanitarian Intervention: A Joke and a Fraud

In the aftermath of the collapse of the Warsaw Pact and the disintegration of the Soviet Union, there was a great deal of jubilation in the United States and among its European allies organized into the NATO Alliance, supported by their bootlickers in the academic world and their acolytes in the legal profession, enthusiastically promoting "humanitarian intervention" and then R2P. The purpose of this analysis is to examine the so-called doctrines of humanitarian intervention and R2P in accordance with the requirements of international law. Thereunder R2P/humanitarian intervention is a joke and a fraud that has been repeatedly manipulated and abused by a small number of very powerful countries in the North in order to justify wanton military aggression against and prolonged military occupation of weak countries in the South—and typically by White Peoples of the North against Peoples of Color in the South—for political, economic, strategic, and military reasons that have absolutely nothing at all to do with considerations of humanity and humanitarianism. History teaches that powerful states do not use military force for reasons of humanity. Conversely, great military powers do not refrain from the use of military force for humanitarian reasons either.

Indeed, the world's major military powers such as the United States and the members of the NATO Alliance have been behind most of the major humanitarian atrocities and catastrophes in the modern world. Yet today these white racist great military powers have euphemistically retooled the doctrine of "humanitarian intervention" into some evanescent "responsibility to protect" (R2P) —as if they had ever been anything but rapacious and voracious when it comes to their gross exploitation and degradation of Peoples of Color in the Third World in order to steal their natural resources. That is precisely what the recently established U.S. Africa Command (AFRICOM) is all about: seizing and stealing the natural resources of Africa, the very cradle of our shared humanity. Libya was the first victim of AFRICOM. It will not be the last.

State Practice

Obviously in the brief space here I cannot review the historical record of massive abuse of the older doctrine of humanitarian intervention by militarily powerful states of the North. But a few scholarly sources to that effect will be mentioned. The first comprehensive study of humanitarian intervention was published by Antoine Rougier over a century ago in 1910:[1]

> The conclusion which emerges from this study is that it is neither possible to separate the humanitarian from the political grounds for intervention nor to assure the complete disinterestedness of the intervening States...
>
> ....
>
> Whenever one power intervenes in the name of humanity in the domain of another power, it cannot but impose its concept of justice and public policy on the other State, by force if necessary. Its intervention tends definitely to draw the [other] State into its moral and social sphere of influence, and ultimately into its political sphere of influence. It will control the other State while preparing to dominate it. Humanitarian intervention consequently looks like an ingenious juridical technique to encroach little by little upon the independence of a State in order to reduce it progressively to the status of semi-sovereignty.

During the subsequent course of the next century, nothing in state practice has altered Rougier's sound conclusions.

In my *Foundations of World Order* (1999), this author examined the entire history of numerous United States military interventions into the Western Hemisphere and the "Pacific" Basin from shortly before the Spanish-American War of 1898 up to the so-called Good Neighbor Policy of President Franklin Roosevelt's administration starting in 1932. At the time, almost all of these military interventions were publicly justified on some type of humanitarian grounds by the United States government—whether Democrats or Republicans. But when the actual historical records were later declassified, released, and published, they established that this specious rationale was nothing more than mere propaganda disseminated for the purpose of building public support for military intervention on the actual grounds of geopolitics, economic exploitation, military strategy, and hegemonic domination.

To the same effect, writing in 1963 Professor Ian Brownlie of

Oxford concluded that "the state practice justifies the conclusion that no genuine case of humanitarian intervention has occurred, with the possible exception of the occupation of Syria in 1860 and 1861."[2] Even that one "possible" exception is debatable. And in a seminal treatise published in 1961, Professor Myres McDougal and Florentino Feliciano of the Yale Law School branded the doctrine of humanitarian intervention to be "amorphous."[3] It is noteworthy that fifty years ago the world saw a consensus of scholarly opinion against R2P/humanitarian intervention by the leading archetypes of the two most important and competing schools of international legal studies in the West: International Legal Positivism and the New Haven School of policy-oriented jurisprudence. Third World legal scholars of Color have typically been vehement in their denunciation of humanitarian intervention precisely because their respective countries and peoples and resources have been its primary victims.

The best recent scholarly treatise on this subject was by Sean D. Murphy, *Humanitarian Intervention* (1996). To his credit, this book was written by Professor Murphy while he was a Lawyer working for the United States Department of State. There is only space here to quote two of Professor Murphy's most compelling conclusions: "In conclusion, unilateral humanitarian intervention finds little support in the rules of the U.N. Charter and in state practice in the post Charter era, including those incidents discussed in Chapter 5."[4] Chapter 5 of Professor Murphy's book dealt with several incidents of military intervention after the termination of the Cold War on alleged humanitarian grounds: Liberia, Iraq, Bosnia and Herzegovina, Somalia, Rwanda, and Haiti. Later on at the very end of his book, Professor Murphy summed up: "Recent events show a striking willingness of states to forego unilateral humanitarian intervention in favor of Security Council authorization, thereby reinforcing the views of those that regard unilateral humanitarian intervention as unlawful."[5]

Despite Professor Murphy's prognostication, after his book was published in 1996 the world witnessed the illegal war of aggression by the neoliberal Clinton administration and the NATO member states against Serbia over Kosovo that was justified on alleged humanitarian grounds. In this regard, the reader is referred to the excellent book by Professor Noam Chomsky of M.I.T. entitled *The New Military Humanism* (1999), which definitively refuted the humanitarian motivations alleged by the United States and the NATO states operating under the auspices of the Clinton administration. Of course this comment is not intended to justify, condone, or diminish any of the hideous atrocities that Serbia and the Milosevic regime inflicted upon the Kosovar Albanians, whom this author had advised and assisted in the past *pro bono publico,* as well as upon the Bosnians, and especially the Mothers of Srebrenica and Podrinja, the author's current *pro bono* clients. On behalf of the latter, I convinced the Prosecutor for the International Criminal Tribunal for the Former Yugoslavia Carla Del Ponte to indict Milosevic for every crime in the I.C.T.Y. Statute, including two counts of genocide—one charge for genocide against Bosnia in general, and the second charge for the genocide at Srebrenica in particular.

Professor Chomsky supplemented his viewpoints on the illegal Clinton/NATO war against Serbia in his next book *Rogue States* (2000), where he also set forth trenchant critiques of United States human rights foreign policies toward East Timor, Colombia, Cuba, Iraq, Turkey, etc. As Professor Chomsky has decisively established in his compendium of publications, humanitarian considerations have absolutely nothing at all to do with the conduct of foreign policy by the United States, the United Kingdom, and Israel except in a mere propagandistic sense.

The reader might also want to read the excellent book of almost the same name by William Blum, entitled *Rogue State* (2000). As the book made clear, this title is Blum's reference to the United States of America. Blum is one of those exceedingly rare and truly courageous humanitarians who quit the United States Department of State as a matter of principle.

There very well could be some itty-bitty "rogue states" lurking out there somewhere in the Third World. But since the end of the Cold War, the United States of America has become the Rogue Elephant of world politics and international law. And the cry of "humanitarian intervention" and now R2P have become its mantra and its mating call—as witnessed during the illegal Clinton/U.S./NATO war against Serbia as well during the Bush Junior administration's wars of aggression against Afghanistan and Iraq. The world must never again be deluded by the United States and the NATO states to believe that they are using military force against some other state for humanitarian reasons or as part of some Orwellian "responsibility to protect" their premeditated victims such as Libya, now Syria, and perhaps someday soon Iran.

International Law Versus R2P/Humanitarian Intervention

Now consider what contemporary international law has to say about the alleged doctrines of R2P/humanitarian intervention. Of course there is not enough space here to discuss all the institutions, procedures, and rules of the international legal regime governing the transnational threat and use of force that was set up by the United States government, inter alia, as of 1945. Of course its essential component was the United Nations Organization and its Charter. Then came the so-called regional organizations that were brought into affiliation with the United Nations by means of Chapter 8 of the United Nations Charter: i.e., the Organization of American States (O.A.S.); the League of Arab States; the

Organization of African Unity (O.A.U.), which has now been superseded by the African Union thanks in significant part to the herculean efforts by Colonel Qaddafi; and perhaps someday the Organization for Security and Cooperation in Europe (O.S.C.E.) together with the European Union, as well as the Association of Southeast Asian Nations (A.S.E.A.N.). These institutions were joined by the so-called collective self-defense agreements concluded under Article 51 of the United Nations Charter, the foremost exemplar of which is NATO As such, NATO had absolutely no legal authority whatsoever to wage war against Serbia over Kosovo, or to invade Afghanistan.[6]

Strikingly, even as conceived by the founders of the United Nations under the direction of U.S. hegemony, the only legitimate justifications and procedures for the perpetration of violence and coercion by one state against another state became those set forth in the U.N. Charter. The Charter alone contains those rules which have been consented to by the virtual unanimity of the international community that has voluntarily joined the United Nations Organization. Succinctly put, these rules include the U.N. Charter's Article 2(3) and Article 33(1) obligations for the peaceful settlement of international disputes; the Article 2(4) prohibition on the threat or use of force; and the Article 51 restriction of the right of individual or collective self-defense to repel an actual "armed attack" or "*aggression armée*," according to the French-language version of the U.N. Charter, which is equally authentic with the English.

Related to this right of self-defense are its two fundamental requirements for the "necessity" and the "proportionality" of a state's forceful response to the foreign armed attack or armed aggression. And in regard to defining this first requirement of "necessity," as definitively stated by U.S. Secretary of State Daniel Webster in the famous 1837 case of *The Caroline*, self-defense can only be justified when the "necessity of self-defense is instant, overwhelming, and leaving no choice of means, and no moment for deliberation."[7] The Nuremberg Tribunal later endorsed this *Caroline* test for self-defense, thus enshrining it as a basic principle of the contemporary international legal order. Consequently, the Nuremberg Tribunal rejected the neoconservative Bush Junior doctrine of "preventive warfare" when the lawyers for the Nazi defendants tried to use it in order to avoid their conviction and execution for committing "crimes against peace," among other international crimes.[8]

Likewise, there exist several institutions and procedures that function as integral components of this international law regime to prevent, regulate, and reduce the transnational threat and use of force. To mention only the most well-known: (1) "enforcement action" by the U.N. Security Council as specified in Chapter 7 of the Charter; (2) "enforcement action" by the appropriate regional organizations acting with the authorization of the Security Council as required by article 53 and specified in Chapter 8 of the Charter; (3) the so-called peacekeeping operations and monitoring forces organized under the jurisdiction of the Security Council pursuant to Chapter 6 of the Charter; (4) peacekeeping operations under the auspices of the U.N. General Assembly acting in accordance with its Uniting for Peace Resolution (1950); and (5) peacekeeping operations and monitoring forces deployed by the relevant regional organizations acting in conformity with their proper constitutional procedures and the U.N. Charter. To this list should also be added the International Court of Justice; the Permanent Court of Arbitration; the "good offices" of the U.N. Secretary General; and numerous other techniques and institutions for international arbitration, mediation, and conciliation, etc.

The World Court Rejected Humanitarian Intervention the First Time

In the historical era prior to the conclusion of the United Nations Charter, some Western imperialist powers of the North asserted that there existed supposed principles of customary international law that permitted them to engage in the unilateral threat and use of military force against other states, peoples, and regions of the world. In particular, these alleged "principles" included the so-called doctrines of intervention, protection, and self-help. Yet, these three supposed doctrines were **unanimously** rejected by the International Court of Justice in the seminal *Corfu Channel Case* (United Kingdom v. Albania) of 1949 as being totally incompatible with the proper conduct of international relations in the post World War II era. Rebutting the British arguments in support of these three atavistic doctrines in order to justify its military intervention into Albanian territorial waters, the World Court ruled:[9]

> The Court cannot accept such a line of defence. The Court can only regard the alleged right of intervention as the manifestation of a policy of force, such as has, in the past, given rise to most serious abuses and such as cannot, whatever be the present defects in international organization, find a place in international law. Intervention is perhaps still less admissible in the particular form it would take here; for, from the nature of things, it would be reserved for the most powerful States, and might easily lead to perverting the administration of international justice itself.
> The United Kingdom Agent, ..., has further classified "Operation Retail" among methods of self-

protection or self-help. The Court cannot accept this defence either. Between independent States, respect for territorial sovereignty is an essential foundation of international relations. The Court recognizes that the Albanian Government's complete failure to carry out its duties after the explosions, and the dilatory nature of its diplomatic notes, are extenuating circumstances for the action of the United Kingdom Government. But to ensure respect for international law, of which it is the organ, the Court must declare that the action of the British Navy constituted a violation of Albanian sovereignty.

Even more significantly, the World Court unanimously repudiated these three so-called doctrines— including and especially "intervention" (humanitarian and otherwise) —without explicitly relying upon the U.N. Charter because Albania was not yet a contracting party thereto while Great Britain was. Hence, the World Court's decision rejecting these three doctrines—including and especially "intervention" (humanitarian and otherwise) —constituted an authoritative declaration of the requirements of customary international law binding upon all members of the international community irrespective of the requirements of the U.N. Charter. A fortiori, when all states parties to an international dispute are members of the United Nations, Charter articles 2(3), 2(4), and 33 absolutely prohibit any unilateral or multilateral threat or use of force that is not specifically justified by the article 51 right of individual or collective self-defense, or else as authorized by the United Nations Security Council.

To be sure, in regard to this last point on February 27, 1998 the International Court of Justice issued two Judgments on Preliminary Objections raised by the United States and the United Kingdom as Respondents (i.e., defendants) in the *Lockerbie* bombing cases filed against them by Libya at the instance of this author, making it crystal clear that the U.N. Security Council is definitely not the Judge, the Jury, and the Lord-High Executioner of International Law. Under article 24(2) of the U.N. Charter, the Security Council is bound to "act in accordance with the Purposes and Principles of the United Nations," which are set forth in Chapter I, articles 1 and 2 of the Charter. Security Council action to the contrary is *ultra vires* (i.e., beyond the powers) of the Security Council and thus illegal and void *ab initio*. These two World Court Judgments in the *Lockerbie* bombing cases have been analyzed at length in the preceding chapter.

The U.N. General Assembly Rejected R2P/ Humanitarian Intervention

Next, three seminal U.N. General Assembly Resolutions have

a distinct bearing on the so-called doctrines of R2P/humanitarian intervention: the Declaration on the Inadmissibility of Intervention in the Domestic Affairs of States and the Protection of Their Independence and Sovereignty (1965); the Declaration on Principles of International Law Concerning Friendly Relations and Cooperation among States in Accordance with the Charter of the United Nations (1970); and the Definition of Aggression (1974). Considered together, these three resolutions stand for the general proposition that, in the emphatic opinion of the member states of the U.N. General Assembly, non-consensual military intervention by one state into the territorial domain of another state is absolutely prohibited for any reason whatsoever.

Just to quote only one paragraph from this foundational 1970 Declaration on Principles of International Law Concerning Friendly Relations and Cooperation among States in Accordance with the Charter of the United Nations (1970):[10]

> No State or group of States has the right to intervene, directly or indirectly, for any reason whatever, in the internal or external affairs of any other State. Consequently, armed intervention and all other forms of interference or attempted threats against the personality of the State or against its political, economic and cultural elements, are in violation of international law.

A specific instance of so-called R2P/humanitarian intervention would probably be most properly classified as a "breach of the peace" and an "act of aggression" within the meaning and purpose of U.N. Charter article 39 as interpreted by reference to these three U.N. General Assembly resolutions. Such was the case for the 1999 Clinton/U.S./NATO war against Serbia over Kosovo on spurious humanitarian grounds as well as the 2001 Bush Junior/NATO war against Afghanistan and the 2003 United States/United Kingdom invasion of Iraq.[11] Ditto for the 2011 U.S./NATO/R2P war against Libya.

The World Court Rejected R2P/Humanitarian Intervention the Second Time

In the seminal decision of *Nicaragua v. United States of America* (1986), the International Court of Justice found that this aforementioned 1970 Declaration on Principles of International Law concerning Friendly Relations and Cooperation among States etc. sets forth rules of customary international law establishing an absolute prohibition against military intervention by one state against another state except in a case of legitimate self-defense at the express request of the victim state itself. The Reagan administration had publicly attempted to justify its Contra terror war against Nicaragua in substantial part on humanitarian grounds. Consequently, this author spent one week in Nicaragua during the Contra war from November 16-23, 1985 as part of a Lawyer's Delegation in order to investigate the human rights situation there. This Delegation consisted of former U.S. Attorney General Ramsey Clark, the noted American Civil Rights Attorney Leonard Weinglass, and two French Canadian human rights lawyers from Montreal, Robert Saint-Louis and Denis Racicot.

At the request of my colleagues, this author drafted our final Report that was endorsed by the entire Delegation. To quote only one sentence from this Report that is the most directly relevant here: "... Contrary to press reports in the United States, [we] found that the counterrevolutionary army created by the U.S. Central Intelligence Agency in Honduras constitutes nothing more than a mercenary band of cowards, terrorists and criminals who attack innocent Nicaraguan civilians—old men, women, children, invalids and religious people..."[12] If anything, it was the People and the State of Nicaragua who desperately needed and warranted R2P/humanitarian intervention against the United States and its Contra terrorist surrogate thugs.

Our Delegation visited Nicaragua in the face of a publicly announced Contra death threat against all U.S. citizens. Pursuant thereto, Reagan's Contra terrorists would later murder Ben Linder from neighboring Urbana, Illinois. Ben was a hydrologist who went to Nicaragua in order to bring potable water supplies to the *campesinos* living in the countryside. Ben was martyred for peace and human rights by Reagan's Contra terrorists. R.I.P.

The Reagan administration's Contra -terror war against Nicaragua was soundly condemned by the International Court of Justice in this seminal decision of 1986. Moreover, for technical procedural reasons not relevant here, like unto the *Corfu Channel* case, in the *Nicaragua* case the International Court of Justice had to condemn this U.S. military aggression as a matter of customary international law instead of by directly applying the prohibitions found in the United Nations Charter per se. Furthermore, in the *Nicaragua* case the World Court explicitly reaffirmed the above-quoted rulings from the *Corfu Channel* case that rejected intervention (humanitarian and otherwise), protection, and self-help. It also held: "The Court concludes that acts constituting a breach of the customary principle of non-intervention will also, if they directly or indirectly involve the use of force, constitute a breach of the principle of non-use of force in international relations."[13]

Finally, in the *Nicaragua* case the World Court expressly rejected the assertion by the United States that it had some putative right of military intervention against Nicaragua on the grounds of alleged human rights violations:[14]

> 268. In any event, while the United States might form its own appraisal of the situation as to respect for human rights in Nicaragua, the use of force could not be the appropriate method to monitor or ensure such respect....The Court concludes that the argument derived from the preservation of human rights in Nicaragua cannot afford a legal justification for the conduct of the United States...

The *Corfu Channel* case and the *Nicaragua* case are the two leading and most conclusive juridical authorities under international law that soundly condemn in no uncertain terms the so-called doctrines of humanitarian intervention and R2P. Not surprisingly, traveling all over the world one will find that the only significant source of opposition to the World Court's decision in the *Nicaragua* case has always come from the international lawyers and law professors in the United States. Nevertheless, today the transnational threat or use of military force and military intervention by one state against another state is only permissible in cases of individual or collective self-defense where the victim state of an armed attack has expressly requested such assistance from another state or states. Or as lawfully authorized by the U.N. Security Council acting within the proper scope of the powers delegated to it by the U.N. member states under the terms of the United Nations Charter.

The Rule of Law (ROL) against R2P

After their Kosovo aggression, the United States and the NATO states made a concentrated effort to get the member states of the United Nations General Assembly to recognize and approve the R2P doctrine as an exception to the normal rules of both customary and conventional international law regulating the threat and use of force, especially those set forth in the United Nations Charter. The U.N. General Assembly expressly *refused* to do this in their 2005 World Summit Outcome Document:[15]

> 138. Each individual State has the responsibility to protect its populations from genocide, war crimes, ethnic cleansing and crimes against humanity. This responsibility entails the prevention of such crimes, including their incitement, through appropriate and

necessary means. We accept that responsibility and will act in accordance with it. The international community should, as appropriate, encourage and help States to exercise this responsibility and support the United Nations in establishing an early warning capability.

139. The international community, through the United Nations, also has the responsibility to use appropriate diplomatic, humanitarian and other peaceful means, in accordance with Chapters VI and VIII of the Charter, to help protect populations from genocide, war crimes, ethnic cleansing and crimes against humanity. In this context, we are prepared to take collective action, in a timely and decisive manner, through the Security Council, in accordance with the Charter, including Chapter VII, on a case-by-case basis and in cooperation with relevant regional organizations as appropriate, should peaceful means be inadequate and national authorities manifestly fail to protect their populations from genocide, war crimes, ethnic cleansing and crimes against humanity. We stress the need for the General Assembly to continue consideration of the responsibility to protect populations from genocide, war crimes, ethnic cleansing and crimes against humanity and its implications, bearing in mind the principles of the Charter and international law. We also intend to commit ourselves, as necessary and appropriate, to helping States build capacity to protect their populations from genocide, war crimes, ethnic cleansing and crimes against humanity and to assisting those which are under stress before crises and conflicts break out.

In other words, R2P creates no exception to the general rules of conventional and customary international law governing the threat and use of force that have been discussed and analyzed above. From the perspective of international law, the "responsibility to protect" (R2P) doctrine is nothing more than imperialist propaganda for wars of aggression in the name of human rights.

Most recently, on September 24, 2012 the United Nations General Assembly convened their "High Level Meeting on the Rule of Law at the National and International Levels." The General Assembly's

Declaration on this subject did not utter even one word in support of the "responsibility to protect" doctrine or any variant thereof.[16] A deafening silence! Undoubtedly a reaction by the world community of states against the 2011 Obama/Clinton/NATO/R2P war against Libya in order to steal its oil and exterminating about 50,000 Libyans/Arabs/Muslims/Blacks/Africans in the process. R2P is antithetical to the Rule of Law (ROL). ROL versus R2P!

The United States and NATO: The Axis of Genocide

That being said, how should the world respond to major human rights atrocities and catastrophes that undeniably do occur today? Certainly, the world must not accord the great military powers such as the United States, the NATO states, Russia, China, and Israel, etc., some fictive right of R2P/humanitarian intervention that these powerful states will only abuse and manipulate in order to justify military aggressions against less powerful states and peoples. There is no need to alter or update presently existing international law in order to expand the possibilities for R2P/humanitarian intervention in alleged response to purportedly new exigencies of the day as selectively pre-determined by the great military powers in order to advance their own narrow self-interests at the expense of innocent human lives. The demand to do so reflects a great power political agenda seeking legal legitimacy, not a deficit in existing law. There are more than enough international laws and international organizations to deal effectively with major human rights atrocities and catastrophes going on around the world today.

Indeed, behind most of the major human rights atrocities and catastrophes in the world today humankind has seen in operation the Machiavellian machinations of the great military powers. So it should have come as no surprise that the world witnessed outright genocide inflicted by Serbia and its Milosevic government against the Kosovar Albanians immediately after the United States and the NATO states launched their illegal war against Serbia in March of 1999, a genocide which NATO admittedly anticipated but which in actuality transpired as the direct result of its aggression. Of course the nominally "Christian" United States and NATO states could not care less about the basic human rights of the Kosovar Albanians, most of whom are Muslims. Just previously, the "Christian" United States and NATO states had stood by and done nothing while Bosnian Serb "Christian" men genocidally raped 40,000 Bosnian Muslim women, who had been my clients when I was the Lawyer for the Republic of Bosnia and Herzegovina during Serbia's war of extermination against them.[17] Soon thereafter, the world witnessed once again outright genocide inflicted by Indonesia against the people of East Timor after decades of military and economic support to the genocidal military dictatorship ruling Indonesia by the United States and Britain – "our kind of guy," as the neoliberal Clinton administration publicly referred to the genocidaire Suharto when he came to visit the United States.

Also in this regard, the world must never forget that the indigenous peoples of Canada, the United States, and Latin America have been subjected to continuing acts of genocide for over the past 520 years. How can the United States and its NATO ally, Canada, talk about a "humanitarian mission" in Afghanistan when both states have a long history of practicing "humanitarian extinction" at home? Despite the slogan and the rhetoric of "Never again!" that was used with respect to the Nazi Holocaust against the Jews, toward the start of the twentieth-first century, genocide has become an increasingly familiar and acceptable tool for powerful states to wield against weaker states and peoples. The 2009 genocide by the Government of Sri Lanka against about 80,000 Tamils while the entire world stood by and did absolutely nothing for reasons of racism and realpolitik is yet another example of the validity of this proposition.[18]

No state has the right or standing under international law to launch an illegal military attack upon another U.N. member state in the name of R2P/humanitarian intervention. This principle applies to both the United States and Canada, which are today continuing to extinguish the indigenous peoples who live within their imperial domains under concepts similar to humanitarianism, if not so-labeled. It applies to Britain's prolonged colonial and genocidal occupation of Ireland as well as its mass deportation of the people of Diego Garcia.[19] It applies to the outright genocides Italy inflicted against the peoples of Libya and Ethiopia; those perpetrated by Spain and Portugal against the indigenous peoples of Latin America; the monstrous genocide committed by Belgium in the Congo; and the genocides committed by France in Algeria and Vietnam.

How could NATO member Turkey ever credibly claim some fictitious right of R2P/humanitarian intervention anywhere given its longstanding campaign to submerge the Kurds as well as its previous extermination of the Armenians, a genocide which it still denies today? As demonstrated by Turkey's current war-making against its former colony, Syria, the Ottoman Empire is now seeking to return with a vengeance! Only the Nazi-German genocide against the Jews in Germany and elsewhere has been universally recognized for what it truly was. Yet today, a generation later, the gullible world was supposed to believe the NATO fairy-tale that the German Wehrmacht was on some type of "humanitarian" mission against Afghanistan. The wanton aggression by the U.S.-U.K. and their "Coalition of the Willing" against Iraq in the name of bringing human rights and democracy resulted in four million refugees, over a million Iraqi deaths, and the wholesale destruction of the country's infrastructure—outright genocide.

The United States and its NATO Alliance constitute the greatest collection of genocidal states ever assembled in the entire history of the world. If anything the United Nations Organization and its member states bear a "responsibility to protect" the U.S.' and NATO's intended victims from their repeated aggressions as it should have done for Haiti, Serbia, Afghanistan, Iraq, Somalia, Yemen, Pakistan, Libya, now Syria, and perhaps tomorrow, Iran. The United States and the NATO Alliance together with their de facto allies such as Israel constitute the real Axis of Genocide in the modern world. Humanity itself owes a "responsibility to protect" the very future existence of the world from the United States, the NATO states, and Israel.

The United States Promotes Israeli Genocide Against the Palestinians

Sociologically, large numbers of people, NGOs, and media who promote R2P are die-hard supporters of Israel. This high degree of correlation is no coincidence. R2P neatly coincides with Israel's aggressive agenda and policies against the Arab and Muslim worlds. But sauce for the goose is sauce for the gander. What about the responsibility to protect the Palestinians from Israeli genocide?

Article II of the Genocide Convention defines the international crime of genocide in relevant part as follows:

> In the present Convention, genocide means any of the following acts committed with intent to destroy, in whole or in part, a national, ethnical, racial or religious group as such:
> (a) Killing members of the group;
> (b) Causing serious bodily or mental harm to members of the group;
> (c) Deliberately inflicting on the group conditions of life calculated to bring about its physical destruction in whole or in part;
> ....

As documented by Israeli historian Ilan Pappe in his seminal book *The Ethnic Cleansing of Palestine* (2006), Israel's genocidal policy against the Palestinians has been unremitting extending from before the very foundation of the state of Israel in 1948, and is ongoing and even intensifying against the 1.6 million Palestinians living in Gaza as this book goes to press. As Pappe's analysis established, Zionism's "final solution" to Israel's much touted and racist "demographic threat" allegedly posed by the very existence of the Palestinians has always been genocide, whether slow motion or in bloody thirsty spurts of violence. Indeed, the very essence of Zionism requires ethnic cleansing and acts of genocide against the Palestinians. In regard to the 2008-2009 Israeli slaughter of Palestinians in Gaza – so-called Operation Cast-Lead – U.N. General Assembly President Miguel d'Escoto Brockmann, the former Foreign Minister of Nicaragua during the Reagan administration's Contra terror war of aggression against that country condemned it as "genocide."[20]

Certainly, Israel and its predecessors in law – the Zionist agencies, forces, and terrorist gangs – have committed genocide against the Palestinian people that actually started on or about 1948 and has continued apace until today in violation of Genocide Convention Articles II(a), (b), and (c). For over the past six decades, the Israeli government and its predecessors in law – the Zionist agencies, forces, and terrorist gangs – have ruthlessly implemented a systematic and comprehensive military, political, and economic campaign with the intent to destroy in substantial part the national, ethnical, racial, and different religious (Jews versus Muslims and Christians) group constituting the Palestinian people. This Zionist/Israeli campaign has consisted of killing members of the Palestinian people in violation of the Genocide Convention Article II(a). This Zionist/Israeli campaign has also caused serious bodily and mental harm to the Palestinian people in violation of Genocide Convention Article II(b). This Zionist/Israeli campaign has also deliberately inflicted on the Palestinian people conditions of life calculated to bring about their physical destruction in substantial part in violation of Article II(c) of the Genocide Convention.

The world has not yet heard even one word uttered by the United States and its NATO allies in favor of R2P/humanitarian intervention against Zionist Israel in order to protect the Palestinian people, let alone a "responsibility to protect" the Palestinians from Zionist/Israeli genocide. The United States, its NATO allies, and the Great Powers on the U.N. Security Council would not even dispatch a U.N. Charter Chapter 6 monitoring force to help "protect" the Palestinians, let alone even contemplate any type of U.N. Charter Chapter 7 enforcement actions against Zionist Israel – which are actually two valid international legal options for R2P/humanitarian intervention! The doctrine of "humanitarian intervention" and its current "responsibility to protect" transmogrification so readily espoused elsewhere when U.S. foreign policy interests are allegedly at stake have been clearly proven to be a sick joke and a demented fraud when it comes to stopping the ongoing and accelerating Zionist/Israeli campaign of genocide against the Palestinian people.

Rather than rein in the Zionist Israelis – which would be possible just by turning off the funding pipeline – the United States government, the U.S. Congress, the U.S. media, and U.S. taxpayers instead support the "Jewish" state to the tune of about 4 billion dollars per year, without whose munificence this instance of genocide – and indeed conceivably the State of Israel itself – would not be possible. Without the United States, Israel is nothing more than a typical "failed state." In today's world genocide is permissible so long as it is done at the behest of the United States and its de jure allies in NATO or its de facto allies such as Israel.

I anticipate no fundamental change in America's support for the Zionist/Israeli ongoing campaign of genocide against the Palestinians during the tenure of the Obama administration and its near-term successors, whether neoliberal Democrats or neoconservative Republicans. Tweedledum versus Tweedledee. What the world witnesses here is (yet another) case of bipartisan "dishumanitarian intervention" or "humanitarian extermination" by the United States and Israel with the support of the NATO states, against the Palestinians and Palestine. While at the exact same time these white racist cowards and hypocrites preach R2P/humanitarian intervention in order to subjugate Libya, now Syria, and perhaps someday soon Iran.

Conclusion

As Machiavelli so astutely counseled his *Prince* on "how to be a fine liar and hypocrite" in Chapter XVIII of that manual for statesmen that over the last half-millennium has become the Bible for foreign policy decision-makers in the United States, the NATO states, and Europe: "...one who deceives will always find one who will allow himself to be deceived."[21] Such holds true for all those who preach the doctrines of humanitarian intervention/R2P. Fine liars and hypocrites indeed!

ENDNOTES

1   **Louis B. Sohn & Thomas Buergenthal, International Protection of Human Rights** 140-141 (1973).
2   *Id.* at 179.
3   **Francis A. Boyle World Politics and International Law** 315 note 43 (1985).
4   **Sean D. Murphy, Humanitarian Intervention** 387 (1996).
5   *Id.* at 393.
6   *See* **Francis A. Boyle, Destroying World Order** 118–39 (2004).
7   Bartram S. Brown, *Humanitarian Intervention at a Crossroads,* 41 **William & Mary Law Rev.** 1714 (May 2000).
8   *See* **Francis A. Boyle**, **Destroying World Order** 147 (2004).
9   1949 **International Court of Justice Reports** 35.
10   American Society of International Law, 9 **International Legal Materials** 1292 (1970).

11   *See* **Francis A. Boyle, Destroying World Order** 140–57 (2004) *and* **Breaking All the Rules: Palestine, Iraq, Iran and the Case for Impeachment** 45–83 (2008).

12   **Francis A. Boyle, Defending Civil Resistance under International Law** 198 (1987).

13   1986 **International Court of Justice Reports** 106-112, par. 209.

14   *Id.* at 134-35.

15   U.N. General Assembly, 2005 World Summit Outcome Document, paras. 138-39, U.N. Doc. A/60/150/2005, at http://www.who.int/hiv/universalaccess2010/worldsummit.pdf. *See also* U.N. Security Council 1674 (2006), paragraph 4, that: "*Reaffirms* the provisions of paragraphs 138 and 139 of the 2005 World Summit Outcome Document regarding the responsibility to protect populations from genocide, war crimes, ethnic cleansing and crimes against humanity."

16   A/67/L.1 (20 Sept. 2012).

17   *See* **Francis A. Boyle, The Bosnian People Charge Genocide** 29-35, 43 (1996).

18   **Francis A. Boyle, The Tamil Genocide by Sri Lanka** (2010).

19   **Francis A. Boyle, United Ireland, Human Rights, and International Law** 13-98 (2012)

20   Al Jazeera News, *Israel Accused of Genocide*, Jan. 14, 2009.

21   **Machiavelli, The Prince** 147 (M. Musa trans. & ed. 1964).

CHAPTER 6

THE 2011
U.S./NATO WAR
AGAINST
LIBYA

"…The United States government will seek direct military control and domination of the hydrocarbon resources of the Arab and Muslim world until there is no oil and gas left for them to steal, using Israel as its regional "policeman" towards that end. Oil and Israel were behind both the Bush Sr. and Bush Jr. wars against Iraq. And now Bush Jr. is threatening to attack Syria, Lebanon, and Iran in conjunction with the genocidal apartheid regime in Israel. As the oil and gas in the Arab and Muslim world proceed to run out, the United States and Israel will become even more predatory, aggressive, destructive, and genocidal toward Arab and Muslim states and peoples…"

Arab Strategy Forum, Dubai, U.A.E.
13 December 2004

Unlimited Imperialism

In the above speech given in Dubai on December 13, 2004 before the Arab Strategy Forum at the request of the Crown Prince of Dubai that is quoted *in extenso* at the end of Chapter 4, I predicted (1) the Israeli war/slaughter against the Palestinians in Gaza in 2006 with support by the Bush Junior administration; (2) the Israeli war of aggression against Lebanon in 2006 with the support of the Bush Junior administration; (3) Israel's "Cast-Lead" genocide against the Palestinians in Gaza during 2008-2009 with the support of the Bush Junior administration and with the acquiescence of the incoming Obama administration; (4) the Obama administration's 2011 war of aggression against Libya; (5) the Obama administration's contemporaneous covert war against Syria starting in 2011; (6) Israel's Cast-Lead-Lite operation against Gaza in November of 2012 with the proverbial "green light" from President Obama himself; (7) repeated acts of overt warfare by both the Bush Junior administration and the Obama administration against Yemen and Somalia; and (8) repeated acts of economic warfare, so far covert warfare, and publicly threatened outright warfare against Iran by both the Bush Junior administration and the Obama administration as well as by Israel.

Elsewhere, in early 2009 I had also predicted that the incoming Obama administration would wage war under the pretext and rubric of the humanitarian intervention/responsibility to protect (R2P) doctrines[1]: viz., Libya and Syria so far. In early 2009 I had also predicted that the incoming Obama administration would implement "their long-planned massive military escalation into Afghanistan"[2]—from the 34,000 illegally sent to that benighted country by the Bush Junior administration starting in October of 2001 to the astronomical figure of 100,000 U.S. troops plus an approximately equal number of mercenary contractors peaking under President Obama. And in early 2009 I had also predicted that the incoming Obama administration would escalate Bush Junior's war against Pakistan "thus further accelerating its ongoing disintegration" deliberately and on purpose in order to produce the "destabilization and fragmentation of this nuclear-armed Muslim state...When it comes to the Muslim world, the Obama/Clinton administration will be only one step removed from the Neoconservatives—at best."[3] Hard to tell them apart. Only the rhetoric and propaganda have improved.

As I had prognosticated shortly after the Obama administration had come into office in January 2009: "Despite their presidential campaign rhetoric promoting 'change,' three weeks into the Obama/Clinton administration the continuity of policies across the board with the Bush administration is striking notwithstanding their change in atmospherics. It very well could be that despite our best efforts, hopes, and expectations for instituting real political 'change' by means of the 2008 U.S. national elections, the American people are going to see in operation a Third Bush Term or at least a hybrid Obama/Bush/Clinton administration."[4] A Third Bush Term was more like it. Just recently President Obama ominously boasted and promised in his victory speech over Romney in the aftermath of his November 6, 2012 presidential re-election win: "The best is yet to come!"

Historically this latest eruption of American militarism at the start of the 21st Century is akin to that of America opening the 20th Century by means of the U.S.-instigated Spanish-American War in 1898. Then the Republican administration of President William McKinley stole their colonial empire from Spain in Cuba, Puerto Rico, Guam, and the Philippines; inflicted a near genocidal war against the Filipino people; while at the same time illegally annexing the Kingdom of Hawaii and subjecting the Native Hawaiian people (who call themselves the Kanaka Maoli) to near genocidal conditions. Additionally, McKinley's military and colonial expansion into the Pacific was also designed to secure America's economic exploitation of China pursuant to the euphemistic rubric of the "open door" policy. But over the next four decades America's aggressive presence, policies, and practices in the so-called "Pacific" Ocean would ineluctably pave the way for Japan's attack at Pearl Harbor on Dec. 7, 1941, and thus America's precipitation into the ongoing Second World War. Today a century later the serial imperial aggressions launched and menaced by the neoconservative Republican Bush Junior administration and the neoliberal Democratic Obama administration are now threatening to set off World War III.

By shamelessly exploiting the terrible tragedy of 11 September 2001, the Bush Junior administration set forth to steal a hydrocarbon empire from the Muslim states and peoples living in Central Asia and the Middle East and Africa under the bogus pretexts of (1) fighting a war against "international terrorism" or "Islamic fundamentalism"; and/or (2) eliminating weapons of mass destruction; and/or (3) the promotion of democracy; and/or (4) self-styled humanitarian intervention/ responsibility to protect (R2P). Only this time the geopolitical stakes are infinitely greater than they were a century ago: control and domination of the world's hydrocarbon resources and thus the very fundaments and energizers of the global economic system—oil and gas. The Bush Junior/ Obama administrations have already targeted the remaining hydrocarbon reserves of Africa, Latin America (e.g., the Pentagon's reactivization of the U.S. Fourth Fleet in 2008), and Southeast Asia for further conquest or domination, together with the strategic choke-points at sea and on land required for their transportation. Today the U.S. Fourth Fleet threatens Cuba, Venezuela, and Ecuador for starters.

In the Western Hemisphere, as the alternative imperial ideology to its specious "war against terrorism" waged elsewhere around the globe, the United States government has traditionally relied upon its bogus, lucrative, and thus never-ending "war on drugs" that it has deployed to militarize, dominate, and control Latin America and the Caribbean. Under that rubric and pretext the United States recently destabilized the neighboring hydrocarbon-rich Mexico, a long-time target of U.S. imperialism and capitalism. The White racist U.S. financial power elite have also turned its "war on drugs" into a war against Black, Latino and poor populations in the United States, creating a prison-industrial complex to supplement their military-industrial complex as a secondary profit-center. The United States now has the highest rate of incarceration in the entire world, predominantly consisting of imprisoned People of Color. The United States of America has literally become the "prison house of nationalities" as Lenin perceptively and derisively referred to the Tsarist Russian Empire before its collapse. Lenin started out as a lawyer.

Meanwhile, on the opposite side of the Atlantic Ocean, in late 2006 the neoconservative Bush Junior administration announced the establishment of the U.S. Pentagon's Africa Command (AFRICOM) in order to better control, dominate, steal, and exploit both the natural resources and the variegated peoples of the continent of Africa, the very cradle of our human species. In 2011 Libya then proved to be the first victim of AFRICOM under the neoliberal Obama administration, thus demonstrating the truly bi-partisan and non-partisan character of U.S. imperial foreign policy decision-making. Let us put aside as beyond the scope of this book the American conquest, extermination, and ethnic cleansing of the Indians off the continent of North America.[5] Since America's instigation of the Spanish-American War in 1898, U.S. foreign policy decision-making has been alternatively conducted by reactionary imperialists, conservative imperialists, and liberal imperialists for the past 115 years and counting.

Today U.S./NATO/AFRICOM/CENTCOM (U.S. Central Command) are quite busy recolonizing Africa as well as re-carving up the Middle East in conjunction with Israel. A combination, respectively, of the Berlin Conference of 1884-85 together with the Sykes-Picot Agreement of 1916 all over again and in spades and at the same time. With no end in sight. Not even a proverbial light at the end of the tunnel of global warfare launched by the White racist Western colonial imperial powers in the U.S./NATO/Europe/Israel de facto criminal alliance against Arab and Muslim and African States and Peoples in order to steal their hydrocarbon resources under one superficial pretext or another, or under several pretexts combined, shifting opportunistically back and forth among them. Whatever propaganda it takes to "manufacture consent" for America's serial wars of aggression in order to achieve absolute global domination. Inexorably implementing the Pentagon's 2000 "Joint Vision" of obtaining "full-spectrum dominance" over all humanity by 2020.[6]

This world-girdling burst of U.S. imperialism at the start of humankind's new millennium is what my teacher, mentor, and friend the late, great Professor Hans Morgenthau denominated "unlimited imperialism" in his seminal book *Politics Among Nations:*[7]

> The outstanding historic examples of unlimited imperialism are the expansionist policies of Alexander the Great, Rome, the Arabs in the seventh and eighth centuries, Napoleon I, and Hitler. They

all have in common an urge toward expansion which knows no rational limits, feeds on its own successes and, if not stopped by a superior force, will go on to the confines of the political world. This urge will not be satisfied so long as there remains anywhere a possible object of domination–a politically organized group of men which by its very independence challenges the conqueror's lust for power. It is, as we shall see, exactly the lack of moderation, the aspiration to conquer all that lends itself to conquest, characteristic of unlimited imperialism, which in the past has been the undoing of the imperialistic policies of this kind....

The factual circumstances surrounding the outbreaks of both the First World War and the Second World War currently hover like twin Swords of Damocles over the heads of all humanity.

Since September 11, 2001, it is the Unlimited Imperialists *à la* Alexander, Rome, Napoleon, and Hitler who have been in charge of conducting American foreign policy decision-making. Right after the terrorist attacks on 9/11/2001, the Bush Junior administration's Zionist neoconservative operative Deputy Secretary of Defense Paul Wolfowitz publicly boasted, threatened, and promised that the United States was going to get into the business of "ending states."[8] So far: Afghanistan, Iraq, Somalia, Sudan, Libya, and Syria. Notice all these U.S. victims were Muslim states and Muslim peoples. Add Palestine and the Palestinians to their hit-list.

As confirmation and implementation thereof, in November 2001 retired U.S. General Wesley Clark—NATO's Mad Dog Bomber of Serbia in 1999—paid a visit to the Pentagon. There he was told by a senior military staff officer that the Bush Junior administration's Pentagon— over which the Neo-con Zionist Wolfowitz then presided—was plotting a five-year military campaign plan against seven Muslim states, starting with Iraq and then moving on to Syria, Lebanon, Libya, Iran, Somalia, and Sudan.[9] Libya was on this 2001 Zionist Neo-con Pentagon kill-list: "Mission accomplished!" Ditto for Afghanistan, Iraq, Somalia, and Syria.

U.S./NATO/Israel planned, promoted, and brokered the secession of the oil-laden South Sudan in 2011, thus permanently debilitating the remainder of that now amputated country. Lebanon is currently being massively destabilized as part of the neoliberal Obama administration's not-so-covert war against Syria. Iran has already been targeted as the next victim of the Pentagon's Zionist Neo-Con/Neo-Lib murder list.

Murdering Muslim states and the Muslim peoples who live in them. Otherwise known as the international crime of genocide in violation of article 2 of the 1948 Genocide Convention:

> In the present Convention, genocide means any of the
> following acts committed with intent to destroy, in
> whole or in part, a national, ethnical, racial or religious
> group, as such:
> (a) Killing members of the group;
> (b) Causing serious bodily or mental harm to
> members of the group;
> (c) Deliberately inflicting on the group conditions
> of life calculated to bring about its physical
> destruction in whole or in part;....

Hijacking the "Arab Spring" in Benghazi

So the 2011 U.S./NATO/AFRICOM war against Libya did not come forth as the proverbial "bolt-out-of-the-blue." Nor was it the direct result of the so-called "Arab Spring" having spontaneously gravitated to Libya from right next door in neighboring Tunisia and Egypt. There the Obama administration had backed-up the pro-U.S. military dictatorships ruling those two countries until the bitter ends of Ben Ali and Mubarak, respectively. Ditto and *pari passú* for the still reigning homicidal King of Bahrain. Why not Qaddafi? Libya's undefendable massive quantities of oil and gas ripe for the picking and plunder by U.S./NATO/ AFRICOM made all the difference, and thus doomed Qaddafi, his family, his Revolution, the Libyans, and Libya to suffer their cataclysmic demise.

In addition, the Zionist apparatchiks dominating the Neo-lib Obama administration had long personally detested Qaddafi because of his strident and uncompromising support for the Palestinians against Israel. There was a strong element of typical Zionist vindictiveness put into operation by the Obama administration and the U.S. news media in their gleeful vendetta against Qaddafi and his family, though the Palestinians had nothing to do with the Nazi Holocaust against the Jews. Psychiatrists call this phenomenon "transference." Zionism is a mental illness—evident among some more than others.[10]

This is not a book about the "Arab Spring."[11] Nor is it a book about the "Arab Spring" in Libya. [12] But I do assert that the United States, France, Britain, and NATO immediately hijacked a legitimate but very brief "Arab Spring" in Benghazi in order to promote their own imperial agenda of (1) stealing Libya's oil and gas; (2) reversing the anti-imperial and anti-colonial Qaddafi Revolution; (3) re-establishing a neo-colonial outpost on the north coast of Africa and a beach-head on the southern rim of the Mediterranean—right next door to the strategically pivotal Egypt—in order to better control and dominate the Maghreb, the southern Med, and the Sahel; and (4) from Libya they felt they could then better project their imperial power southwards onto the rest of the African continent. They are doing this right now to Mali with its former colonial power France again taking the lead as the U.S./NATO cat's-paw, just as France did to Libya. *Vive La France?*

Northern Mali was predictably destabilized as a direct result of the Tuaregs who had fought for the defeated Qaddafi Jamahiriya fleeing Libya with advanced weapons systems for their ancestral homeland where they had always sought to create their own state of Azawad. Now the United States and France are cajoling the neighboring hydrocarbon-laden Algeria to serve as a base of military operations for staging their imperialist intervention into Mali. But this will only re-destabilize Algeria. There in 1992 the ruling F.L.N. government had cancelled elections because they were being democratically won by the Islamic Salvation Front (F.I.S.). The ensuing civil war killed about 200,000 Algerians. U.S./France/NATO have no problem with reigniting the Algerian civil war in order to fragment that country and accomplish their other imperial objectives in North Africa and the Sahel. Algeria will become just another destroyed Muslim State à la the Zionist Wolfowitz's Neo-con agenda as continued by the Zionist Neo-lib Obama administration.

The entire Maghreb and Sahel have now been discombobulated by the 2011 U.S./N.A.T.O war against Libya that will only serve as additional pretexts for further Western military penetration and intervention into North Africa, the Sahel and the Sahara under guise of the need to combat "international terrorism," which they had deliberately fomented in the first place by relying upon, importing, and arming religious extremists in order to oust Qaddafi, the long-time foe of the fundamentalists. Likewise, the U.S. covert war against Syria is now destabilizing the entire Levant in order to benefit NATO and Israel. The U.S./NATO are now exporting and transporting their proxy mercenary religious extremists from Libya and elsewhere into Syria through Turkey, Lebanon, and Jordan in order to overthrow the Assad government and thus to remake and further balkanize the Levant in their own image and that of Zionist Israel.[13] A truly hideous visage indeed!

Going all the way back to its original organization and sponsorship of Al Qaeda and other religious extremist groups in Afghanistan in order first to provoke and then to oppose the invasion of that country by the Soviet Union in 1979 under the neoliberal Carter administration, the United States government has never had any problem with deploying "Muslim fundamentalists" in conjunction with religiously extremist Saudi Arabia in order to prosecute its geopolitical objectives around the world. September 11, 2001 was the ultimate case of C.I.A. "blowback."[14] Some say it was an inside-job.[15] At the very least, *The 9/11 Commission Report* (2004) was a white-wash and a cover-up.[16]

The same holds true for the F.B.I.'s "investigation" that covered up the U.S. governmental origins of the immediately following anthrax attacks in October of 2001.[17] A one-two punch against the American Republic. There still remains lurking somewhere in the bowels of the U.S. military-industrial complex a stockpile of superweapons-grade anthrax ready to be used once again when the malefactors in the Pentagon/C.I.A. deem it useful to scaremonger the American people yet again for yet another nefarious purpose such as their previously pushing the stalled totalitarian "USA Patriot Act" through the U.S. Congress after 9/11/2011. A homegrown anti-American weapon of mass destruction (W.M.D.) that needs to be located and neutralized immediately.

America's Global War on Terrorism (GWOT) has always been based upon the combined *Frankenstein* and boogeyman of "Islamic fundamentalism," scaremongering, blackmailing, and persecuting peoples and governments around the world, including and especially in the United States itself—reflected most recently in the Holy Land Foundation Five prosecution. With the definitive collapse of the Warsaw Pact and the Soviet Union as of 1991, America's financial power elite *cum* military–industrial complex had to manufacture some mythical monster to replace "communism" in order to mobilize the American people to support their unlimited imperial objectives abroad together with their construction of a U.S. police state at home to undergird them. The U.S. empire abroad necessarily requires a police state at home. Empire is antithetical to democracy and *vice versa*. In fact, from the very moment of its inception in 1787 the United States of America has been a plutocracy and not a real democracy.[18]

The 2011 U.S./NATO/Europe War against Libya was the opening shot of White racist Western colonial imperialism's scramble for the natural resources of Africa in competition against the already present Asian neoliberal and now only nominally "communist" China that had not resorted to military force and had been making quite remarkable strides at extracting natural resources for itself while in the process of benefiting Africans and African countries by fostering major infrastructure development projects. In a similar vein, Qaddafi had utilized Libya's enormous hydrocarbon wealth gratuitously in order to improve Africa, Africans, and African countries for their own benefit against Western colonial imperialism. Yet another strike against Qaddafi in the view of the racist U.S./NATO/European predatory powers.

Of course, there was indeed a legitimate but very brief "Arab Spring" in Benghazi in mid-February of 2011.[19] It did not surprise me at all. On my first lecture tour of Libya in 1985 I had spent some time in Benghazi where I lectured and debated at the then-named Garyounis University, now called the University of Benghazi. Afterwards, the President of the

University and several of the Faculty members took me out for dinner at a government sea-side guest resort where they had just slaughtered and roasted a lamb in my honor—a real tribute in the Arab and Muslim worlds. When the Garyounis President informed me of this fact in the midst of eating dinner while looking out over the Med from the beach, I recall thinking that if I had been given the choice between "my" lamb and sea-food for dinner, I would have preferred the sea-food. Nevertheless, I sincerely thanked the President of Garyounis University for this great honor and continued to munch upon "my" lamb.

From my readings and preparations for my 1985 Libyan lecture tour, I was fully aware of the historical, geographical, economic, political, and tribal hostilities and tensions existing between Cyrenaica in the East (where most of the oil is located) and Tripolitania in the West, which were conjoined together with the other Ottoman Province of Fezzan in the south in order to produce the modern-day state of Libya after World War II. Even then I could sense an undercurrent of condescension and resentment toward what these sophisticated Benghazians deemed to be Qaddafi's Bedouin rule from Tripoli. So I do not doubt the sincerity of those lawyers who peacefully took to the streets of Benghazi in February of 2011 in order to protest against Qaddafi with a demand for democratic reform. I suspect I had dealt with some of their professors during my 1985 visit to Garyounis University. Perhaps some of these protesting lawyers had heard my lecture and debate as students?

In any event, as far as I could tell in 1985, their standard of living in Benghazi was about on a par with southern Europe thanks to the Qaddafi Revolution. But the grass is always greener on the other side of a new revolution. Yet in 2011 this mirage proved to be the classic bait-and-switch operation perpetrated by U.S./NATO against the Libyan people. How could it have been otherwise?

Even some of my Libyan friends were bamboozled into supporting the 2011 U.S./NATO war against Libya. Not surprisingly, their former Foreign Minister and long-time world-renowned diplomat *extraordinaire,* Dr. Ali Treiki, was not so fooled. Like me, Dr. Treiki made a last ditch attempt to save Libya and the Libyans from the U.S./NATO destruction and depredation. Then he retired from public life and retreated into self-imposed exile in Cairo. I wish Dr. Treiki well. Perhaps someday he and I could work together again for the good of Libya and the Libyans.

Libya now lies in ruins. In 2011 the racist genocidal imperialists of U.S./NATO exterminated about 50,000 Libyans from off the face of Africa. *Qaddafi delendus est!* Or as Obama's Secretary of State Clinton jocularly paraphrased it on C.B.S. News, deliberately mimicking the Roman Imperial General Gaius Julius Caesar: "We came! We saw! He died!" A truly sadistic performance that is now readily available for permanent viewing on *YouTube*! This gets back to my previous point about the collective mental illness of the Neo-lib Obama administration, let alone the Neo-con Bush Junior administration. Socio-pathic and sickening American genocidal imperialistic "group-think."

In this regard, we now know that President Obama himself personally approves the murder of each and every human being selected from the two separate murder-lists generated by the C.I.A. and the Pentagon's Joint Special Operations Command (JSOC), respectively. As of last count these Obama-murders included at least three United States citizens targeted by drones in Yemen in gross and impeachable violation of the Fifth Amendment to the United States Constitution guaranteeing that: "No person shall...be deprived of life, liberty, or property without due process of law..."

America's Murderer-in-Chief. Once again, with no end in sight. President Obama's murder-lists are currently being institutionalized as a permanent feature of the United States empire *cum* police state.[20] **Right now the only thing that can save humanity from a Third World War is the disintegration of the United States of America along the lines of the late Union of Soviet Socialist Republics in 1991. *The sooner the better!***

Nuremberg Crimes Against Peace

Chapter 5 demolished any alleged legal basis for the doctrines of "humanitarian intervention" and "responsibility to protect" (R2P), and proved that they each violate several foundational requirements of both conventional and customary international law in the post-World War II era of international relations. I will not bother to repeat any of that legal analysis here, but will simply incorporate it by reference and refer the reader back to Chapter 5. But those Professors of International Law who support the doctrines of humanitarian intervention/R2P are merely imperialistic and neocolonial wolves dressed up in the sheep's clothing of "human rights." These "law professors" are a disgrace to my profession! The reader would be well advised to discount anything they have to say about anything else. The doctrines of humanitarian intervention/R2P are completely incompatible with and indeed antithetical to World Order.

As definitive proof thereof, the 2011 U.S./NATO war against Libya constituted a "crime against peace" as defined by the 1945 Nuremberg Charter, which provides in relevant part as follows:

> Article 6
> ....
> The following acts, or any of them, are crimes coming within the jurisdiction of the Tribunal for which there

shall be individual responsibility:

(a) *CRIMES AGAINST PEACE: namely, planning, preparation, initiation or waging of a war of aggression, or a war in violation of international treaties, agreements or assurances, or participation in a common plan or conspiracy for the accomplishment of any of the foregoing;*

(b) WAR CRIMES: namely, violations of the laws or customs of war. Such violations shall include, but not be limited to, murder, ill-treatment or deportation to slave labor or for any other purpose of civilian population of or in occupied territory, murder or ill-treatment of prisoners of war or persons on the seas, killing of hostages, plunder of public or private property, wanton destruction of cities, towns or villages, or devastation not justified by military necessity;

(c) CRIMES AGAINST HUMANITY: namely, murder, extermination, enslavement, deportation, and other inhumane acts committed against any civilian population, before or during the war; or persecutions on political, racial or religious grounds in execution of or in connection with any crime within the jurisdiction of the Tribunal, whether or not in violation of the domestic law of the country where perpetrated.

Leaders, organizers, instigators and accomplices participating in the formulation or execution of a common plan or conspiracy to commit any of the foregoing crimes are responsible for all acts performed by any persons in execution of such plan.

Article 7

The official position of defendants, whether as Heads of State or responsible officials in Government Departments, shall not be considered as freeing them from responsibility or mitigating punishment.

Article 8

The fact that the Defendant acted pursuant to order of his Government or of a superior shall not free him from responsibility, but may be considered in mitigation of punishment if the Tribunal determines that justice so requires.

....

[Emphasis added.]

As Associate Justice Robert Jackson—then on leave from the United States Supreme Court—stated as Chief Prosecutor before the Nuremberg Tribunal at the conclusion of his opening argument: "And let me make clear that while the law is first applied against German aggressors, the law includes, and if it is to serve a useful purpose, it must condemn, aggression by any other nation, including those which sit here now in judgment."[21] Those judging states at Nuremberg consisted of the United States, Britain, France, and the Soviet Union. It is only a fair and reasonable exercise to take Mr. Justice Jackson at his word and thus to so adjudge these first three NATO state allies accordingly today for what they did to Libya in 2011.

On the basis of the Nuremberg Charter, the Nuremberg Tribunal found that several of the Nazi defendants "planned and waged aggressive wars against twelve nations, and were therefore guilty of this series of crimes."[22] As briefly mentioned above in this chapter, immediately after 9/11/2001 the Zionist neoconservative operative U.S. Deputy Secretary of Defense Paul Wolfowitz publicly bragged that the United States government was going to get into the genocidal business of "ending states." Soon thereafter, pursuant thereto, and as confirmation thereof, retired U.S. Four-Star General and past Commander of NATO Wesley Clark later related as found on page 130 of his *Winning Modern Wars* (2003):

> As I went back through the Pentagon in November 2001, one of the senior military staff officers had time for a chat. Yes, we were still on track for going against Iraq, he said. But there was more. This was being discussed as part of a five-year campaign plan, he said, and there were a total of seven countries, beginning with Iraq, then Syria, Lebanon, *Libya*, Iran, Somalia, and Sudan. [Emphasis added.]

That number of planned and then implemented U.S.-destroyed states is only five fewer than the twelve states against which the Nazi defendants committed aggression and for which they were were convicted for crimes against peace at Nuremberg. To that list of U.S. "ended" states must also be added Afghanistan and Palestine for a sum total of nine—and still counting. Today the United States and the NATO/European Union member states and Israel are now waging a combination of economic warfare and covert warfare against Iran with a view to actually implementing the Pentagon's 2001 war plan of aggression against that revolutionary Muslim state. U.S./NATO/Israel bear special antipathy towards revolutionary Muslim states.

Libya was on the Pentagon's state-murder-list as far back as at least November of 2001. Iraq too! Syria three! Iran four! Just like the Nazis: "...planning, preparation, initiation or waging of a war of aggression, or a war in violation of international treaties, agreements or assurances, or participation in a common plan or conspiracy..." In October of 2011 Libya finally fell victim, then after fighting valiantly, succumbed to the U.S. government's long-standing "common plan" and "conspiracy" to wage aggressive warfare against Libya and seven other Muslim states that was formulated and implemented at the Pentagon no later than November of 2001 as confirmed by General Clark.

NATO: An International Criminal Conspiracy

Libya/2011 was a Nuremberg crime against peace perpetrated by the United States, France and Britain that was aided and abetted and facilitated by the NATO Alliance and its other member states. Today, these three nuclear-armed NATO allies consisting of the United States, Britain, and France are legally akin to the criminal 1940 Tripartite Part among Hitler's Nazi Germany, Mussolini's Fascist Italy, and Hirohito's Imperial Japan that led inevitably to World War II. The original Axis-of-Evil. But even existentially far worse, these three NATO allies currently threaten to use thermonuclear weapons whose destructive power far exceeds even the wildest fantasies of Hitler and the Nazis, and thereby menace all humanity. I have been to Dachau in 1982 and Stalingrad (now Volgograd) in 1989, and toured the front lines at Leningrad in 1986 where the Germans had starved to death one million Russians during World War II. The savagery of the Germans thrice took my breath away. It still does today. But there will be no equivalent to a Nuremberg War Crimes Tribunal after a thermonuclear World War III.

Indeed, the NATO Alliance and its member states today constitute an ongoing international criminal conspiracy to commit sequential and numerous Nuremberg crimes against peace, Nuremberg war crimes, and Nuremberg crimes against humanity as defined by article 6(a), article 6(b), and article 6(c) of the 1945 Nuremberg Charter that are quoted above. As the Nuremberg Tribunal ruled in its October 1, 1946 *Judgment* while convicting several Nazi defendants on the charge of waging wars of aggression among other international crimes:[23]

The charges in the Indictment that the defendants

> planned and waged aggressive war are charges of the
> utmost gravity. War is essentially an evil thing. Its
> consequences are not confined to the belligerent states
> alone, but affect the whole world. To initiate a war
> of aggression, therefore, is not only an international
> crime; *it is the supreme international crime, differing
> only from other crimes in that it contains within itself
> the accumulated evil of the whole.*

It was the United States, Britain, France and the other member states of the NATO alliance that committed a Nuremberg crime against peace and then consequent and ineluctably ensuing Nuremberg war crimes and Nuremberg crimes against humanity as well as genocide against Libya and the Libyans during 2011.

U.S./NATO Genocide Against Libya and the Libyans

This penultimate international crime of genocide—in terms of severity coming right after "the supreme international crime" of aggression—was committed by the U.S./NATO surrogate terrorist army proxies against Libya's Black citizens and Black foreign guest-workers in violation of article 2 of the 1948 Genocide Convention, cited above. [24] Because the U.S./NATO states organized, armed, equipped, supplied, and directed their surrogate terrorist army proxies in Libya, the U.S./NATO civilian leaders and military officers bear "command responsibility" for their agents' commission of all acts of genocide, war crimes, and crimes against humanity under both conventional and customary international criminal law during 2011. For example, U.S. Army Field Manual 27-10, *The Law of Land Warfare* (1956) sets forth the generally recognized rule of international criminal law on command responsibility that applies to all civilian leaders at the top of the U.S./NATO military chains-of-command (e.g., Presidents and Prime Ministers; "Defense" Secretaries, Deputy Secretaries, Ministers, Deputy Ministers; etc.) as well as to all their subordinate military commanders:

> Chapter 8
> REMEDIES FOR VIOLATION OF INTERNATIONAL LAW;
> WAR CRIMES
> ....
> Section II. CRIMES UNDER INTERNATIONAL LAW
> ....
> 501. Responsibility for Acts of Subordinates
> In some cases, military commanders may be responsible

for war crimes committed by subordinate members of the armed forces, or other persons subject to their control. Thus, for instance, when troops commit massacres and atrocities against the civilian population of occupied territory or against prisoners of war, the responsibility may rest not only with the actual perpetrators but also with the commander. Such a responsibility arises directly when the acts in question have been committed in pursuance of an order of the commander concerned. *The commander is also responsible if he has actual knowledge, or should have knowledge, through reports received by him or through other means, that troops **or other persons subject to his control** are about to commit or have committed a war crime and he fails to take the necessary and reasonable steps to insure compliance with the law of war or to punish violators thereof.*
[Emphases added.]

The U.S./NATO states exercised "control" over their surrogate terrorist army proxies in Libya during 2011. Indeed, if not for the U.S./NATO states, the latter would have never even come into existence in the first place, let alone have survived to "win victories."

U.S./NATO Perpetrated Aggressive "Regime Change" Against Libya

As was true for almost every previous invocation of the doctrine of so-called "humanitarian intervention" in modern history going all the way back to the mid-19th Century, the application of R2P to Libya in 2011 was based upon outright lies, falsehoods, propaganda, and half-truths that were systematically manufactured, concocted, and disseminated by the U.S./NATO states, their ground-feeding news media, their sycophantic NGOs, and their prostituted academics and "intellectuals" such as Michael Berubé in the United States, Bernard Henri Levy in France, and Gilbert Achcar in Britain, etc.[25] This is not to excuse any violation of international human rights law that might have been threatened or committed by Colonel Qaddafi. But they pale into insignificance before the 50,000 Libyans exterminated in 2011 by the U.S./NATO states and their genocidal surrogate terrorist army proxies. Under basic principles of international law, any government has the right to use force in order to suppress an armed rebellion against it, especially when the rebel terrorist army has been organized, armed, equipped, supplied, and directed by foreign military powers striving aggressively and illegally to overthrow that government.

In fact, the leaders of the U.S./NATO states quite quickly and readily admitted that the real purpose of their 2011 military intervention into Libya was not R2P, but "regime change" against Colonel Qaddafi and his Revolution—an objective that clearly constituted an illegal armed aggression against Libya for all the reasons detailed in Chapter 5 above. This is exactly the same type of unlawful behavior that the International Court of Justice soundly condemned in its 1986 *Nicaragua* Judgment when the neoconservative Reagan administration deployed its own Contra terrorist proxy army in a failed attempt to overthrow the socialist government of Nicaragua and perpetrate "regime change" against the Sandinistas while exterminating about 35,000 Nicaraguans in the process. I am not going to belabor the legally obvious here. All the reader has to do is examine the World Court's 1986 *Nicaragua* Judgment and substitute "Libya" for "Nicaragua" in order to comprehend the elemental lawlessness and criminality of this 2011 U.S./NATO aggression against Libya.

Ditto and *pari passu* for the Zionist Neo-con 2001 Pentagon war plan for perpetrating "regime change" against the Assad government in Syria and its longstanding socialist Baath Revolution that has always been anathema to the voraciously capitalist American Empire. Today the unholy NATO triumvirate of the United States, France, and Britain are striving to do to Syria and its President Bashar al-Assad and their Baath Revolution exactly what they did to Libya and its Leader Muammar Qaddafi and his Green Revolution in 2011.

R2P was just a flimsy pretext for perpetrating "regime change" against Colonel Qaddafi and his Revolution by U.S./NATO in order to steal Libya's oil and gas. In fact, for at least the past three decades, the United States, Britain, France, and the NATO states together with their apologists and prostitutes in the news media, academia, and the Western "*intelligentsia*" have never demonstrated a tinker's dam about the human rights of the Libyan People and the well-being of Libya. Openly, publicly, repeatedly, and consistently since 1981, I have done so—knowingly and at great cost to my professional career. At one point the United States government even threatened to prosecute me for standing up for Libya and the Libyans against it. I stood my ground and toughed it out.

United Nations Complicity with U.S./NATO Against Libya and the Libyans

If anything, the world community of states and the entirety of the United Nations Organization itself bore the "responsibility to protect" Libya and the Libyans from the predatory United States and the NATO states during 2011. Instead, the United Nations became an accomplice to, and an aider and abettor of, U.S./NATO international crimes against,Libya and the Libyans during 2011 and beyond. This United Nations complicity with U.S./NATO and their international crimes against Libya and the Libyans continues today.

As documented in this book, the United Nations Organization and its member states have *never* defended Libya and the Libyans from repeated acts of aggression by the United States and its allies since at least 1981. In fact, as their criminal Lockerbie economic sanctions demonstrated starting in 1992, the United Nations Security Council and its numerous and serial member states since then historically facilitated the illegal attempt by the United States and Britain to perpetrate "regime change" against and decapitation upon Colonel Qaddafi and his Revolution while in the process inflicting terrible economic harm upon and gross human rights violations against the completely innocent people of Libya. The 2011 invocation of the doctrine of some chimerical "responsibility to protect" the Libyan people by the United States, Britain, France, the NATO states, the United Nations, and its Security Council was a fraud!

In their mad rush to destroy Colonel Qaddafi and his Revolution as well as to steal Libya's oil and gas, the United States, Britain, and France have reduced the U.N. Secretary-General and the entire U.N. Secretariat to functioning as their servile lackeys against Libya and the Libyans in violation and absolute negation of Chapter 15 of the U.N. Charter that guarantees and requires the total independence of the U.N. Secretariat from manipulation by U.N. member states. Today the United Nations has become a legal front organization for the U.S./NATO crime syndicate— their Potemkin Village on the banks of the East River in New York City and a fitting successor to the morally bankrupted League of Nations now sitting forlornly next to Lake Geneva in Switzerland.

The United States, Britain, and France Violated Chapters 6 and 8 of the United Nations Charter

Under the impetus of three of its five Permanent Members— the United States, France, and Britain—the United Nations Security Council deliberately made absolutely no effort whatsoever to obtain a peaceful settlement of the originally internal dispute in Benghazi that was required by U.N. Charter article 2(3) and Chapter 6 mandating the "Pacific Settlement of Disputes." Because the U.S./NATO objective from the very get-go was to inflict "regime change" against Colonel Qaddafi and his Revolution, the whole purpose of the U.S./U.K./France exercise at the Security Council was to precipitate the violent escalation of the Benghazi situation into Qaddafi's deposition and decapitation. They accomplished that objective by using the U.N. Security Council as their imperialist tool and vehicle. I will opine below why Russia and China did not veto this N.A.T.O. Axis-of-Evil triumvirate at the Security Council on behalf of Libya and the Libyans in 2011.

Furthermore, these three N.A.T.O. Permanent Members of the U.N. Security Council nonchalantly brushed aside all efforts by the African Union to obtain a peaceful resolution of this originally internal dispute at Benghazi. The African Union is the relevant and concerned regional organization for the continent of Africa that under Chapter 8 of the United Nations Charter should have been given the first crack at resolving the internal dispute at Benghazi by the Security Council. Instead, these three NATO Permanent Members of the Security Council short-circuited, by-passed, and violated the entirety of Chapter 8 of the U.N. Charter as well as Chapter 6 and Chapter 15. The United States, Britain, and France debased the United Nations Charter into "a scrap of paper" reminiscent of the outbreak of the First World War in the summer of 1914.[26]

The Arab League Gives U.S./NATO Approval to Destroy Libya

Today the League of Arab States effectively constitutes a regional talking-shop for tin-pot Arab dictators who reside securely and happily in the imperial pockets of the United States. The primary function of the Arab League is to serve as an international public relations agency designed to deceive and to mislead the Arab people into believing that their respective "leaders" are actively doing something to help solve critical problems in the Arab world experienced by Palestinians, Iraq, Lebanon, Libya, Al Quds, Syria, etc., while in fact behind the scenes most Arab leaders do exactly what the Americans tell them to do. Furthermore, many of these Arab League dictators are also in cahoots with Israel.

That is exactly why Colonel Qaddafi decided to pull Libya out from active participation in the Arab League and to concentrate his efforts instead upon building up the Organization of African Unity, then its successor the African Union, and ultimately pursued his vision of founding a "United States of Africa."[27] Yet another strike against Colonel Qaddafi in the eyes of the U.S./NATO salivating over the prospect of stealing the abundant natural resources of Africa. Thus, it came as no surprise that at the behest of the United States in 2011, a handful of Arab League dictators turned against Libya and the Libyans to give the Americans an Arab good-housekeeping seal of approval for their war of aggression to perpetrate a regime change upon and decapitation of Colonel Qaddafi and his Revolution.

U.S./U.K./France Perverted Chapter 7 of the U.N. Charter

The United States, Britain, and France maliciously pressured the U.N. Security Council to skip the entirety of Chapter 6 of the U.N. Charter calling for the peaceful resolution of the originally internal dispute at Benghazi, and move immediately into adopting a resolution under Chapter 7 of the Charter providing for "enforcement action" against Libya. Nevertheless, a required factual predicate to such Chapter 7 "enforcement action" resolutions is that the Security Council must make a formal determination therein under article 39 of the U.N. Charter that there existed a 'threat to the peace, breach of the peace, or act of aggression." Of course there was none of that until the U.S./NATO states attacked Libya in mid-March of 2011. Finally, then, at that point there definitively existed a "threat to the peace" and a "breach of the peace" and an "act of aggression" by the United States, Britain, France, and the other NATO states against Libya. The United Nations Security Council should have defended Libya and the Libyans from its three Permanent Members the United States, Britain, France and their NATO allies. But the U.N. Security Council, the U.N. Secretariat and the U.N. General Assembly have never done that for well over three decades.

Moreover, article 2(7) of the United Nations Charter specifically barred the entirety of the United Nations Organization from intervening "in matters which are essentially within the domestic jurisdiction of any state" which was the case with Benghazi in February-March 2011. The only exception to this hard-and-fast rule of international law is "the application of enforcement measures under Chapter VII" of the Charter by the U.N. Security Council. But these required a prior and formal determination by the Security Council that the domestic situation had risen to the level of constituting a "threat to the peace, breach of the peace, or act of aggression" under article 39 of the U.N. Charter. The Security Council never made such a determination with respect to Benghazi in 2011.

Resolution 1970, the first adopted by the U.N. Security Council in reaction to the "Arab Spring" in Benghazi on February 26, 2011, never made that required article 39 determination of "the existence of any [1] threat to the peace, [2] breach of the peace, or [3] act of aggression." How could any one of the 15 member states of the U.N. Security Council so have so determined with a straight face? None of these three disjunctive conditions existed in Libya until the U.S./NATO aggression commenced on March 19, 2011. Instead of determining the legally and factually impossible, U.N.S.C. Resolution 1970 (26 February 2011) summarily declared that the Security Council was "acting under Chapter VII of the Charter of the United Nations" without the requisite determination set forth in article 39.

Furthermore, by means of Resolution 1970 (26 February 2011) the Security Council then stated that it was "taking measures under its article 41." But the Security Council ignored, short-circuited, by-passed, and violated the immediately preceding U.N. Charter article 40 that required the Security Council first to adopt "provisional measures" under article 40 before moving on to "enforcement measures" under article 41 "[i]n order to prevent an aggravation of the situation." To the contrary, the Security Council acquiesced to the entire collective purpose of the U.S., Britain, and France to aggravate the situation at Benghazi, and to continually escalate their violent aggravation of the situation in Benghazi to the point of perpetrating regime change.

These nefarious U.S./NATO objectives were finally accomplished on October 20, 2011 when their surrogate army of terrorists sadistically and sexually tortured to death Libya's Head of State, Colonel Qaddafi, an international crime in its own right. Their obscenity can now also be viewed on *YouTube* along with Mrs. Clinton gloating and chortling over the crimes of her surrogate gang of sexual sadists and perverts. As the atrocities at the Abu Garab Prison in Iraq demonstrated, the most bogus U.S. "war on terrorism" is based in significant part on inflicting torture and sexual sadism and perversions on Arabs and Muslims. All the better to terrorize them into submission!

International Criminal Court: The White Man's Court

Paragraph 4 of U.N. Security Council Resolution 1970 (26 Feb. 2011) referred the situation in Libya since February 15, 2011 to the Prosecutor of the International Criminal Court for action despite the fact that Libya was not a contracting party to the I.C.C. Rome Statute. Then, paragraph 6 of U.N.S.C. Resolution 1970 (2011) deliberately exempted the United States from prosecution for any war crimes, crimes against humanity, and genocide it might then commit in the future against Libya and the Libyans from the jurisdiction of the I.C.C. It:

> Decides that nationals, current or former officials or personnel from a State outside the Libyan Arab Jamahiriya which is not a party to the Rome Statute of the International Criminal Court, [e.g., U.S.A.] shall be subject to the exclusive jurisdiction of that State for all alleged acts or omissions arising out of or related to operations in the Libyan Arab Jamahiriya established or authorized by the Council, unless such exclusive jurisdiction has been expressly waived by the State...

In other words, U.N.S.C. Resolution 1970 (2011) gave the United States the proverbial "green light" to inflict all the war crimes, crimes against humanity, and genocide it wanted to its heart's content against Libya and the Libyans with absolute legal impunity. U.N.S.C.

Resolution 1970 (2011) thereby aided and abetted and facilitated the U.S./NATO extermination of about 50,000 Libyans and all the international crimes incidental thereto, including a Nuremberg crime against peace, Nuremberg war crimes, Nuremberg crimes against humanity, and genocide, as previously explained above.

U.N.S.C. Resolution 1970 (2011) proved what a total farce and an elaborate charade the International Criminal Court has been since its foundation. The I.C.C. is nothing more than an imperialist tool selectively wielded by the racist and genocidal colonial imperialist powers who bought and paid for it. So far the I.C.C. and its vaunted Prosecutors have primarily and almost exclusively gone after Black tin-pot-dictators in Africa, earning the well-deserved sobriquet of "the White man's court." Meanwhile, the I.C.C. and its pathetic Prosecutors have deliberately failed and refused to proceed against the White racist genocidaires running the United States, Britain, France, Israel, and the NATO states for inflicting international crimes upon Arab and Muslim Peoples of Color around the world. How could it have been otherwise? From the very moment of its conception at the 1998 Rome Conference, the United States and the NATO states together with their allies in racist and genocidal Japan (e.g., their still unrequited "comfort women" sex slaves), inter alia, had fashioned the I.C.C. into yet another weapon of aggression in their imperialist arsenal.

The "Perm 5" Law of Power Politics

Paragraph 9 of U.N.S.C. Resolution 1970 (26 Feb. 2011) then imposed a comprehensive arms embargo upon Libya. Not that it made the least bit of difference to the United States, Britain, France, and the other NATO states who were engaged in establishing, manning, arming, equipping, supplying, training, and directing their terrorist fundamentalist proxy army in Libya to overthrow Qaddafi on the ground while they provided air support. U.N. Security Council Resolutions have never been intended or designed to apply to its Five Permanent Members: United States, United Kingdom, France, Russia, and China. The so-called "Perm 5" believe they are a "law" unto themselves that is above and beyond the terms of the United Nations Charter and the basic requirements of international law: The Hobbist and Machiavellian "law" of power politics— might makes right—was built into the founding mechanism, in reflection of the orientation of those at whose instigation it came into being.[28]

U.S./NATO Thievery

Paragraphs 17 through 21 of U.N.S.C. Resolution 1970 (2011) imposed a self-styled "asset freeze" upon Libya that enabled the United

States and the NATO states to seize and steal the enormous sovereign wealth funds that Libya had invested abroad. The U.S./N.A.T.O. states acted no differently from primitive marauding tribes of the medieval era, all to the grave detriment of Libya and the Libyans. The U.S./N.A.T.O. alleged "responsibility to protect" the Libyans was in actuality their License to Steal from Libya and the Libyans. How could it have been otherwise? The so-called U.N. "Security Council" has in operative fact become the Insecurity Council for all states in the world but its Five Permanent Members.

Russia and China Sold Out Libya

U.N. Security Council Resolution 1973 of 17 March 2011 then established "safe areas" for civilians in and imposed a "No Fly Zone" upon Libya. As the lawyer for the Republic of Bosnia and Herzegovina during Yugoslavia's genocidal war against the Bosnians, I procured a U.S./NATO "no fly zone" for Bosnia/Herzegovina on 8 April 1993: The Serbs could no longer exterminate the Bosnians from the sky! So I have direct, practical experience with U.S./NATO no-fly-zones and their enforcement and the deliberate lack thereof. [29]

Furthermore, as the Attorney for the Mothers of Srebrenica and Podrinja in Bosnia and Herzegovina, I know all about so-called "safe areas" established by the U.N. Security Council such as Srebrenica was supposed to have been. In that capacity, I personally toured the "killing fields" of Srebrenica with one of the few male survivors of that genocidal massacre as my guide. [30] From my work with Bosnia/Herzegovina and the Bosnians for the past two decades I learned from their sad and tragic experience the genocidal hypocrisy and double-standards behind the U.S./NATO/U.N. doctrines of "humanitarian intervention," "responsibility to protect," "no fly zones," and "safe areas." [31] LOL! Laughing out loud!

At the time of its adoption by the Security Council it was clear to me from reading through U.N.S.C. Resolution 1973 (17 March 2011) that it would be used and abused by the United States and the NATO states as the legal fig-leaf for their pre-planned massive military offensive against Libya and Qaddafi and then substitute a quisling dictatorial regime to take his place. [32] Yet, in the aftermath of this U.S./NATO Armageddon inflicted upon Libya and the Libyans, Russia and China falsely claimed that they had been misled and deceived by the U.S./NATO states exceeding the terms of the authority granted to them by U.N.S.C. Resolution 1973 (2011). To the contrary, Russia and China knew full well that by failing and refusing to veto Resolution 1973 (2011) they had consigned the fate of Colonel Qaddafi, his family, his Revolution, Libya and the Libyans to the bloody hands of the U.S./NATO states.

Like Pontius Pilate, Russia and China washed their hands of

Colonel Qaddafi, Libya, and the Libyans at the U.N. Security Council during 2011. Then Russia and China shed some great power crocodile tears over Libya and the Libyans for domestic and international public relations purposes. A most cynical exercise of Hobbist and Machiavellian power politics by Russia and China. Why?

The Russians are well-known around the world as passionate and consummate chess-players. In this case, Russia decided to sacrifice the Libyan Pawn on the international chess-board in the geopolitical game of power politics in order to protect the Syrian Rook and the Persian Queen as well as its own King. Russia figured that it could divert U.S./NATO to the West and away from its own borders and those of its allies and friends in Syria and Iran. And that Russia could also tie down the U.S./NATO in Libya for a period of time and also dissipate their military strength and aggressive momentum before being brought to bear upon Syria, Iran, and then Russia itself. Russia and China know full well that they are the ultimate objectives of the Unlimited Imperialists running the American Empire along the lines of Alexander, Rome, Napoleon, and Hitler.

The Russians are painfully and acutely aware of the historical facts of their invasions by Napoleon, Hitler, U.S. President Woodrow Wilson, and the Mongols, inter alia. If the Soviets/Russians had not held at Stalingrad, all of Europe would today be speaking German and saluting "Heil Hitler!" A near-death experience for Western civilization—such as it is. As for the comparatively far more ancient Chinese civilization, the Chinese are neuralgic about having been invaded by Japan and overrun by hordes of White racist western colonial imperialist barbarian armies including the United States. So in 2011 Russia and China decided to buy themselves some time and some space by throwing Libya and the Libyans to the U.S./NATO pack of wolves and hyenas. As Socrates observed in Plato's *Phaedo:* "And those who have chosen the portion of injustice, and tyranny, and violence, will pass into wolves, or into hawks and kites; whither else can we suppose them to go?"

These geopolitical calculations and historical dynamics behind their 2011 Libyan sell-out were reminiscent of those manifested at the Munich Conference in 1938. There British Prime Minister Neville Chamberlain and French Prime Minister Edouard Daladier sacrificed Czechoslovakia to Hitler in order to divert Nazi Germany eastwards towards the Soviet Union and away from Britain and France. Of course Stalin saw right through their Machiavellian machinations. So he decided to protect the Soviet Union by entering into the Ribbentrop-Molotov Pact with Hitler on August 23, 1939. That unholy pact in turn became the proverbial "green light" for Hitler to invade Poland on September 1, 1939, starting the Second World War. Sixty million people died. Tragic modern history is repeating itself in a thermonuclear age. How many people will survive World War III to count the myriad bodies buried beneath the radioactive rubble while the planet Earth sempiternally hurtles through the universe as a radioactive wasteland?

Obama's War Against Libya Was an Impeachable Violation of the U.S. Constitution

In the previous chapter I had identified several uncanny resemblances between the Clinton administration's "humanitarian intervention" bombing of Serbia in 1999 and the Obama administration's "responsibility to protect" bombing of Libya in 2011. There is one more similarity that is critical for the analysis here: In both cases President Clinton and President Obama went to war against Serbia and Libya, respectively, with absolutely no authorization from the United States Congress to do so, as required by the Article I, Section 8 War Powers Clause of the United States Constitution as well as by Congress's own War Powers Resolution of 1973.

In other words, President Obama's war against Libya was unconstitutional and illegal. It was also an impeachable offense under Article II, Section 4 of the U.S. Constitution: "The President, Vice President, and all civil Officers of the United States, shall be removed from Office on Impeachment for, and Conviction of, Treason, Bribery, *or other high Crimes and Misdemeanors*." (Emphasis added.) Of course the same was true for President Clinton's unconstitutional war against Serbia.

So much for those neoliberal law professor supporters of President Clinton's "humanitarian intervention" against Serbia and/or of President Obama's "responsibility to protect" against Libya and Syria. These legal charlatans were and still are supporting unconstitutional and illegal wars in gross violation of "the supreme Law of the Land" under Article VI of the U.S. Constitution: "This Constitution, and the Laws of the United States which shall be made in Pursuance thereof; and all Treaties made, or which shall be made, under the Authority of the United States, shall be the supreme Law of the Land..." Like me, most American law professors take an oath to uphold the Constitution and Laws of the United States when we are sworn-in as lawyers and officers-of-the-court. So much for that.

Today we have American law professors for unconstitutional wars! American law professors for torture! American law professors for the Gitmo kangaroo courts! American law professors for indefinite detention! American law professors for drone strikes! American law professors for assassinations! American law professors for war crimes! American law professors for murdering United States citizens! American law professors for murder courts! How much lower can American law professors descend into the criminal muck of Neo-Nazi legal nihilism? Since 9/11/2001, the shades of Nazi "crown jurist" law professor Carl Schmitt have been running amok in the hallways, classrooms, faculty offices, conferences, and publications of the American legal academy and among their now practicing lawyer former students. Arabs and Muslims have become their new Jews.

The fact that President Obama—unlike President Clinton—importuned a U.N. Security Council Resolution from its member states cannot be invoked to excuse his most grievous violations of the United States Constitution and Congress's own War Powers Resolution of 1973. By comparison, even President George Bush Junior got approval from the United States Congress for his 2003 war of aggression against Iraq. Constitutionally speaking, President Obama is worse than President Bush Junior!

All the more so, because President Obama knows better than President Bush Junior, who is not a lawyer. President Obama used to teach Constitutional Law at the University of Chicago, where I had attended College. He also graduated from Harvard Law School after me. That is what these "elite" institutions of higher education in America will do to you. After ten years of elitist imperial brainwashing as a student at the University of Chicago and Harvard from 1968 through 1978, I was most fortunate to have come out with my head screwed on straight: "There but for the grace of God go I!"

Now President Obama is preparing to engage in yet another unconstitutional war against Syria that constitutes yet another impeachable offense in its own right. Anticipating his next aggression, I issued a public call for President Obama to be impeached on October 29, 2011 and offered my professional services free of charge to any Member of the U.S. House of Representatives who might seek to introduce a Bill of Impeachment against Obama into Congress and start the impeachment ball rolling.[33] At that time I cited two basic grounds for the impeachment of President Obama: (1) his unconstitutional and illegal war against Libya as explained above; and (2) his murdering three United States citizens in Yemen by means of drone strikes in violation of the Due Process Clause of the Fifth Amendment to the U.S. Constitution as also explained above.

Of course there are many other good grounds that warrant President Obama's impeachment and removal from Office that are too numerous to list here: In a nutshell, President Obama has ratified, condoned, continued, compounded, and aggravated almost every atrocity that President Bush Junior inflicted upon the United States Constitution after September 11, 2001 in order to construct and further consolidate an American police state. But even President Bush Junior did not go so far as to arrogate for himself the "right" to murder United States citizens.

So my proposed two Articles of Impeachment against President Obama simply used President Bush Junior as the lowest common denominator of presidential deportment. On both counts—his unconstitutional Libyan war and his murdering U.S. citizens—President Obama is constitutionally far worse than President Bush Junior. Sad but true. President Obama is just the Black velvet glove covering the White racist iron fist of U.S. imperialism and capitalism.

The American people must never forget that President Obama and his Democratic Party apparatchiks are the direct and lineal Sons and Daughters of David Halberstam's *The Best and the Brightest* (1972) from Harvard who gave us the Vietnam War. If we do not stop President Obama and his Ivy Leaguer confederates now, they will usher in World War III. For once they have devoured and partially digested Syria, this Obama pack of wolves and hyenas will move on to Iran. Unlimited Imperialism indeed along the lines of Alexander, Rome, Napoleon, and Hitler. To repeat what Hans Morgenthau presciently said about them all:

> ....They all have in common an urge toward expansion which knows no rational limits, feeds on its own successes and, if not stopped by a superior force, will go on to the confines of the political world. This urge will not be satisfied so long as there remains anywhere a possible object of domination—a politically organized group of men which by its very independence challenges the conqueror's lust for power. It is, as we shall see, exactly the lack of moderation, the aspiration to conquer all that lends itself to conquest, characteristic of unlimited imperialism, which in the past has been the undoing of the imperialistic policies of this kind....

After September 11, 2001 the United States has vilified and demonized Muslims and Arabs almost to the same extent that America inflicted upon the Japanese and Japanese Americans after Pearl Harbor. As the Nazis had previously demonstrated with respect to the Jews, a government must first dehumanize and scapegoat a race of people before its citizens will tolerate if not enthusiastically approve their elimination. Witness Hiroshima and Nagasaki in August of 1945!

In post-9/11/2001 the world is directly confronted with the prospect of a nuclear war of state annihilation and human extermination conducted by the American and NATO and Israeli White racist Judeo-Christian financial power elites against the Muslim and Arab worlds in order to steal their oil and gas. It's the Crusades all over again. But this time nuclear Armageddon stares all of humankind directly in the face!

ENDNOTES

1   Francis A. Boyle, Tackling America's Toughest Questions 158-59
        (2009).
2   *Id.* at 158.
3   *Id.* at 159.
4   *Id.* at 174 (footnote omitted).
5   *See* Editorial El Coqui, USA on Trial: The International Tribunal on
        Indigenous Peoples' and Oppressed Nations in the United States
        (1996).
6   Jim Garamone, *Joint Vision 2020 Emphasizes Full-Spectrum Dominance*,
        D.O.D. American Forces Press Service, June 2, 2000; F. William Eng-
        dahl, Full Spectrum Dominance (2009).
7   *See* Hans Morgenthau, Politics Among Nations 52-53 (4th ed. 1968).
8   *See* Francis A. Boyle, The Criminality of Nuclear Deterrence 24-25
        & n. 17 (2002).
9   *See, e.g.*, Sydney H. Schanberg, *The Secrets Clark Kept*, Village Voice,
        Sept. 30, 2003, *quoting from* Wesley Clark, Winning Modern Wars 130
        (2003).
10   *See, e.g.*, Joel Kovel, Overcoming Zionism (2007).
11   *See, e.g.*, Tariq Ramadan, Islam and the Arab Awakening (2012).
12   *See* Vijay Prashad, Arab Spring, Libyan Winter (2012).
13   *See, e.g.*, Tony Cartalucci, *NATO Using Al Qaeda "Rat Lines" to Flood
        Syria with Foreign Terrorists*, Global Research, Oct. 26, 2012.
14   Chalmers Johnson, Blowback (2002).
15   David Ray Griffin, The New Pearl Harbor (2004).
16   David Ray Griffin, The 9/11 Commission Report: Omissions and
        Distortions (2005).
17   Francis A. Boyle, Biowarfare and Terrorism (2005).
18   *See, e.g.*, Charles A. Beard, An Economic Interpretation of the
        Constitution of the United States (1935 ed.); Robert A. Dahl, How
        Democratic Is the American Constitution? (2d ed. 2003); Michael
        Parenti, Democracy for the Few (6th ed. 1995).
19   *See, e.g.*, Mike Raffauf, *Chronology of the NATO-Led Assault on the
        Great Socialist People's Libyan Arab Jamahiriya,* in Dignity, The Illegal
        War on Libya 275, 280 (Cynthia McKinney ed.: 2012) (hereinafter cited
        as *Chronology*);Vijay Prashad, Arab Spring, Libyan Winter 148-49
        (2012).
20   *See, e.g.*, Greg Miller, *Plan for Hunting Terrorists Signals U.S. Intends to
        Keep Adding Names to Kill Lists*, Washington Post, Oct. 23, 2012.
21   Joseph E. Persico, Nuremberg 137 (1994).
22   *The Nurnberg Trial*, 6 F.R.D. 69, 106 (1946).
23   *Id.* at 86.
24   *See, e.g.*, T West, *America's Black Pharoah and Black Genocide in Libya*,
        in Dignity, The Illegal War on Libya 63 (Cynthia McKinney ed.: 2012).
25   *See generally* Dignity, The Illegal War on Libya (Cynthia McKinney ed.
        2012).
26   *See* Francis A. Boyle, Foundations of World Order 134 (1999); Barbara
        W. Tuchman, The Guns of August 153 (1962).
27   *See generally* Dirk Vandewalle, A History of Modern Libya 194-98 (2d
        ed. 2012).
28   *See* Francis A. Boyle, *The Law of Power Politics*, 1980 Univ. Ill. L. F.
        901.
29   *See* Francis A. Boyle, *Trying to Stop Aggressive War and Genocide*

Against the People and the Republic of Bosnia and Herzegovina, in **The Tamil Genocide by Sri Lanka** 71 (2010) *and* in **The Palestinian Right of Return under International Law** 105 (2011). *See generally* **Francis A. Boyle, The Bosnian People Charge Genocide** (1996).

30   B.B.C. Europe, *Mothers Demand Arrest of U.N. Officials*, Feb. 4, 2000.

31   Francis A. Boyle, *Is Bosnia the End of the Road for the United Nations?*, 6 **Periodica Islamica**, No. 2, at 45 (1996) (yes!).

32   *See, e.g.*, Francis A. Boyle, *U.N. Resolution on Libya Allows Invasion*, **The Real News Network**, March 20, 2011 (interview); Francis A. Boyle, *Attack on Libya Is "War of Plunder and Aggression,"* **Black Agenda Report**, March 28, 2011 (interview with Glen Ford).

33   *See Prof. Francis Boyle Offers to Draft Bill to Impeach Obama*, Executive Intelligence Review News Service, Nov. 1, 2011; *Legal Expert Says Impeach Obama; Warns of War Danger*, **Executive Intelligence Review**, Nov. 18, 2011, at 41-46.

CONCLUSION

What is the upshot of the tragic U.S./France/AFRICOM/NATO aggression on Libya in the name of responsibility to protect, and where will it lead to? On January 11, 2013 France invaded Mali with the assistance of the United States, Britain, Canada, and several other NATO states at the supposed request of a military junta whose strongman was trained in the United States and had recently deposed the democratically-elected government of that country in March of 2012. Of course all this was just a coincidence. The Western imperial states said they were operating under the bogus pretext of fighting "Islamic terrorists"—many of whom they had just deployed in 2011 to overthrow Colonel Qaddafi in Libya and were simultaneously employing their fundamentalist confederates from Libya in order to overthrow the Assad government in Syria. The real reason behind France's re-invasion of Mali was to re-establish its direct colonial stranglehold on the Sahel and West Africa in order to better plunder the natural resources of these abundant countries and their surrounding hydrocarbon-rich seas, ousting China in the process. Toward that end, on January 23, 2013 France landed Special Forces in neighboring Niger in order to grab the Nigerois uranium mines that fuel the French nationwide nuclear power industry and its genocidal nuclear weapons complex. Then AFRICOM announced that it is considering opening up a drone base in Niger from which it can terrorize the Muslim peoples of the Sahel just as the C.I.A. and the Pentagon have terrorized the Muslim peoples living in Afghanistan, Pakistan, Somalia, Yemen, and Libya by means of drones—so far.

Since 9/11/2001 murderous drones have become America's preferred weapon of choice for the widespread and systematic extermination of Muslims all over the world. Hence the U.S. drone campaign against Muslims violates the 1948 Genocide Convention to which America is a contracting party:

> Article II: In the present Convention, genocide means any of the following acts committed with intent to destroy, in whole or in part, a national, ethnical, racial *or religious group* [i.e., Muslims], as such:
>   (a) Killing members of the group;....
> [Emphasis added.]

We know for a fact that President Obama personally selects his Muslim victims for drone-murder, which renders Obama a *genocidaire*. There is no statute of limitations for the commission of international crimes such as genocide, war crimes, and crimes against humanity. So Obama will be liable to such prosecution for the rest of his life by any government in the world and by the International Criminal Court.

Previously in 2011 France had intervened militarily into the Ivory Coast in order to overthrow the government there in the alleged name of promoting "democracy." Yet in its 1986 Judgment on the merits in the *Nicaragua* case, the International Court of Justice emphatically decreed that military intervention on the purported grounds of promoting "democracy" is clearly illegal by means of the following language:

> 205....In this respect it [the Court] notes that, in view of the generally accepted formulations, the principle [i.e., non-intervention] forbids all States or groups of States to intervene directly or indirectly in internal or external affairs of other States. A prohibited intervention must accordingly be one bearing on matters in which each State is permitted, by the principle of State sovereignty to decide freely. *One of these is the choice of a **political**, economic, social and cultural system, and the formulation of foreign policy. Intervention is wrongful when it uses methods of coercion in regard to such choices, which must remain free ones.* The element of coercion, which defines, and indeed forms the very essence of, prohibited intervention, is particularly obvious in the case of an intervention which uses force, either in the direct form of military action, or in the indirect form of support for subversive or terrorist armed activities within another State. As noted above (paragraph 191), General Assembly resolution 2625

(XXV) equates assistance of this kind with the use of force by the assisting State when the acts committed in another State "involve a threat or use of force." *These forms of action are therefore wrongful in the light of both the principle of non-use of force, and that of non-intervention....* [Emphases added.]

Notice that the above ruling by the World Court in the *Nicaragua* case also soundly condemns the U.S./NATO/France proxy surrogate war against Syria. Especially by means of the following language: "...or in the indirect form of support for subversive or terrorist armed activities within another State... These forms of action are therefore wrongful in the light of both the principle of non-use of force, and that of non-intervention...."

As part of this U.S./NATO/France not-so-covert war against Syria, on January 30, 2013 the rogue state Israel illegally bombed Syria, a longtime victim of Zionist aggression and land-grabbing. Pursuant thereto, Israel had illegally invaded the airspace of Lebanon, a daily occurrence that U.S./NATO routinely tolerate. This is because Israel serves as the U.S./NATO attack-dog against the Arab and Muslim worlds. Israel's latest aggression upon Syria could be a harbinger of all-out aggressive warfare by U.S./NATO/France/Israel/Turkey along the lines of 2011 Libya in order to destroy this longtime impediment to their imperial and Zionist agendas in the Levant. Syria will become the ante-chamber to their cataclysmic assault upon the Islamic Republic of Iran.

France is the Western colonial power that formerly ruled over Syria and Lebanon. Previously, after the First World War imperial France and imperial Britain had supplanted the colonial Ottoman Empire throughout the Middle East. The latter's successor-in-law Turkey is aggressing against its former colony in Syria in order to promote its own modern imperial agenda with the Turkic-speaking people and lands of Central Asia.

I am very proud of my French ancestry on my Mother's side traceable all the way back to Paris in the early nineteenth century. I am especially proud of the fact that I am the descendant, inheritor, beneficiary, and product of three separate Revolutions: American (1776), French (1789), and Irish (1916). But given the long history of French neo-colonialism supporting mercilessly bloodthirsty dictators all over Africa, it is hard to take any of this French palaver about promoting "democracy" and "human rights" in Africa without howling out loud. Instead, France decided to brush aside its *Black Skin, White Masks* (1952) comprador classes in Africa in order to re-establish direct colonial control and exploitation over Francophone Africa under the jackboots of the French Foreign Legion, its long-time imperial-enforcer shock-troops. France is now using the Atlantic ocean port in Ivory Coast as the disembarkation point and staging area for its rapidly expanding military invasion into and colonial re-occupation of Mali. There is no way France could have deployed and then immediately thrown into armed combat an Expeditionary Force of 4000 troops with all of their heavy weapons, equipment and supplies on a blitzkrieg offensive reminiscent of Rommel's Afrika Corps in order to conquer the vast expanse of northern Mali in just three weeks without having previously developed and implemented a well-honed war plan with extensive diplomatic and military preparations being laid that had all been coordinated with and approved by NATO, AFRICOM, and the United States government. Hence also the pre-planned U.S. drone base in Niger.

Mali became the second victim of France/AFRICOM/U.S./ NATO after Libya. Yet another of their destroyed Muslim states. The hydrocarbon-laden Algeria seems to be next on their hit-list for destabilization and disintegration as manifested by the January 2013 terrorist attack on the Western gas facility near the border with Libya in purported retaliation for Algeria giving France overflight rights to illegally bomb Mali. The more Algeria intervenes into Mali at the behest of Western colonial imperialism, the more destabilized it will become. U.S./France/NATO/AFRICOM know this full well. That is their imperial game-plan. *Divide et impera* like the Romans before them.

Will Africa and the Middle East witness a second round of national liberation movements erupting in order to resist this latest re-imposition of direct Western colonial rule? Or after a generation spent in governmental power marked by gross Western co-optation together with its concomitant economic and political corruption, have not African and Middle Eastern national liberation movements and leaders shot their wads of legitimacy in the eyes of their own peoples? Rather, this attempted re-imposition of Western colonial imperialism in Africa, the Middle East and elsewhere has produced a wave of locally-based Islamic resistance movements (IRMs) along the lines of al-Shabab in Somalia.[1] Islam has now become the primary force that resists the post-9/11/2001 resurgence of Western colonial imperialism around the world. Witness al-Shabab in Somalia; Hamas and Islamic Jihad in Palestine; the Taliban in Afghanistan; Hezbollah in Lebanon; the Islamic Republic of Iran; the A.I.G./F.I.S. in Algeria; Jordan's Muslim Brotherhood against its U.K. then C.I.A. stooge-Monarchy; the Nation of Islam in the United States, etc.

With all due deference to and sincerest respect for secular Third World National Liberation movements and leaders (many of whom I have supported and assisted), their glorious days of courage, integrity, and principle are now behind them. To the contrary, if anything can resist and defeat Western unlimited imperialism intruding upon Muslim lands and peoples today, it is Islam. Witness the spectacular successes of Islamic resistance movements in Iraq, Afghanistan, Gaza, and Southern Lebanon. The verdict is still out in Somalia and Yemen. The battle has just begun in the Sahel. Western imperialism's overt war against the Islamic Republic of Iran might soon be joined. U.S./Europe are currently waging economic warfare against Iran all over the globe.

Contemporary world politics have been literally shaped to realize Sam Huntington's *Clash of Civilizations* (1996). The West's criminal clash against Islamic civilization in order to steal their oil and gas and other natural resources. Huntington's book seems to have served as the de facto "blueprint" for the conduct of American foreign policy decision-making since its thesis was first articulated in his 1993 article under that name published by the American imperial establishment's Council on Foreign Relations in their foremost propaganda journal, *Foreign Affairs*.

Huntington's screed originally appeared during the height of "Christian" Serbia's war of extermination against the Bosnian Muslims while the "Christian" United States, France, Britain, NATO, and Europe aided and abetted this instance of genocide against Muslims. As the Lawyer for the Republic of Bosnia and Herzegovina at the time, I did everything humanly possible to prevent all of these good "Christians" from annihilating my clients. If Bosnian Muslim men had raped 40,000 Christian women as the Serbs had done to Bosnian women, the U.S./ NATO would have bombed them all to hell the very next day.[2] Yet another glaring example of the genocidal hypocrisy and double standards behind Western colonial imperialism's doctrines of "humanitarian intervention" and "responsibility to protect."

As a matter of historical fact elided over by Huntington, white racist Western colonial imperialism commenced its "clash of civilizations" against the Arab and Muslim worlds in 1948 when it stole Palestine from the Palestinians and illegally gave Palestine to white racist European Zionists who have continued to occupy Palestine since then and have continually tortured and tormented the Palestinians until today. I went through the same Ph.D. program in political science at Harvard that produced Huntington before me—as well as Kissinger and Brzezinski. But as a matter of principle I and many other Harvard students refused to study with Huntington because of his die-hard support for the genocidal Vietnam War. Huntington was just a typical, genocidal Harvard "inner-outer" living on the frequent-flyer shuttle commuting between Cambridge, Mass. and Washington, D.C. Ditto for Kissinger and Brzezinski.

I do not believe these diverse and for the most part geographically-based Islamic resistance movements will band together in order to found some sort of worldwide "Islamic Caliphate." Since 9/11/2001 that chimerical specter has become a boogeyman that was maliciously concocted by Western Islamophobes to serve as ideological propaganda to publicly justify their serial wars of aggression against Muslim states and peoples in order to steal their oil and gas and other natural resources. But after 9/11/2001 opposition to these Western unlimited imperialists has increasingly come to be based upon Islam and its IRMs as an alternative to, or else as a superseding supplement to nationalism.

After all, nationalism is a construction of "Western civilization" — such as it is. The Muslim world cannot beat the West at its own game and on its own terms. The Muslim world must force the West to play its game and on its own terms when the West is on Islam's turf. Thus, at the fallacious "end of history" I respectfully submit that Islam will perhaps constitute the one force that can defeat Western unlimited imperialism attacking and encroaching upon Muslim lands and peoples.

> "Say: 'O God, Master of the Kingdom, Thou givest the Kingdom to whom Thou wilt, and seizest the Kingdom from whom Thou wilt. Thou exaltest whom Thou wilt, and Thou abasest whom Thou wilt; in Thy hand is the good; Thou art powerful over everything." – *Sadaqa Allahu Al-Azim*

February 11, 2013

ENDNOTES

1   *See* Interview with Francis A. Boyle, *Application of International Law in Africa*, **Heart of Africa**, Oct. 25, 2012.
2   *See* Francis A. Boyle, *Letter to the Editor*, Champaign-Urbana News Gazette, Aug. 26, 2012, at C-3; *Id.,* **The Bosnian People Charge Genocide** (1996); *Id., Trying to Stop Aggressive War and Genocide Against the People and the Republic of Bosnia and Herzegovina,* **The Tamil Genocide by Sri Lanka** 71-95 (2010) *and in* **The Palestinian Right of Return under International Law** 105-33 (2011).

INDEX

A

Abu Ghazala, Abd al-Halim, 59, 90
Abu Nidal, 45, 66-7, 72
Achcar, Gilbert, 187
Achille Lauro, 59
Afghanistan, 159-60, 163, 168-169,
    174, 177, 179, 184, 201, 204-5
African Union, 160, 190
air defense identification zone(ADIZ),
    51, 56
al-Assad, Bashar, 188
al-Assad, Hafez, 82, 94
Albania, 161-2
Ali, Ben, 178
Allende, Salvador, 49
Al Qaeda, 13, 179
America (Aircraft Carrier), 46-7
*American Journal of International
    Law*, 22
Arab League, 190
Arab spring, 89, 178, 180, 191
Arafat, Yasser, 42, 67
Arms Export Control Act, 78
Ayatollah Khomeini, 82

B

Baker, James, 109
Basic Popular Congress (Libya), 12
Baxter, Richard, 81
Bedjaoui, Mohammed
    *The New World Order and the
      Security Council*, 135-7
Begin, Menachem, 41, 94-5
Belgium, 79, 168
Berlusconi, Sylvio, 11-12
Berubé, Michael, 187
Best and the Brightest, The (Halbers-
    tam), 155, 198
Biological Weapons Convention
    (1972), 99-100
Blair, Tony, 142

Blum, William
    Rogue States, 159
Boyle, Francis A.
    Foundations of World Order, 157
    Law of Power Politics, The, 199
Brockmann, Miguel d'Escoto, 170
Brownlie, Ian, 157-8
Bush, George H.W. (President), 71,
    98, 110-11, 143
Bush Jr. Administration, 20, 23-5,
    30-5, 142-4, 159-60, 163, 173-7,
    182, 197-8
Bush Sr. Administration, 13, 35, 99,
    101, 107-8, 112-18, 173

C

Camp David Accords, 92
capitalism, 13
Caroline test, 160
Carter Administration, 35, 38-9, 49,
    58, 89-90, 179
Carter, Jimmy (President), 38
Casey, William, 12, 39, 48, 83
Castro, Fidel, 49, 69, 82, 85
Chamberlain, Neville, 195
Chayes, Abram
    Cuban Missile Crisis, The, 37
Chicago Convention, 51, 56
China, 101, 111, 114-15, 167, 175,
    180, 189, 193-5
Chomsky, Noam, 159
    Manufacturing Consent, 84
    New Military Humanism, 158
Christian Science Monitor, 94
Clark, Ramsey, 12, 97-8, 111, 164
Clark, Wesley, 177, 185
    Winning Modern Wars, 184
Clinton Administration, 35, 154-5,
    158-9, 163, 167-8, 174, 196
Clinton, Bill (President), 35, 155,
    196-7
Clinton, Hillary, 155, 181, 192

closing line, 46, 52, 54-7
Colonel Qaddafi. *See* Qaddafi
    (Colonel)
communism, 13, 88, 180
Concept of Law, The (Hart), 21
Convention on International Civil
    Aviation. *See* Chicago Conven-
    tion
Convention on the Territorial Sea
    and Contiguous Zone, 55-6
Cuba, 69, 82, 85, 159, 175
Cuban Missile Crisis, The (Chayes),
    37

D

Daladier, Edouard, 195
Del Ponte, Carla, 159
Denton, Jeremiah, 82
D'Estaing, Valery Giscard, 89
Diem, Ngo Dinh, 49
Dole, Robert, 82

E

Egypt, 13, 45, 47, 58-9, 69, 85, 88-
    95, 99, 178
Egypt-Israeli Peace Treaty, 89-90,
    92, 94-5
El Al, 45, 47
El Houderi, Ahmed, 110, 113
Ethnic Cleansing of Palestine, The
    (Pappe), 169

F

Feliciano, Florentino, 158
Fhima, Lameen, 141
Financial Times (London), 74, 108
First World War, 82, 95-6, 100, 177,
    190, 203
Fisher, Roger
    *Improving Compliance with Inter-
    national Law*, 26
Foundations of World Order (Boyle),
    157
France, 47, 100-01, 120, 128-9, 168,

178-9, 184-95, 201-05
Fuller, Lon
    Morality of Law, The, 21

G

Ganschow, Manfred, 73-4
Geneva Convention on the High Seas
    (1958), 55
Geneva Conventions (1949), 41, 55-
    6, 67, 117
    Common Article 1, 41
Geneva (Gas) Protocol (1925), 99-
    100
Genocide Convention, 117, 169-70,
    177-8, 186, 202
German Press Agency (G.P.A.), 73
Germany, 44, 66, 74, 83, 168, 185,
    195
Great Green Charter of Human
    Rights of the Jamahiriyan Era,
    The, 12
Greece, 66, 94
Green Book (Qaddafi), 9-10, 13, 84,
    86-8

H

Hague Regulations, 80, 117
Haig, Alexander, 60
Halberstam, David
    Best and the Brightest, The, 155,
    198
Hannay, David, 110
Harsch, Burkhard, 74
Hart, H.L.A.
    Concept of Law, The, 21
historic bays/waters, 55-8
History of Modern Libya, A (Vander-
    walle), 15
Hobbes, Thomas
    Hobbism, 17-9, 23, 29, 31, 33
    Leviathan, 18, 21, 23-4
Holocaust, 11, 168, 178
humanism, 18
humanitarian intervention, 35, 154-
    71, 174-5, 182, 187, 194, 196,

205
Humanitarian Intervention (Murphy), 158
Hurd, Douglas, 109
Hussein (Jordanian King), 94-5
Hussein, Saddam, 82, 156

I

Idris (King), 85, 87
Improving Compliance with International Law (Fisher), 26
internal waters, 49-50, 53-7
International Civil Aviation Organization, 39, 122
International Committee of the Red Cross (I.C.R.C.), 39
International Court of Justice (ICJ), 13-14, 53-4, 57-8, 81, 108-10, 119, 123, 125-6, 130-40, 161-4, 188, 202
    Corfu Channel Case, 161-2, 164-5
    Nicaragua v. United States of America, 53-4, 57, 131, 163-5, 170, 188, 202-03
International Criminal Court, 192-3, 202
international enforcement mechanisms, 23-4
    international terrorism
    discotheque (West Berlin), 46, 72-77
    El Al ticket counters in Rome and Vienna, 45, 48, 60, 66-8, 72,
    Lockerbie bombing, 13-14, 35, 107-44, 162, 189
    September 11, 2001, 35, 66, 175, 177, 179, 197-8
    T.W.A. flight between Rome and Athens, 46, 72
Iran, 30, 82, 87, 92, 96, 100, 107-08, 117-18, 143, 156, 159, 169, 171, 173-4, 177, 184-5, 195, 198, 203-05
Iraq, 23, 31, 82, 92, 94, 99-100, 107, 143, 158-9, 163, 168-9, 173, 177, 184-5, 192, 197, 205

Islamic Salvation Front (F.I.S.), 179
Israel, 39-42, 45, 50, 66, 78-9, 89, 91-100, 143-4, 155, 159, 167, 169-71, 173-9, 184-5, 190, 193, 198, 203
Italian Holocaust, 11
Italy, 11-12, 66, 69, 74, 79, 99, 168, 185

J

Jackson, Robert, 184
Jamahiriya, 10, 14, 68, 93, 130, 179, 192
Japan, 87, 175, 185, 193, 195, 198
Jenkins, Brian, 92
Jervis, Robert
    Perception and Misperception in International Politics, 97
Johnson Administration, 20, 75, 78
Jordan, 94-6, 179, 204

K

Kahler, Miles, 95
Kellogg-Briand Pact, 44
Kelso, Frank II, 71
Kennan, George, 20
Kennedy Administration, 49, 85
Keohane, Robert
    Power and Interdependence, 26
Khalil, Mustafa, 95
al-Kidwa, Nasser, 101
Kissinger, Henry, 30, 205
Klinghoffer, Leon, 59
Koechler, Hans, 140-1
Kohl, Helmudt, 74
Kosovo, 154-5, 158, 160, 163, 165

L

Law of Land Warfare (U.S. Army Field Manual), 81, 186
Lebanon, 41-3, 45, 50, 66-7, 92-4, 96, 143, 173, 177, 179, 184, 190, 203-4
Legwell, Ibrahim, 139-41

Leviathan (Hobbes), 18, 21, 23-4
Levy, Bernard Henri, 187
Linder, Ben, 164
Lockerbie (Bombing), 13-14, 35, 107-44, 162, 189
Los Angeles Times, 74
Lumumba, Patrice, 49

M

Machiavelli, Niccolo
    The Prince, 171
Maghour, Kamal, 111, 140-1
Mali, 179, 201, 204
Malta, 54, 79, 108, 112-13, 142
Manufacturing Consent (Chomsky and Herman), 84
McDougal, Myres, 158
McKinley, William (President), 174-5
Megrahi, Abdel Basset, 141-2
Metzenbaum, Howard, 46
Milosevic, Slobodan, 158-9, 167
Montreal Sabotage Convention, 108-10, 112, 116, 120, 124, 130-2, 134-8
Morality of Law, The (Fuller), 21
Morgenthau, Hans, 17, 19-20, 29, 41, 198
    Politics Among Nations, 176-7
    Purpose of American Politics, The, 29
Mubarak, Hosni, 58-9, 89-90, 178
Mukhtar, Omar, 14
Murphy, Sean
    Humanitarian Intervention, 158
Muslim fundamentalists, 13, 179

N

NATO (North Atlantic Treaty Organization), 12-14, 35, 76, 88, 95, 113, 154-60, 165, 167-71, 173-98, 201, 203-05
Nasser, Gamal Abdel, 13
neoconservativism, 18-20, 23-4, 28-9, 31, 33, 35-6, 40-1, 78, 91, 160,
171, 174-7, 184, 188
neoliberalism, 35, 89, 113, 143, 154-5, 158, 168, 171, 175-7, 179-80, 196
New Military Humanism, The (Chomsky), 158
Newsweek, 70
New World Order and the Security Council, The (Bedjaoui), 135-7
New York Times, 72, 76, 89
Nixon Administration, 20, 30
Noriega, Manuel, 118
Nuremberg Charter, 98, 182, 184-5
Nuremberg Tribunal, 44, 160, 184-5
Nye, Joseph
    Power and Interdependence, 26

O

Obama Administration, 35, 113, 143, 154-5, 167, 171, 173-8, 181-2, 196-7, 202
Obama, Barack (President), 144, 174, 182, 196-7,202
Obama, Michelle, 155
Ortega, Daniel, 82

P

Pact of Paris. *See* Kellogg-Briand Pact
Pakistan, 169, 174, 201
Palestine, 78, 100-01, 144, 169, 171, 177, 184, 204-5,
Palestinian Liberation Organization (P.L.O.), 39, 42, 45, 67, 95
Pan Am, 13, 108, 118, 134,
Pappe, Ilan
    The Ethnic Cleansing of Palestine, 169
Paris Peace Conference, 83
Peng, Li, 110
Pentagon, The, 43, 73, 155, 175-7, 180, 182, 184-5, 188, 201
Perception and Misperception in International Politics (Jervis), 97

Peres, Shimon, 93-4
Pickering, Thomas, 110, 127,
Pigs, Bay of, 69
Poindexter, John, 58, 70
Politics Among Nations (Morgen-
thau), 176-7
positivism, 18, 20, 158
Power and Interdependence (Keo-
hane & Nye), 26
Prince, The, (Machiavelli), 171
Purpose of American Politics, The,
(Morgenthau), 29

Q

Qaddafi (Colonel), 11-14, 35, 38,
45-60, 66-90, 96-8, 110-11, 113,
132, 142-3, 154-6, 160, 178-81,
187-95, 201
Green Book, 9-10, 13, 84, 86-8

R

Rabin, Yitzhak, 94
Racicot, Denis, 164
Reagan, Ronald (President), 12, 38-
60, 66-101, 164,
Reagan Administration, 11-13, 20,
24, 30-1, 33-5, 38-60, 66-101,
110-11, 117-18, 142, 164, 170,
188
Contra "Psyops" Manual, 49
realism, 19-20
regime theory, 26-8
Responsibility to Protect (R2P), 35,
96, 113, 154-171, 174-5, 182,
187-8
retorsion, 69
Revolutionary Command Council
(R.C.C.) (Libya), 84-5
Rogue State (Blum), 159
Rome Conference (1998), 193
Romney, Mitt, 144, 174
Roosevelt (Franklin) Administration,
157
Rostow, Eugene, 78
Rougier, Antoine, 157

Russia, 39, 83, 87, 167, 176, 189,
193-6

S

Sadat, Anwar, 58, 89, 95
Saint-Louis, Robert, 164
Salafists, 13
Sandinista (Nicaraguan Government),
49, 188
Santayana, George, 35, 83
Saudi Arabia, 79, 86, 99, 179
Schmitt, Carl, 98, 197
Scotland, 118
Second World War, 11, 17, 19, 44, 96,
175, 177, 195,
Self-defense, 44, 59, 71, 76-9, 94,
160, 162, 164-5
Senegal, 101, 108
September 11, 2001, 35, 66, 175,
177, 179, 197-8
Serbia, 83, 154-6, 158-60, 163, 167,
169, 177, 196, 205,
Shamir, Yitzhak, 93-4
Sharon, Ariel, 41, 94-5
Shultz, George, 43, 76, 83
Sidra, Gulf of, 35, 38-60, 69-71, 75,
88, 93
Sixth Fleet (Navy). *See* United States
Military
socialism, 18
Social Contract, 22, 86-7
Sofaer, Abraham, 43-8, 79
Sohn, Louis B, 112
Somalia, 13, 158, 169, 174, 177, 184,
201, 204-5
Soviet Union, 39, 48, 59, 72, 82, 87-8,
101, 156, 179-80, 184, 195
state terrorism, 40
Strauss, Franz Joseph, 74
Supreme Court of the United States,
Valentine v. Neidecker, 117, 122
Syria, 67, 72, 82, 93-6, 99, 107, 143,
155, 158-9, 168-9, 171, 173-4,
177, 179, 184-5, 188, 190, 195-8,
203

T

terrorism. *See* International Terror-
ism.
Thatcher, Margaret, 12, 66, 76-7, 90,
97
Thucydides, 35-6
Tonkin, Gulf of, 48, 75
Trans World Airlines (T.W.A.), 46, 72
Turkey, 159, 168, 179, 203

U

United Kingdom, 12-14, 35, 80, 90,
108-13, 116-42, 159, 193
United Nations
Charter, 24, 30, 42, 52, 59, 69, 71,
76-9, 95, 98-9, 124, 126, 127, 130,
132-7, 159, 161-2, 164-5, 189-91,
193
Committee on International Ter-
rorism, 38
General Assembly, 22, 58, 83,
140, 161-3, 165-6, 170, 191, 202
Security Council, 22-4, 58, 69, 78,
101, 108-19, 124-44, 158, 160,
170, 189-97
Universal Declaration of Human
Rights, 139
*World Summit Outcome Docu-
ment*, 165
United States Constitution, 82, 182,
196-198
United States Military Maneuvers
America (Aircraft Carrier), 46-7
Coral Sea, 47, 69
Fourth Fleet (Navy), 175
John F. Kennedy, 98
Saratoga, 69
Sixth Fleet (Navy), 13, 49-50, 52,
55, 57, 70-1, 88, 98, 111, 113
Theodore Roosevelt, 99
U.S. Fleet, 68, 71
Vincennes, 117
United States Supreme Court. *See*
Supreme Court of the United
States

U.S. Africa Command (AFRICOM),
156, 176, 178, 201, 204
use-it-or-lose-it doctrine, 52-3
utilitarianism, 18

V

Vanderwalle, Dirk
History of Modern Libya, A, 15
Versailles, Treaty of, 83
Vietnam War, 17, 20, 78, 82, 100,
155, 198, 205

W

Wall Street Journal, 107
Walters, Vernon, 74
War Powers Resolution, 82, 196-7
Warsaw Pact, 156, 180
Washington Post, 59, 83
Webster, Daniel, 160
Weinberger, Caspar, 12, 43, 59
Weinglass, Leonard, 164
Whitehead, John, 66
Winning Modern Wars (W. Clark), 184
Wolfowitz, Paul, 177, 179, 184
World Court. *See* International Court
of Justice
World Summit Outcome Document
(United Nations), 165
World War I. See First World War
World War II. See Second World War

X

Y
Yemen, 169, 174, 182, 197, 201, 205

Z
Zionism, 178

Printed in Great Britain
by Amazon.co.uk, Ltd.,
Marston Gate.